Learning Mobile App and Game Development with Solar2D

Brian G. Burton, Ed.D.

Learning Mobile App and Game Development with Solar2D

By Brian G. Burton, Ed.D.

Published by Burtons Media Group, Abilene, Texas, United States of America. See http://www.BurtonsMediaGroup.com/books for more information.

ISBN:
Digital: 978-1-937336-19-6
Paperback: 978-1-937336-25-7
Hardback: 978-1-937336-26-4

Version 1.0.2 (8/2024)

Contents

About the Author

Brian Gene Burton, Ed.D. is a professor, author, and game developer. Besides writing *Beginning Mobile App Development with Corona*, *Learning Lua*, several books on Unity, and contributing to academic books on serious games and learning in the metaverse, Dr. Burton has created game development degrees at two universities and enjoys researching and playing virtual environments.

Dr. Burton presents and publishes internationally on his research and enjoys sharing what he has learned about game and mobile development. When not traveling or teaching, he can be found with his beautiful wife of over 35 years, Rosemary.

Dedication

I dedicate this book to my loving wife whose support and encouragement kept me focused and writing. Thank you for keeping me focused and not running off on rabbit trails!

Foreword

From our first edition "Learning Mobile App & Game Development with Corona' (2015):

Welcome to Corona!

Whether you are just beginning or are an experienced programmer, Corona SDK is a fantastic way to develop rich interactive mobile apps. I designed Corona with the principles of play and experimentation. In that way, you'll be able to iterate and build something quickly. For example, in just a few lines of code, you can get objects bouncing off each other.

Today, Corona SDK is the leading mobile development platform for building #1 cross-platform games, apps and eBooks. As a result there's a thriving and supportive developer community that you can join. They come from all backgrounds and experience levels, from indies to game studios, from teenagers to octogenarians, from publishers to agencies.

In this book, you will see that Corona gives you a simple and powerful platform so you can take your idea and build great apps. If you have used other technologies, I think you'll be surprised at how quickly you'll see something interesting on the screen.

Okay, it's time to get started. With Corona's help, I hope you have fun bringing your ideas to life.

Happy coding!

Walter Luh
Creator of Corona SDK

Preface

Welcome

Welcome to Learning Mobile App and Game Development! This book is an update that has been years in the making. It is based on the popular textbooks that I wrote years ago on the Corona SDK, which is now known as Solar2D. When I began writing *Beginning Mobile App Development with Corona* in 2011, it was with a specific audience in mind; my current and future students who were experienced programmers. But before I had even finished that textbook, I had begun hearing from another vocal group; those who did not have any programming experience but had fantastic ideas for apps that they wanted to develop. Since that time Corona went through many iterations, eventually reaching its current state as open-source software known as Solar2D.

Solar2D/Corona SDK (https://solar2d.com) was developed from the beginning around the concept that anyone can make apps. Using the Lua scripting language, Solar2D is easy to learn yet powerful enough to allow you to create great, apps and fast, responsive games. Finally, the international community that has formed around Solar2D is one of the best, developer-friendly environments that I have ever experienced in my 40+ years of programming.

Best wishes and looking forward to seeing your app in the stores,

Brian G. Burton, Ed. D.

Who This Book Is For

While my focus and impetus for writing this book is that it be used as a textbook, I have also written it with the understanding that many (hopefully) are just interested in learning more about the Solar2D SDK and want to develop for multiple mobile devices at the same time. As I wrote this book, it was with the expectation that this is are new to app and game development.

How This Book Is Organized

While writing this book, I have kept the traditional 16-week U.S. college semester and an 18-week high school semester in mind. While that doesn't work for everyone, it should be enough for most people to get started with mobile development using Solar2D. My first draft ended up with more than 28 chapters. After reorganizing content and continuing to develop, we are now down to 18 chapters.

Conventions Used In This Book

To better separate scripts used in this book, we have surrounded all programming code with a

```
box
```

to distinguish it from the descriptive information in the book

Using Code Examples and Fair Use Laws

This book was written to help you learn to develop applications and games with the Solar2D SDK. In general, you may use the code in this book in your programs and documentation. You do not need to contact us for permission to reproduce a portion of the code. You also don't need to ask permission to write an app that uses large chunks of code.

I don't have any issues with using the examples as a starting point, but take the app further; be original! Answering questions by citing this book or quoting examples does not require permission (but I appreciate the citation).

I reserve all rights for selling or distributing the examples in any format this book provides. If you're not sure if your use falls outside of the fair use laws, please feel free to contact me at: DrBurton@BurtonsMediaGroup.com.

How to Contact Us

Please address any comments or questions to DrBurton@BurtonsMediaGroup.com. Any sales questions or purchases for schools should be directed to sales@BurtonsMediaGroup.com.

Supporting Solar2D

Solar2D is an Open-source, community-supported project. It is funded by the community and developed by a small group of developers led by Vlad Shcherban.

Please help continue the great work that is being done by contributing to the Solar2D project either via Patreon or Github Sponsors:

Patreon: https://www.patreon.com/shchvova

Github Sponsors: https://github.com/sponsors/shchvova

GitHub repository for code examples

All chapter examples can be downloaded from
https://github.com/drburton/LearningMobileGamewithSolar
2D

Chapter 1 Introduction to App Development

Learning Objectives

In Chapter 1 we will learn:

- The different mobile operating systems
- The life-cycle of a mobile app project
- Software needed to make a mobile app
- How to make your first app
- Troubleshooting basics
- An Introduction to Objects, Methods, and Properties

Introduction to Mobile Application Development

You have been working on your killer mobile app idea for days. It is completely original; no one has done anything like what you have planned before! Just one problem... How do you get your idea on the tablet or smartphone?

Don't worry! You are in the right place! This book was specifically written for you! In the following pages, we will walk through all the decisions and processes that you will need to address to develop and sell your app.

To begin, we will examine the various options you have for developing your app.

Mobile Operating Systems

The smartphone and tablet world is divided by the operating system (OS) that runs on the device. An operating system handles all of the directions from the apps that are running and what the user is tapping on as well as connecting to the Internet, handling text messages and phone calls. It is a busy system! As we begin to develop applications for smartphones and tablets, it is important that we keep in mind the devices that our apps will be running on. Below I have listed the four most popular Operating Systems for mobile devices:

Android

The Android OS was developed by Google. The first beta was released in 2007 and it has been regularly updated every few months. At the time of this writing, Android 14 is the current stable release.

Native development for Android devices is done with Google's APK (Android Programming Kit). But many tools (including Solar2D) also allow you to build Android applications.

The Android OS is available on smartphones and tablets. It is the foundation of Amazon's Kindle Fire, Google Pixel, and Samsung Galaxy to name a few. Android enjoys a devoted following. Android Apps can be sold on Amazon and Google Play.

Apple iOS

Apple's iOS was first released in 2007. Apple iOS can only run on Apple hardware according to the licensing agreement that you sign when you download the software.

Apple iOS runs on the iPhone and iPad. Currently, Apple iOS apps can only be sold through the iTunes store.

Apple iOS native app development is done with xCode. However, like Android, there are many tools, such as Solar2D that allow you to build multiple operating systems/devices at the same time.

Desktop

Solar2D now allows you to build for Windows and Macintosh desktops. While there are a few minor differences that are required in programming, you will find creating a desktop game for Windows or Mac as easy as creating a game for mobile.

HTML5
Publishing to desktop or mobile devices is a great way to create innovative apps, but you also have the freedom to publish to the web with the HTML 5 build option in Solar2D.

Cross-Platform Development
Perhaps I am just lazy, but I don't like to do things twice. When I have created a great app (or even a not-so-great app) for the iPhone or iPad, I don't want to spend weeks completely re-writing all of the programming code just so that it can be deployed to a different set of devices. When I first started in app development, this was exactly what you had to do. Fortunately, there are now many tools that allow the developer to create apps for more than one operating system.

We will be using the Solar2D as our development tool. Corona Labs was created in 2008 as a venture-backed company in Palo Alto, California. Before Solar2D, the Corona Labs team was responsible for creating many of the industry standard tools that I am sure you are familiar with. In the time that I have been developing apps with Solar2D/Corona, I have found them to be one of the most friendly and helpful businesses that I have had the pleasure of working with. In addition, their online community is unusually friendly and supportive. If you decide to join the Solar2D community, be sure to continue this great spirit of helpfulness!

Developing Mobile Applications
From concept to store, an app development project goes through eight distinct stages:

1) **Design phase** – This is the entry point that many apps never get past: you have an idea for an app and what you want the app to do. The first thing to determine is if the device you hope to place the app on can even do the tasks that you require of it. If it can, is the project feasible? There are many considerations including development costs, software costs, web hosting expenses, and development time.

   Creating a good design document is critical. If the project appears to be capable of being completed, then you move on to the next stage. Remember to include in this initial design phase how to make money from your app and include any social networking/marketing ideas.

   The most successful apps plan for marketing and sales from the beginning. One final consideration in the design phase is legal. Be sure to investigate the intellectual property and regional/national laws where you plan to sell your app.

2) **Gather Requirements** – This phase details exactly what functionality the app will contain and the design of what the various views will look like. Many people use tools like Figma for layout. This is an essential phase. If you, the developer, are unsure what the app will look like when it is completed, how can you communicate what you are developing to others? Be sure to keep these initial designs and develop a webpage around the development process. It will help with your marketing efforts!

3) **Code and Graphic development** – This is where you get started programming and developing the graphics for your project. The best teams are composed of programmers and artists.

4) **User Testing** – Too many people skip the testing phase or do not conduct a thorough enough test of their app. Deploy your app to a few test devices and have people in

your target audience use the app. Listen to their feedback (remembering that they might be overly kind) and implement their suggestions.

5) **System Tests**- Before releasing your app into the wild, run a systems test. Is your app connecting to a remote server, the cloud, Facebook, X/Twitter, or TikTok? Make sure that all of these features and services are capable of supporting the additional demand your app might place on it.

6) **Documentation/Marketing** – Before you can release your work to an app store, you must have a supporting webpage in place with contact emails and screenshots. This is also part of your marketing effort, so ensure everything is perfect!

7) **Production** – Create your app for release and place it in the stores where you want to sell it.

8) **Maintenance** – If you haven't noticed, the operating systems for devices are constantly changing with more, newer devices becoming available on almost a regular basis. You should expect to refresh and update your app at least every few months at the very least. On the bright side, in most app stores, releasing a new version could get you a higher ranking in the search engine!

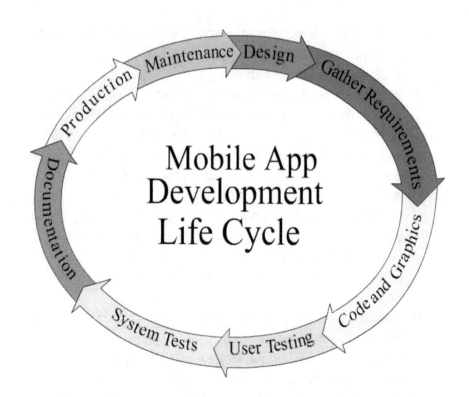

The above list is based on the traditional software development lifecycle. I have made one adjustment. In the traditional lifecycle, Documentation and Marketing are placed after Production. In app development, that would be a mistake. Documentation and marketing are too important and not being completed will delay the submission of your app to the stores.

Software That You Will Need
It's no surprise that you will need Solar2D to get started https://solar2d.com/#download.

In addition to Solar2D, you will need an editor. I will be using Microsoft Visual Studio Code https://code.visualstudio.com/download, but feel free to use any editor you like.

Hardware

Solar2D isn't too demanding on your development computer. As long as you are running at least OSX 10.11 or later on the Mac side, or Windows 7 with a 1 GHz processor, and OpenGL 2.1 or newer on the PC side, you should be fine.

If you are planning to develop and deploy to iPhone and/or iPad, you can do the development for the iOS app on a Windows computer, but you must have a Mac with Xcode to publish your apps. This is an Apple requirement. To keep in everyone's good graces, Solar2D will only publish for an iOS device if you are using a Mac computer to deploy the app.

If you only have a Windows system, you will be able to develop and deploy for Android, HTML5, and Windows desktops. You will also be able to develop for iOS devices, but not deploy your finished app to an iOS device or the iTunes store. Personally, I use both a Mac mini and a PC, regularly switching back and forth during the app development process.

Development Hardware Matrix:

Development Hardware	Android OS		Apple iOS	
	Develop	Deploy	Develop	Deploy
Mac	√	√	√	√
Windows	√	√	√	

Test Devices

If you are going to develop and sell apps for mobile devices, you should have a mobile device to test your creation. I have been on projects where I was expected to develop for mobile devices that I didn't have. It was like herding cats. Using the app simulator will get you 75% of the way home, but it won't allow you to spot all potential problems. On one of the aforementioned projects, the app worked fine on the simulator but crashed on the mobile device and was rejected by Apple. The experience was more than just a little frustrating and taught me a valuable lesson: If you are developing for a platform, have test devices!

Android

Solar2D only builds for Android 4.0.3 and newer. Any devices that you plan to develop for must use the ARM V7 processor. There are plenty of devices that meet this requirement, so you shouldn't have any problem finding one to perform your tests.

iOS

For deploying to an iOS device, you will need a developer's license and either an iPhone or iPad. Having an older phone or iPad is a good idea for testing FPS (Frames Per Second) for graphically intensive apps. It is recommended that you use the newest iOS on your devices. To be able to deploy to an iOS device, you will need a Mac computer and a developers account from Apple.

Book Examples and Graphics

If you don't want to create your own graphics or you would like to double-check what you have programmed against the sample code, I have created a repository of code samples, graphics, and other tools that you might want to use with the projects that are listed in this book. They are all available at
https://github.com/drburton/LearningMobileGamewithSolar2D

Editors

The editor that you decide to use is a personal decision. Solar2D isn't impacted by the editor selection, so you need to use an editor that you are comfortable with. I recommend one that allows the integration of Lua to make your editing easier.

Some of the most popular editors in use with Solar2D include (but are not limited to) Sublime, Notepad++, TextMate, TextWrangler, and Xcode. Editor screenshots will be from Visual Studio Code.

Notepad++ (Win) Open source, $0
A popular open source language editor for the PC environment.
http://notepad-plus-plus.org/

Sublime Text 4 (Mac/Win) free trial, $99
You can download Sublime at: http://www.sublimetext.com

TextMate (Mac) by Micromates, ??.
Textmate is very popular in the Solar2D community.

Visual Studio Code (Mac/Win) Free.
Visual Studio Code from Microsoft is a very popular free editor.

Xcode (Mac) by Apple, $0*.
Xcode is an integral part of the iOS SDK. If you are used to developing using Objective-C, Xcode is a natural choice.

If you do not have access to a system to do development, you can use the Solar2D playground to test your code:
https://www.solar2dplayground.com/

Our First Project: Hello World

I always hated books and classes that spent the first chapter or week covering things I didn't care about. I purchased the book or took the class because I wanted to create, not to go over some syllabus or a review of all the different ages of computer development. So let's skip all of that and make an app that will help you learn your way around Solar2D: a "Hello World" project. Stop with the rolling of your eyes! Before I lose you, let me guarantee that you will get a valuable resource out of this Hello World project, something that you will use the rest of the time you develop in Solar2D.

Was that enough to get your attention? Then let's get started!

Project Setup

Launch the Solar2D Simulator. You should see the Corona Simulator Console and the Solar2D Simulator.

We will use the Console soon. To get started in the Solar2D Simulator, click on the New Project button.

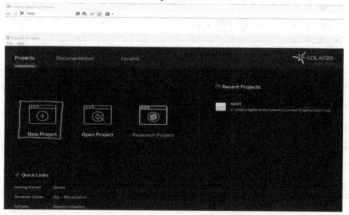

Name the project "HelloWorld." Select the Blank template then select the screen size of your choice. Optionally, you can also

set the project folder to a different location.   When you have the
new project configured, click the OK button.

Solar2D will create a folder for your project in your Documents
folder, launch your default editor, and a simulator that will show
the output from your project. We will cover all of the files and
folders in the project later, but for now, we will focus on the editor.

There should now be a main.lua file in your HelloWorld folder.

In your editor type:

```
print("Hello World")
```

and save your file (Click File on the menu bar and then Save). The Solar2D Simulator should ask you if you wish to relaunch the simulator. Confirm that you want it to relaunch.

main.lua ✕

C: > Users > bgb07a > Documents > Corona Projects > HelloWorld > main.lua

```
1    ---------------------------------------------------------------
2    --
3    -- main.lua
4    --
5    ---------------------------------------------------------------
6
7    -- Your code here
8    print("Hello World")
```

Hello World project in the editor

Did you notice? That's right, nothing happened...in the simulator. Look at the Terminal (Mac) or Corona Simulator Console (Windows).

On the last line of the text in the Console, you should see your Hello World displayed.

```
22:28:12.686
22:28:12.686   Copyright (C) 2009-2023 C o r o n a   L a b s   I n c .
22:28:12.686      Version: 3.0.0
22:28:12.686      Build: 2023.3700
22:28:12.686   Platform: SM-G991x / x64 / 10.0 / Intel(R) UHD Graphics 770 / 4.6.0 - Build 31.0.101.4644 /
               | en_US | en
22:28:12.686   Loading project from:    C:\Users\bgb07a\Documents\Corona Projects\HelloWorld
22:28:12.686   Project sandbox folder: C:\Users\bgb07a\AppData\Local\Corona Labs\Corona Simulator\Sandbox
               \helloworld-1F546A6EB93190F50A340C97E80FC926\Documents
22:28:12.717   Hello World
```

Hello World in the Solar2D Terminal window

Congratulations! You just made your first Solar2D app! Now before you become disappointed, you just learned a very important tool for troubleshooting your applications. When something doesn't seem to be working correctly or displaying the way you want, you can send yourself messages through the Solar2D console. Believe me when I tell you that this one command will save you hours of troubleshooting headaches!

I am sure you also noticed that Solar2D generates a great deal of additional information before giving you the results of your print command. The first few lines provide information about the version of Solar2D and the location of the simulation files.

Note: If you didn't see anything, there are two areas that people commonly make a mistake:
1) they didn't save their main.lua file (I still make this mistake) or
2) when saving the main.lua file, it wasn't saved as a text file type.

Debugging

One of the key methods for debugging is the liberal use of the print() command. With the print() command, you can pass a variety of text or variable values to the NSLog (a file that tracks events for Apple devices) or console window. To be a successful app developer, you will quickly come to depend on using print throughout your program.

Project 1.1: Hello World (v2.0)

Well, that was frustrating! I wanted to make something appear on the screen! Let us make a second attempt at getting something on the simulator screen. Back in your editor (you can use the same main.lua file) type:

```
local textObj = display.newText("Hello World", 100, 100,
native.systemFont, 24)
textObj:setFillColor(1, 1, 1)
```

Lua, the language behind Solar2D, is case sensitive. So newText is a different word than newtext or NewText. Try newtext and look at the error that appears in the Terminal window.

Note: Be sure to use " " and not "" in your apps. "" will cause an error!

So what do you make of everything you just typed? Take a moment and savor the possibilities. What will the screen look like when it launches? Why?

Of course. we expect "Hello World" to be emblazoned somewhere on the screen, but where? Perhaps those two 100's have something to do with where it will be placed on the screen? What will it look like? Looks like some sort of default font will be used for the text, and we are setting the color of the text, but what color shall it be?

I'm sure you have a lot of questions about what you typed in. Time to save and launch your app, and then we will look at what happens.

Save the file, and then relaunch (CTRL + R) your simulator. You should now see Hello World displayed in the simulator:

Hello World on the Droid simulator

Looks like it's an equal distance from the top and the side: *100.
100*? 100 pixels either way, right? It's definitely a system font,
probably Helvetica, and those three 1's somehow add up to white.
Okay, so I'm presuming you know nothing about RGB values. Well,
just in case you did, let's change a couple of those 1 to 0's and see
what happens:

(1, 0, 0)

(0, 1, 0)

(0, 0, 1)

And of course when you add Red, Green, and Blue together in the
additive color system, you get White.

Now that the final number: 24. Let's change it to a larger number
such as 48. What do you think will happen?

What if you want to change the font to say, *Times*? What would
you do?

Well, first off, you would have to get rid of the offending
native.systemFont, but could you just type in *Times*? Let's try it,
change native.systemFont to Times.

15

Hmmmmm. Nothing. No error in the terminal window, but no change on the display either.

I will give you a clue: *you can quote me.*

We have to convert Times to a string (i.e. place it inside of quotes) for it to be understood. Fonts are stored by their literal names and can only be recognized if you tell Solar2D that this is a name, not a variable. Anything placed in quotes is referred to as a string (which we will discuss in greater detail later). The only way the computer in our smartphone knows that we are looking for the name of a font is if we place it in quotes. Try changing the font to "Times" and see what happens.

Now for the technical explanation of what we just accomplished:

First we created a local variable called textObj. A **variable** is just a placeholder or a name for other things in our program. Often we aren't sure what the value or information will be when we are writing our apps, so it is necessary to use a variable to hold our information. Remember back in math (or if you are from the U.K., maths) when you would use x or y to solve an equation? Well, a variable is the same thing, except we are going to name our variables much better than x or y. Good variable naming will make our lives much easier when we get to more complex apps that might have 10 to 20 (or more) variables. It might mean more typing, but you will really appreciate it when you go to revise or update the program at a later date. We do not have to use the variable name textObj, we could use fred for the variable name but after a couple of days, we might forget what fred represents.

We set textObj equal to the **object** (which we will discuss in just a minute) that we create by calling display.newText. display.newText is a command that Solar2D understands. When Solar2D sees display.newText, it knows that we are going to type something to the screen by telling it what we want to type, where we want it placed (the numbers 100, 100, which are the center X and Y of the text), what font we want to use, and how big the text will be.

The display.newText parameters are:

display.newText(*text, center x or width, center y or height, font, text size*)

or
display.newText("Hello World", 100, 100, native.systemFont, 24)

By default, the text object is white, so we didn't really accomplish anything by setting the textObj to white. But I want to get you into the practice of setting the text color when you create a text object. Later we will look at how to fade the text object out (or in).

Now you have made your first REAL mobile app!

Warning: If you copy code from a website (or even from this book), sometimes the quotation marks will change from straight quotation marks to smart quotes. This WILL cause an error in Solar2D. Make sure your quotes are always " " and not " ".

Introducing Objects
You may have noticed the use of the term **object** sprinkled throughout the book. When I use the term 'object' it is to represent anything that is used in our project. Text, buttons, or sounds; are all objects. Just as in the real, physical world, I can move or interact with an object (a lamp, table, or car). An object in your software is anything that you or the people using your app can interact with, including viewing, tapping, dragging, listening to, or just a pretty picture that is on the display.

Real-world objects all have **properties** that help to describe the object's location, color, or anything that can be changed about the

17

object. If I have a car, I might describe the car's location by its longitude and latitude.

In programming, we are able to interact with each object's properties to make changes; such as when the textObj was created, we set the center X, center Y, font, and size properties as well as the string that would be displayed.

Most objects can have their property changed just by setting it to a new value:

textObj.x = 100

would move the Hello World that was displayed on the screen to pixel location 100 (or to the right 50 pixels of the original location). Properties always have a period between the object name and the name of the property.

A few valid properties for display.newText include:

object.size – set the font size of the text
object.text – set or change the text
object.x – set or change the x location of the object (based upon the center of the text)
object.y – set or change the y location of the object (based upon the center of the text)

Objects can also have **methods.** A method is something that changes the current state of an object. Think of a lamp. A lamp can be turned on or off. If we were going to have a method for a lamp, we might call it setLight so that we could have it on or off.

To use a method, we put a colon between the object's name and the method we are going to use. In the case of our text, the primary method that we are concerned about right now is

18

setFillColor. To change the color of the text we would use the command

object:setFillColor(R, G, B)

If it seems confusing, do not worry about it, it is confusing when you are first getting started! Give yourself a little bit of time to get used to the ideas that we covered. Remember: 75% of any new skill is learning the vocabulary.   If you get used to the idea that an object can be anything in our app and a variable is just the name that we are going to use to refer to that object, you are most of the way there already!

Summary
This has been a busy chapter! Solar2D should now be installed on your system, you have been introduced to editors, hardware considerations, and publishing information. We even managed to develop two apps (okay, maybe not saleable apps, but they are apps)! The first app introduced the critically important print command; the second app actually displayed text to the Solar2D simulator, our original goal. Finally, the concept of a variable and an object in programming was briefly introduced. If the idea of an object and variable doesn't seem natural yet, don't worry, it will make more sense as we learn more material.

Programming Vocabulary
Method
Object
Property
String
Variable

Questions:
1. What is a method?
    a. A method holds an attribute or setting of an object.

b. A method changes the current state of an object.

c. A method is used to hide an object.

2. What is an object? Specify its importance and give an example.
3. What is a property? Specify its importance and give an example.
4. How are objects and properties related to one another?
5. What is a variable? Specify its importance and give an example.
6. What is the programming language that Solar2D uses?
7. True or false: I can publish for an iOS device using a PC.
8. True or false: Solar2D allows me to publish to multiple operating systems.
9. List and summarize the eight steps of app development.
10. When developing an app with Solar2D, what should your first file be named?

Assignments

1. Try various typos to see the resulting error messages in the terminal window.
   a. Make a typo in newText. What is the result?
   b. Make a typo in native.systemFont. What is the result?
   c. Try setFillColor. What is the result?
2. Change the text object to red in the Hello World (v2) project.
3. Reposition the text to the bottom of the simulator without letters going off the bottom by changing the x and y values of display.newText in the Hello World (v2) project.
4. Place 5 different messages in different places on the screen, each in a different font, size, and color. Note that fonts will depend upon your system. Remember that the font name must be enclosed in quotation marks. Don't worry, if the font is not available, the system will switch to a default font.

Chapter 2   Introduction to Functions

Learning Objectives
In chapter 2, we will learn

- about Variables
- the difference between a local and global variable
- how to place a comment in your program
- how to determine the screen size of a device
- how to create a routine that can be used later
- what a listener is and how to use one
- about the API and how to use it

Name That Object
In our last chapter we learned about objects. Now it is time to name the object. Whenever we assign an object to a variable, we are essentially giving that object a name. Everything that the object is will be stored and referred to through that assigned name. Just as you are called by a name, so are the objects within our app. When I assign text that will be on the screen to the variable name textObj, we have given it a 'name'. Using this name (in this case textObj), we can give it further instructions later in the app.

It is very important that each object receive its own unique name! Imagine a teacher asking Pat to answer a question in a class. But everyone in the class is named Pat! We have the same problem if we reuse the same variable names. Make your objects feel special; give each one a unique name.

Local vs. Global Variables

Most of us have the experience at one point or another where we are given a 'temporary' name. Perhaps during school, there were two students with the same first name in a class, so they would have their last initial also used: thus two Heathers became HeatherA and HeatherB. Or maybe you were given a nickname in school or in athletics. Usually, these different names were short-lived or only used in limited situations.

There are a few rules to the naming of variables:

- A variable can be any combination of letters, numbers, or underscores
- A variable must not begin with a number
- A variable cannot contain a space or any symbol except underscore
- Variables are case-sensitive. myVariable is not the same as MyVariable

Valid	Invalid
Variable1	1Variable
My_Variable	My Variable
_variable	-variable
variable12345	variable12.345

In programming we have two types of variables: local and global. As we progress through the rest of this book (and any other programming language that you ever learn) think of the differences this way: a local variable is a short-lived name given to an object, much like that short-lived nickname in school. A global variable is a long-lasting name and can be used throughout a program, anywhere in a program.

How do you tell them apart? Easy. A local variable will always have the word **local** in front of it the first time it is used in an app. A global variable will never have the word local.

Declaring a local variable:

local textObject
local myNewPicture
local backgroundImage

Declaring a global variable:

textObject
myNewPicture
backgroundImage

The preference in programming is to always use local variable whenever possible. Local variables use less memory and will help you avoid naming problems in more complex programs.

One last thing before we move on: while you can place text and images on the screen without using a variable, you won't be able to move, hide, change, or remove them later. It is best to always use a variable name for your objects.

```
display.newText("Can't Touch This", 100, 10, nil, 16)

local myObject = display.newText("Can Touch This", 100, 50, nil, 16)

myObject.y = 100
```

How to Code Comments

If you have never written a program before, placing comments might seem like a silly waste of time, especially when you are working on a simple program. Let me assure you that comments are as important as any line of code that you write! While good commenting is needed in all software development, it is especially critical in mobile app development. Mobile apps have a very short cycle before they have to be updated. Usually, you will be updating a successful app every 6 to 12 months; just enough time to completely forget why you wrote a line in the program to do a specific operation or how you used a special command to fix a bug.

Comments are a gift you give the future you (or the programmer who comes after you to update the software). Taking a few minutes to leave good comments in your program will potentially save you hours of work later. Learn the habit of commenting now. Believe me, you will thank yourself later!

There are two ways to comment in Solar2D: line comment and block comment.

Line comments convert the remainder of the current line into a comment. By placing two dashes: -- you tell Solar2D that everything after the dashes is a comment and can be ignored.

A block comment also begins with two dashes and is followed by two brackets: --[[You end the comment with:]]-- usually placed on its own line in the editor. Everything between the brackets will be ignored by the compiler.

Block commenting is a great way to turn on or off a section of the program when you are doing testing.

```
-- This is a comment.
local myObject = display.newText("Your Text Here", 10, 40, nil,
20) -- everything after the 2 dashes is a comment
--[[
This is a block comment. Everything between the double
brackets is a comment.
--]]
```

Device Boundaries

Developing an app for mobile devices is a little different than traditional programming. One of our considerations, especially when we are developing apps for a number of devices is that each one has a different screen size and pixel count. Even if you are just going to publish to Apple, you have four different resolutions that need to be supported. If you add all the different Android based devices, you could drive yourself crazy making all of the adjustments so that each view that is created looks good.

One way around this problem is to use variables to store the device resolution. Solar2D has built-in commands that will return the display width and height. The command *display.contentWidth* and *display.contentHeight* will return the width and height. These are just two of the commands included in the Solar2D SDK Application Programming Interface (usually abbreviated as API). All programming languages and development kits include an API so that programmers know what commands are available and how to properly use those commands.

Project 2.0 Display Size

For our first project in this chapter, let's create a simple program that will give the screen size of our device. Specifically, I would like to know what the x, y location is for each corner of my screen. For this program, I would like it to display at each corner what that screen location is, shown in the examples below:

0, 0   768, 0

0, 1024   768, 1024

The iPad display resolution (not to scale)

To start our new project, click the New Project like in the previous chapter and name the project ScreenSize.

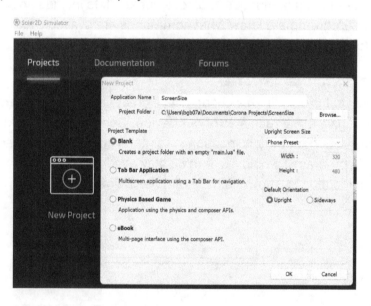

To get started let's hide the status bar. This is done using the display.setStatusBar API command. To make the status bar hidden, we need to pass it as a **parameter.** A parameter is any information that is given to the API (Application Programming Interface). In this case, the parameter is *display.HiddenStatusBar*. This sends the command to hide the status bar from view during the execution of your app: *display.setStatusBar(display.HiddenStatusBar)*

main.lua

```
display.setStatusBar( display.HiddenStatusBar )
```

Now that the status bar is hidden, it is time to find out the height and width of the display. We can store the display's width and height in variables for easy reuse with the display.contentWidth and display.contentHeight commands.:

```
local myWidth = display.contentWidth
local myHeight= display.contentHeight
```

We now know (well, our app knows) the maximum width and height of the display. Displaying it is just a matter of using the display.newText, right? Remember, the top, left corner will be our starting point, so it has an x of 0 and a y of 0.

One last thing: instead of using system.nativeFont as the fourth parameter of display.newText, we will use a short cut: *nil.* Nil is nothing, zero, nada. It is a shortcut way of telling Solar2D that I don't care what system font is used, so it will automatically use the system's native font.

```
local topLeft = display.newText("0, 0", 0, 0, nil, 24)
local topRight = display.newText(myWidth.. ", 0", myWidth, 0, nil, 24)
local bottomLeft = display.newText("0, " .. myHeight, 0, myHeight, nil, 24)
```

```
local bottomRight = display.newText(myWidth ..", ".. myHeight,
myWidth, myHeight, nil, 24)
```

Did you notice my use of two periods in the display.newText
(myWidth.. ", 0")? By placing two periods together, we are telling
Solar2D that we want to **concatenate** or take two strings and
make them one string. In this case, we are taking myWidth and
concatenating it with ", 0" which will place the width beside the
comma in the string (for example: if the width is 360 pixels, the
resulting string would be "360, 0"). We will talk about
concatenation more in chapter 4.

Save your app and run it with the Solar2D Simulator.

Hmmm, the text is only partially showing. That will not work.

iPhone showing only left, top text

Why? As we saw in Chapter 1, display.newText positions the
center of the text at the values we give. So when we assign
topRight to myWidth, 0, the myWidth positions the text partially off

28

of the screen. The same situation for myHeight at the bottom of the screen, it causes the text to be displayed below the bottom. To fix this problem, we need to move the text back on the display by subtracting from the myWidth & myHeight values. Remember that the measurement is in pixels, not characters. Let's replace the last four lines with the following:

```
local topLeft = display.newText("0, 0", 25, 20, nil, 24)
local topRight = display.newText(myWidth.. ", 0", myWidth-100, 20, nil, 24)
local bottomLeft = display.newText("0, " .. myHeight, 50, myHeight-50, nil, 24)
local bottomRight = display.newText(myWidth ..", ".. myHeight, myWidth-120, myHeight-50, nil, 24)
```

Run the app. You can change the device shown by the Simulator by clicking on the View Menu, then View As. Doesn't that look better? Try changing the values in the left and top parameters of the display.newText to see how the text changes location on the screen.

Functions

A function is a small segment of a program that we might need to use at certain times in our program. Say you have created an app that has a button on the screen. In this app, every time the button is tapped, the button is moved to a new location. Now, we don't want this app just randomly moving the button. Nor do we want it continuously moving the button. We only want the button to move after it has been tapped. This can be managed by creating a function.

A function begins with the keyword 'function' (surprised?) followed by the name of the function and any parameters to be passed. A function always ends with the keyword 'end'. In between these two keywords will be the commands and operations you want to execute when the function is called.

Always use an original name for your function (and your variables) that describes what the function accomplishes. It is a common mistake to name a function the same as a variable name that you are already using. While you can sometimes get away with it, it is bad programming practice and will create confusion as you create more complex programs. Think of it like this: how confusing is it in a classroom when you have 5 people named Ashley or Jacob?

A function can be implemented in several ways. The most common is:

function *functionName* *()*

  programming script

end

Functions can receive parameters (contained in the parenthesis) and return information to the command that called them using the keyword **return** (which we will talk about later).

Remember that local variables are limited to their current function. If a variable is declared as local within a function, it is only available when that function is in use. Once the function is done, the variable and any information that was stored in it are gone, poof, no longer available. If a variable is declared as a local variable outside of a function, it is limited to the current file (such as main.lua); thus it would be available to all functions within main.lua, but not in other files that might be a part of the application (something we will talk about in a couple of chapters).

Variable Scope
When you declare a variable inside of a function, the variable is only available inside that function. Think of it like light. Outside, we have sunlight, and it is everywhere. If I walk into a building, I still have sunlight through the windows. Sunlight is like a global

variable; it is everywhere.

A local variable that is declared at the beginning of a file like main.lua is available anywhere in main.lua. It is local to main.lua. This is like turning on a light switch that turns on all the lights in a house. If I declare a local variable inside a function, it is only available inside that function. More like a table lamp, it is only useable on the table.

myGlobalVariable = "Solar2D is great"

would be a global variable and could be used anywhere in our program.

local myLocalVariable = "I am a local variable"

would only be used in the file (like main.lua) that it was created.

```
local function myFunction()
     local anotherLocalVariable = "I am in a function"
end
```

would only be a useable inside the function. Once we were done with the function, the variable anotherLocalVariable would return a nil value, which could crash your program.

How do you avoid crashing your program?

Always try to declare your variables at the beginning of the file if they are going to be used throughout the file (like main.lua). By declaring them at the beginning of the file, you will have use of them everywhere in your file. If you need a temporary variable inside a function to do a calculation, that's fine, that why we have them, just don't plan to use them outside the function!

Event Listeners

Event listeners are essential to every app. An event listener is a function that is constantly running in the background on the device. When the event occurs, the event listener tells the app which function should handle the event. Think of this like your telephone. It is always 'listening' to see if you have an incoming phone call. It only rings when you receive a call. Your phone is like an event listener which then passes control of the phone ringer function when there is a phone call.

Event listeners are usually placed at the end of the program listing since they call functions that must already be declared.

*objectVar:***addEventListener**(*interaction, eventListener*)

Project 2.1: Fun with Buttons

For this project we are going to create an app that will move a text object to a random place on the screen each time the button is tapped. Create a new project and name it Project2.1. You will need to create a button graphic. I just went into Photoshop (or gimp, paint, or any other graphics software) and created a small 100-pixel by 50-pixel rectangle and saved it as **button.png**. Then I copied the button.png file into the Project2.1 folder that was created for this new project.

To load the button.png into our app, we need to create an object to refer to the graphic:

```
local myButton = display.newImage( "button.png" )
```

This creates a local variable called myButton, and then assigns an image to it (the button.png graphic we just created). The command display.newImage will take any image we give it and display it on our screen. I recommend that you always use the

PNG file format. PNG is accepted by Apple and Android. Other graphics file formats are not accepted by both.

If you save the main.lua file and run the simulator, you should see the button you created located in the left top corner of the simulator. You could also set the top left corner location of the graphic by adding a setting for the center x and center y of the object as we did with the textObj in chapter 1:

```
local myButton = display.newImage( "button.png", 100, 100 )
```

We can also set the myButton object location directly by changing the x and y property setting. When you set the x & y values by changing the property, you are setting where the center of the object will be located. Try entering the following code after you create your myButton object and see the difference:

```
myButton.x = 100 -- sets the center 100 pixels from left
myButton.y = 100 -- sets the center 100 pixels from top
```

Great! We can move the myButton object anywhere on the screen we want. But there is a problem. There are a lot of different types of devices that we can build for with Solar2D and each one has a different resolution. Wouldn't it be nice to have it located in about the same place on the screen no matter what type of device it is running on? Fortunately, this is easy with the commands we have already played with: display.contentHeight and display.contentWidth!

Using a little math, we can place the myButton object in the exact center of the screen. Replace the original myButton.x and myButton.y with:

```
myButton.x = display.contentWidth /2
myButton.y = display.contentHeight /2
```

and save, then run your app. The button should now be in the
exact center of your screen, no matter what device it is running on.

myButton is now in the center of the screen

Next, we will make something move to a new location on the
screen. For this, we will simply place some text on the screen that
we can move with our function:

```
local textObj = display.newText("Button Tapped", 100, 50,
native.systemFont, 24)
textobj:setFillColor(1, 1, 1)
```

Now for the function. To begin with, we are going to have the text
object (textObj) move down a few pixels every time the button is
tapped.

```
function moveButtonDown( event )
    textObj.y = textObj.y + 50
end
```

Note: It is considered good programming practice to indent the code in a function to make it easier to read. Either tap or five spaces is considered optimal.

This little function will take the old .y property of textObj and add 50 pixels. (i.e., it will move the text "Button Tapped" down the screen 50 pixels every time the button is tapped).

One last line is required before we test our app. Add this to your program as the last line of code:

```
myButton:addEventListener( "tap", moveButtonDown )
```

This sets up an event listener (but I'm sure you guessed that from the name of the command) that listens for a tap event to occur on myButton. We will talk about other types of events at a later time.

Save your project and run it in Solar2D. With your mouse, you can click on the button at the bottom of your screen, which simulates a 'tap'.

The full program should look like this:

```
local myButton = display.newImage( "button.png" )
myButton.x = display.contentWidth /2
myButton.y = display.contentHeight/2

local textobj = display.newText("Button Tapped", 100, 50,
native.systemFont, 24)
textobj:setFillColor(1, 1, 1)
```

```
function moveButtonDown( event )
   textobj.y = textobj.y + 50
end

myButton:addEventListener( "tap", moveButtonDown )
```

Let's adjust the button a little more. To simplify the interface, I want to move the button to the bottom of the screen.

Again, with a little math, this is easily accomplished. Since we know that the button is 50 pixels in height, that the y property looks at the center of the object, and that the height of the device is in pixels from the variable display.contentHeight, we can easily place the button 50 pixels above the bottom of the screen with: myButton.y=display.contentHeight − 75 (i.e. 50 pixels from the

bottom + 25 pixels for the center of the object).
Replace the myButton.y = display.contentHeight/2 with:

```
myButton.y=display.contentHeight − 75
```

It is important at this point to consider the aesthetics of the app in the sense of the button size. Too small a button and a user's finger might be too big; too big of a button and you will waste limited screen space. Examine some buttons from mobile apps, iOS, Windows phones, etc to get a concept of the right button size for your app. Remember, once you have created a button you like you can reuse it for other projects.

Let's make this project a little more interesting. Using a random number generator we can relocate the text object to a new location with little effort and make the project more interesting at the same time. The random number generator in Solar2D is part of the math command set and is called *math.random(low, high)*. Since we are building for a variety of devices, we will use display.contentWidth and display.contentHeight for our high values.

By adding two lines of code to our function, we can now relocate the text object to a new, random, location.

Your myButton:tap function should now look like:

```
function moveButtonDown( event )
    textObj.x = math.random( 0, display.contentWidth)
    textObj.y = math.random( 0, display.contentHeight)
end
```

Note: Solar2D is case sensitive. If you are getting errors, it is probably caused by a typo in either a variable name or a command name.

Tip: When making major changes to your code, it is often easier to just comment out the line of code that you don't want rather than deleting it. Comments in Solar2D are noted by placing a double hyphen -- at the beginning of the comment. You can begin a comment at any point on the command line. To comment out blocks of code, use --[[ ]].

Save and try it in your Solar2D Simulator.

Throw in a Little Fancy

Did you notice that sometimes the text object (your "Button Tapped" text) goes off the screen? That is because the .x and .y properties are setting the location based on the center of the textObj. The program can't tell where the edges are on the object. For all it knows, we WANT only part of the object to be shown!

There are many ways to keep this from happening. One method is to modify the .x and .y calculations so that the number returned doesn't allow the text to be cut off. Using trial and error, we can adjust the numbers until we finally get:

```
textObj.x = math.random( 85, display.contentWidth -85)
textObj.y = math.random( 20, display.contentHeight – 110)
```

In this case, we are generating a number between 85 and the content width - 85 for x and a number between 20 and the content height -100 for y. I chose the 100 pixels value so that the text

38

object is always above the button. This keeps the text on the screen at all times. You can make these changes, save, and then click on the simulator, File > **Relaunch**.

Relaunch reloads your main.lua with the changes you made. It saves you from having to do it with Open each time (a wonderful feature when you're trying to troubleshoot a project).

A better (and there are other even better methods, but this will do for now) method is to look at the size of the object that you want to keep on the screen. Since you might not know the size of the object when the program is running (for a variety of reasons), it is better to let the program figure out what will keep the object fully on the screen:

```
local w = textObj.width
local h = textObj.height

function moveButtonDown( event )
    textObj.x = math.random( w/2, display.contentWidth − (w/2))
    textObj.y = math.random( h/2, display.contentHeight − (100 +
h/2))
end
```

TIP: Sometimes we have to split the programming script between two lines such as above due to book margins. When you see this happen, the program code should be on one line in your editor.

The .width and .height properties return the size of the object in pixels. This makes it easy to calculate where the object can be placed on the screen. Of course, we don't have to set the text object width and height to a variable, but it does make the random number calculation a little easier to read.

By creating two variables (h & w), we are recording the height and width of textObj. This can then be used in creating a simple formula to keep our text on the screen!

Now textObj.x property is limited to generating a number between half the width of the text object and the content width minus half the width of the text object. Similarly, the textObj.y property is limited to a number between half the height of the text object and the content height minus half the height of the text object plus 100 pixels (to keep it above the button).

Tip: if you have tried to copy and paste from the book into an editor and had strange errors, try retyping the line of code. Sometimes the word processor adds invisible characters. Also, check the quotation marks. Smart quotes will not work, they must be straight quotes.

Keeping Track

Often times in programming and app development it is necessary to keep track of something such as how many times an operation has been performed (such as how many times was the button tapped). In the case of moving a text object down the screen, we added a value to the text object's last location. When we want to count something we use a process called incrementing. Incrementing is adding 1 to the previous value. In Lua programming, it would look like:

```
local number = 0
number = number +1
```

In this example we have created a variable called number and initialized it to the value of 0. It is always a good idea to initialize your variables to their starting value. If you initialize a variable but don't assign a value, it will have the current value of nil. If you then try to do a mathematical operation to the variable you will get an error or might have unplanned results.

After we initialize the variable, we can then begin to count operations by increasing the value of the variable. By using *number = number + 1* we are telling Solar2D that we want to take the original value of number and add 1 to it, storing the new value in the number variable.

How Solar2D reads the main.lua file

Now that you have been introduced to functions, you might be wondering how Solar2D processes the main.lua file. Solar2D processes your file from top to bottom, one time. Solar2D will continue to listen for any event that you have included, so the app will continue to function until it is shut down.

This is why you will usually load any variables and outside files (we will get to that soon) at the beginning of the file, then your functions, and finally, make any needed function calls and add event listeners.

API Documentation

The API (Application Programming Interface) is the list of all commands that are available in a programming environment. The API is your primary reference tool when you are making apps. Experienced programmers can write software in a new program with just the API information. Solar2D's API is broken into three sections: Libraries, Events, and Types, and can be found at: http://docs.coronalabs.com/api/.

The Libraries contain a complete list of built-in Solar2D functions such as display.newText. Here you will find the details for the function: Syntax, an overview of what the function does,

41

parameters that are optional or required, and example code for how the function might be implemented.

The Events column contains all of the different types of events that can be tracked within Solar2D, as well as their associated properties. Events, like Libraries and Types, are broken into different categories to make finding the proper event easier.

The final column, Types, shows the different data types in Solar2D, which includes various objects that are produced by different Library functions. Types include properties and methods when appropriate, as well as an overview and sample code.

Summary

In chapter two we have added to our knowledge base the ability to load graphics, move them around the screen, and turn them into buttons. We learned how to generate a random number, return the width and height of an object, and implement an event listener. Also thrown in, just to move things along was an introduction to commenting, functions, and the API.

Programming Vocabulary

API
Concatenate
Function
Parameter
Syntax

Questions:

1. Explain the difference between a local variable and a global variable. How do you tell them apart?
2. List and explain the two different types of comments you can make in Solar2D.

3. True or false: You should always start a new project for each app you create.
4. What is a function? Give an example of a function.
5. What is an event listener, and how is it important to app development?
6. Which image file format should be used since it is accepted by both Android and Apple?
7. What is a button?
8. True or false: The Solar2D SDK is case-sensitive.
9. What is the purpose of Relaunch in Solar2D simulator?
10. How does Solar2D process the main.lua file?

Assignments

1. Create an application with two buttons; one red and one green. Tapping on the red button places the word "Red" at a random location on the screen. Tapping the green button places the word "Green" randomly on the screen.

2. Create an application that keeps track of how many times the button is tapped and displays a running total on the screen (hint, it is like moving a textObj down the screen).

3. Create 10 number buttons (0 through 9) similar to what you would find on an inexpensive calculator. Write an app that, when a number button is tapped, the corresponding number appears near the top of the screen. The output font should be fairly large. Make the number buttons small enough that another row of buttons can be placed along the right.

4. Create an application that moves a text object down the screen by 50 pixels every time a button is tapped.

Chapter 3 Animation and Orientation

Learning Objectives

In chapter 3 we are going to begin working with animation and handling when the user changes the orientation of their mobile device. To do this we will learn:

- Methods of animation
- How to program a decision
- How to program a loop
- Fading objects in and out
- Handling orientation change

Animation

Animation is the process of moving objects on the screen over a period of time. While there are several ways to create animation effects on mobile devices, in this chapter we are going to look at the most direct method and save a second method for chapter 5. Before we jump into animation, we first need to go over two of the primary building blocks of all programming languages: Decisions and Loops.

Boolean Expression

Decisions and loops are both based upon the answer from a **Boolean expression**. Based on the result generated by the Boolean expression, the program can handle a variety of issues based on a change in the situation. These decisions are just like they sound: you program into your app the ability to make a 'decision' based upon information that is supplied. Unfortunately, computers are not as smart as the movies and television make them out to be. Our mobile device can only make a decision based on information that is either True or False. This is known as a Boolean expression: there are only two possible answers, but that answer can be displayed as True or False, Yes or No, 0 or 1. We can get very complex with Boolean expressions using AND, OR, and NOT in a variety of combinations (which we will discuss later), but at the core, all Boolean expressions must be answerable as true or false.

Boolean expressions usually compare one variable to another. To do the comparison, we use the symbols:

==   - two equal signs to check for equality (two equal signs are used to show that it is a comparison and not assigning a value).
>   - greater than to check that one variable is greater than another.
<   - less than to check that one variable is less than another.
>=   - greater than or equal to checks for one variable being greater or equal to another.
<=   - less than or equal to checks for one variable being less than or equal to the second variable.
~=   - not equal to checks that the variables are not equal (i.e. it is true that they are not equal).

Boolean Practice

Answer the problems below. All problems result in either True or False.

Assume that A = 1, B = 4, C = 5. (Answers are supplied at the end of the chapter)

1. A == B
2. B > C
3. B < C
4. A <= B
5. C == A
6. A+B == C
7. C-A ==B

8. C+A <= B
9. B ~= C
10. B <= C+A

How to Code Decision Statements

if-then

The most basic decision statement is an if-then. The if-then command syntax is:

if *Boolean expression* **then**
    one or more statements/commands
end

The if-then statement is used in all programming languages, though the syntax may vary. In Lua, the decision statement is kept simple, which is to our benefit. An example of an if-then might look like:

```
if (subtotal > 100) then
    discount = 0.1
end
```

In this example, we check to see if the value of the variable subtotal is greater than 100. If it is, then we set a discount rate equal to .1.

TIP: Did you notice that the discount = 0.1 line was spaced over from the left column? This indentation is done for the readability of our programs. If you space over each time you begin a block of code that is under the control of another program segment, it will make your program MUCH easier to read. This is one of those little tips that will win you big points with your future self!

if-then-else

With the addition of an else situation, we can pass additional commands to the computer:

if *Boolean expression* **then**
    one or more statements/commands
else
    one or more statements/commands
end

The addition of else tells our program what to do when the Boolean expression is false. An example of an if-then-else would be:

```
if (subtotal > 100) then
    discount = 0.1
else
    discount = 0
end
```

if-then-elseif

But what if we need to check for a different situation in case the first situation wasn't met? We have two choices, we can nest an if-then inside another if-then or we can use the if-then-elseif:

if *Boolean expression* **then**
    one or more statements/commands
elseif *Boolean expression* **then**
    one or more statements/commands
end

With the if-then-elseif, the second Boolean expression is only evaluated in the event that the first Boolean expression was false. Example:

```
if (subtotal > 200) then
    discount = 0.2
elseif (subtotal > 100) then
    discount = 0.1
end
```

In this case, the discount will only be set to .1 if the subtotal is greater than 100 but less than 200. And yes, it is possible to have multiple elseif statements.

if-then-elseif-else

The final decision statement includes the else catch after the elseif. With this statement, we can test for multiple situations and still provide a final set of commands if none of the conditions are met.

if *Boolean expression* **then**
    one or more statements/commands
elseif *Boolean expression* **then**
    one or more statements/commands
else
    one or more statements/commands
end

Example:

```
if (subtotal > 500) then
    discount = 0.25
elseif (subtotal > 200) then
    discount = 0.2
elseif (subtotal > 100) then
    discount = 0.1
```

```
else
   discount = 0
end
```

Nested if-then

Sometimes we run into the situation where it is necessary to place an if-then within another if-then. This is referred to as a nested if-then. Only if the first condition is true will the second if-then be tested:

if *Boolean expression* **then**

   if *Boolean expression* **then**

      one or more statements/commands

   end

end

Example

```
if (subtotal > 500) then
   discount = 0.25   -- 25% discount if sales over $500

   if (customerID == "employee") then
      discount = 0.35 -- 35% discount if sales > $500 and an
employee
   end

end
```

There is a lot more that we can do with if-then statements, but we will save it for a later chapter.

Loops

Loops are also commonly used to control the flow of your program. Often times we will have the need to do a set of commands multiple times or until some condition is met. Loops provide the means to accomplish these repetitive tasks. There are three ways to create a loop: while-do, repeat-until, and for-next. We will examine for-next first, as it is the simplest to understand.

for-next

The for-next loop is used when we want to execute a block of code a known number of times.

for *name = start number, end number* [, *step*] **do**
   block
end

name - When starting a for-next loop, the first required item is a temporary variable *name* to store the number the loop is on. This can be any variable name, but should not be a variable that you are using elsewhere in your program.

Start number – any number or variable that holds a numeric value.

End number - any number or variable that holds a numeric value.

Step - (Optional) The increment for counting. Example: -1 to count down, 2 to count by evens or odds, 10 to count by 10, etc.

Examples:

```
for count1 = 1, 5 do  -- Count from 1 to 5
    print (count1)    --Output: 1, 2, 3, 4, 5
end
```

```
for count = 0, 10, 2 do  -- Count 0 to 10 by 2's
```

```
    print (count)    --Output: 0, 2, 4, 6, 8, 10
end
```

```
for counter = 10, 1, -1 do   --Count down 10 to 1, print result in
terminal
    print (counter)   --Output: 10, 9, 8, 7, 6, 5, 4, 3, 2, 1
end
```

while-do

The while-do loop repeats a block of code until a Boolean expression is no longer true. If the condition is false on the first loop of the while-do, then the block of code within the loop will never be run.

while *Boolean expression* **do**

  block

end

Example

```
count = 0
while (count < 10 ) do
    print (count)
    count = count + 1
end
```

repeat-until

The repeat-until loop repeats a block of code until a condition becomes true. The repeat-until will always run the block of code at least once since the Boolean expression evaluation comes at the end of the loop.

repeat

   block

until Boolean *expression*

Example:

```
count = 0
repeat
    print (count)
    count = count + 1
until (count > 5)
```

Tip: If you need to keep track of how many loops have happened in a while-do or repeat-until, you can add the variable to the block of code that adds 1 each time the block repeats: e.g. counter = counter + 1

Nested Loops

When you place one type of loop inside another loop, it is called a nested loop. When a nested loop executes, every time the outside (or first) loop does one loop, the inside loop will loop until it completes its required loops.

Example:

```
for outsideloop = 1, 3 do  -- outside loop
    print (outsideloop)

    for insideloop = 4, 1, -1 do   -- inside loop
        print (insideloop)
    end
```

```
end
```

Output: 1, 4, 3, 2, 1, 2, 4, 3, 2, 1, 3, 4, 3, 2, 1

Infinite Loops

An infinite loop is usually created by accident. It is the situation when the condition that will stop the loop is never met:

```
count = 0
while (count < 10) do
    counter = counter + 1
end
```

As you can see from the example above, count will never increase in value, as the variable being changed is counter. Situations like this will cause your app to lock up and potentially crash.

To avoid infinite loops, always double-check that at some point the condition that will end the loop will occur.

Math API

We need to be familiar with one more concept before we start our next program: using the math API. Solar2D provides us with shortcuts so that we are not required to write program code for different mathematical calculations. All of the math API begin with the word 'math' followed by a period, then the function. For example, if you wanted to use Pi in your application, you would only need:

```
local pi = math.pi
```

and the constant 3.1415926535898 would be assigned to your variable.

We will discuss the Math API further in the next chapter. For your next project, we are going to be using the math.random function, which returns a random number. The math.random function has three possible uses:

1. If you do not pass it a value, math.random() will return a number between 0 and 1.
2. If you pass it one number, math.random(x) will return a whole number between 1 and x.
3. If you pass two numbers, math.random(x, y) will return a whole number between x and y.

Project 3.0: Basic Animation

In this project we are going to use a loop to move a square graphic toward the center of the mobile screen. For this example, you will need to create two graphics, a small square (50 x 50 pixels), and just to make it more visually interesting, a graduated white spot that we will place in the center of the screen.

Both of the graphics should be in the PNG format which will give us compatibility between all of the various devices supported by Solar2D SDK.

Create a new project and copy your PNG images into the folder.

To begin, we will load the graduated white dot and then the square into your app. Place the graduated white dot in the center of your display:

```
--Load images into memory and store them in local variables
local center = display.newImage("Ch3Center.png")
local square = display.newImage("Ch3Square.png")

-- Place the center graphic in the middle of the display
center.x = display.contentWidth/2
center.y = display.contentHeight/2
```

To place the square at a random location on the screen, we will use the math.random function, passing it the display width and height for the x and y coordinates. Remember that this will generate a number between 1 and the display width and height.

```
-- Place the square at a random location on the screen
square.x= math.random(display.contentWidth)
square.y= math.random(display.contentHeight)
```

Now for the fun part. We are going to move the square toward the image with a while loop and a couple of if-then statements.   The while loop includes the keyword OR. There are three keywords that can be included in a Boolean expression: AND, OR, and NOT. For now, we will focus on OR and AND.

Including OR in our Boolean expression means that if either condition that we are looking at is true, then the whole expression should be considered true. Using AND means that both Boolean expressions must be true for the expression to be true.

Consider it like this: If someone says "If it rains or snows tomorrow, we will go to the mall." You know that if it rains or snows, you are going to the mall.
However, if someone says "If it rains and snows tomorrow, we will go to the mall." You know that it must both rain and snow before

56

the shopping excursion will occur. It is the same in our if-then, while-do, and repeat-until programming.

```
while (square.x ~= center.x or square.y ~= center.y) do
   if (square.x > center.x) then
      square.x = square.x -1
   elseif (square.x < center.x)then
      square.x = square.x +1
   end

   if (square.y > center.y) then
      square.y = square.y -1
   elseif (square.y < center.y)then
      square.y = square.y +1
   end

end
```

With this while loop, we are telling the program that as long as the x and y of the center of the square are not equal to the x and y of the center graphic, keep doing the two if-then statements. The if-then statements check to see which direction to move the square so that it will always move toward the center.

Save your main.lua and give it a try.

Wow, that was fast! It didn't really animate, did it? Solar2D moved the square object so quickly that we didn't even see the movement.

Let's try a different approach. The problem is that Solar2D will move the square as fast as the processor can process the movement. On an older, slow smartphone, it would still be far too fast.

Fortunately, there are other options that will give us the ability to move the square smoothly from its starting location to its new location in the center of the screen. If you are familiar with Adobe Flash/Animate or other animation software, then you have probably used tweening. In Solar2D, we can create similar transitions using the transition.to command. The transition.to API is:

transition.to(object, {array})

The object is the object we want to move (our square). Within the array of the transition.to, we can pass the parameters we would like to change and how quickly we want that transition to occur.

My new movement code (replacing the old while loop) looks like:

```
transition.to( square, { time=2000, x = center.x, y = center.y } )
```

In this one line of code, I have first passed the variable called square as the object to be transitioned. In the array, I'm passing it a time parameter that is set to 2000 milliseconds (or 2 seconds), and then the x and y variables with the location that I want to move the square.

```
--Load images into memory and store them in local variables
local center = display.newImage("Ch3Center.png")
local square = display.newImage("Ch3Square.png")

-- Place the center graphic in the middle of the display
center.x = display.contentWidth/2
center.y = display.contentHeight/2

-- Place the square at a random location on the screen
square.x= math.random(display.contentWidth)
square.y= math.random(display.contentHeight)

transition.to( square, { time=2000, x = center.x, y = center.y } )
```

Want to see a neat feature of Solar2D SDK? Hold down the CTRL – R (Windows) or Command – R (Macintosh) after you run the app the first time. This will re-launch the app without you having to reload it each time. It will allow you to see the random element for placing the square on the screen.

Alpha
Now You See It, Now You Don't

Being able to hide objects on the screen until they are needed is an easy way to simplify the User Interface (UI) in your apps. In Solar2D, the easiest way to hide an object until needed is with the alpha property. Alpha is also commonly used in game environments to cause objects to not be visible or only partially visible. At 0, an object is invisible or hidden; at 1 (or 100%) an object is fully visible. You can also set the alpha at any decimal between 0 and 1 to partially fade in or out the object.

Project 3.1: Alpha Fun

For this project we are going to load three buttons: Hide, Fade, and Show. Each of these buttons will adjust the square used in the previous project by changing the alpha value in a function.

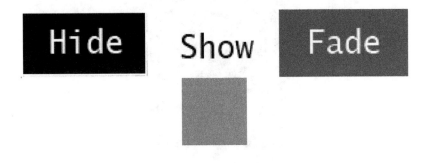

To begin with, we will need to load and place the square and each of the buttons somewhere on the display. For simplicity, I have placed them all in the center of the device.

```
--Load square and locate it toward the top-middle of the device.
local square = display.newImage("Ch3Square.png")
square.x = display.contentWidth/2
square.y = 50

--Load the buttons and place it bottom center of the device.
local hideButton = display.newImage("Ch3HideButton.png")
hideButton.x = display.contentWidth/2
hideButton.y = display.contentHeight - 300
local showButton = display.newImage("Ch3ShowButton.png")
showButton.x = display.contentWidth/2
showButton.y = display.contentHeight - 200
local fadeButton = display.newImage("Ch3FadeButton.png")
fadeButton.x = display.contentWidth/2
fadeButton.y = display.contentHeight - 100
```

Now we will need to set up the function for each button. The first two, hideButton:tap and showButton:tap will set the alpha of the square object to either 0 or 1 (hide or show).

The third function, fade, will need to use the transition.to command to fade the square over 3 seconds.

```
function hideButton:tap(event)
    square.alpha = 0
end

function showButton:tap(event)
    square.alpha = 1
end

function fadeButton:tap(event)
    transition.to(square, {time=3000, alpha=0})
end
```

And finally, after our functions, we will need the three event listeners, one for each button:

```
hideButton:addEventListener("tap", hideButton)
showButton:addEventListener("tap", showButton)
fadeButton:addEventListener("tap", fadeButton)
```

Save your main.lua file and give it a try.

It works pretty well, except the fade button only fades out. It doesn't fade in. Let's adjust the function fadeButton:tap so that it will fade the button in if it is currently faded out.

This can easily be accomplished by adding an if-then statement to check for the current alpha state of the square:

```
function fadeButton:tap(event)
```

```
  if square.alpha == 1 then
     transition.to(square, {time=3000, alpha=0})
  else
     transition.to(square, {time=3000, alpha=1})
  end
end
```

And there we have it! You can now fade in or out an object.
Remember, the alpha property is available for all objects, so
anything can be hidden until it is needed.

Orientation change

Device orientation is a very important issue to mobile app stores.
They (the users and the reviewers/approval department at Apple,
Amazon, Google, and any other app store you submit your app)
expect your app to work correctly in left landscape, right
landscape, and portrait view if it is a phone. On tablets, your app
should work in any orientation, including upside down, if
appropriate.

That isn't to say that you can't limit your app to just landscape or
portrait, but there should be a reason why it only works in that
orientation. Most games and apps have little problem being
approved with having just one or two orientations if it is
appropriate to the app.

There are two issues with orientation change. The first is
detecting that the orientation of the device has changed. The
second is changing the layout of your application for the new
orientation.

As far as simulating the orientation change, it can easily be
accomplished with the Solar2D Simulator. Through the Hardware
Menu, select Rotate Left or Rotate Right.

```
```

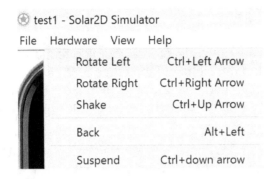

test1 - Solar2D Simulator

File   Hardware   View   Help

Rotate Left	Ctrl+Left Arrow
Rotate Right	Ctrl+Right Arrow
Shake	Ctrl+Up Arrow
Back	Alt+Left
Suspend	Ctrl+down arrow

Please recognize that this is for general rotation. Seldom will this be sufficient to handle all rotation needs of your app. You will usually need to code in the screen size and where you want the object to be located in the new orientation.

If possible, your app should support every orientation based on the device it is going to be deployed. Phones should never support upside-down orientation as it may cause confusion should the phone need to be answered.

Supported Orientations Based Upon Device

	Phones	Tablets
Portrait	√	√
Portrait – Upside-down		√
Landscape-Left	√	√
Landscape-Right	√	√

Project 3.2: A New Orientation

For this project, we are going to create two text objects, one that reads Portrait, the other Landscape. Each only shows in the appropriate orientation. We will remove the incorrect text object by setting its alpha to 0, and change the appropriate object's alpha to 1.

Create a new project.

To get started with our code, create your two text objects; set their color to white and the alpha of landscape to 0 (so that it doesn't show on the screen yet) and portrait's alpha to 1 (yes, we are going to assume that the app starts in the portrait orientation).

```
local portrait = display.newText("Portrait", display.contentWidth/2,
display.contentHeight/2, native.systemFont, 24)

local landscape = display.newText("Landscape",
display.contentWidth/2, display.contentHeight/2,
native.systemFont, 24)

portrait:setFillColor(1, 1, 1)
portrait.alpha = 1
landscape:setFillColor(1, 1, 1)
landscape.alpha = 0
```

If you run the app right now, just 'Portrait' will show. Next, we need to create a function that will fire on an orientation change event and pass the new orientation to the program:

```
local function onOrientationChange (event)

   if (event.type =='landscapeRight' or event.type ==
'landscapeLeft' ) then
      portrait.alpha = 0
      landscape.alpha = 1
   else
      portrait.alpha = 1
      landscape.alpha = 0
         end

end
```

In this case, event is a parameter passed into the function from the event listener (which we will add in a few moments). event.type for an orientation change can pass:

· "portrait"
· "landscapeLeft"
· "portraitUpsideDown"
· "landscapeRight"
· "faceUp"
· "faceDown"

In our function, we are checking for the "landscapeLeft" and "landscapeRight", which simplifies our if-then statement considerably. Of course, it wouldn't be much work to change the if-then statement so that it looks for each of the possible orientation changes.

Finally, we need to add the event listener for the orientation change:

```
Runtime:addEventListener( "orientation", onOrientationChange )
```

Note that **Orientation change is a system event.** So our event listener is using the keyword "Runtime" to tell Solar2D to check for the system event orientation.   We will discuss other types of system events in later chapters.

If you save and run the app right now, you will see that it does work, but maybe not the way that we would like.

To handle the rotation of the text object, we will need to add a few more lines of code to our function. There is a second property to the event object that will help us handle the rotation of any object. event.delta returns the difference between the start and finish angles of the device, allowing the rotation to be handled very easily:

```
local newAngle = landscape.rotation − event.delta

transition.to( landscape, {time= 150, rotation = newAngle})
```

Of course, rotation can be used as a property of any object at any time; we are introducing it here to make adjusting for device orientation easier. There is a rotate method and a rotation property. The rotation property is used to get or set the rotation of the object. The rotate method adds the specified degrees to the current rotation of the object.

The final code onOrientationChange function should now look like:

```
local function onOrientationChange (event)

    if (event.type =='landscapeRight' or event.type ==
```

```
'landscapeLeft' ) then
     local newAngle = landscape.rotation – event.delta
     transition.to( landscape, {time= 150, rotation = newAngle})
     portrait.alpha = 0
     landscape.alpha = 1
   else
     local newAngle = portrait.rotation – event.delta
     transition.to( portrait, {time= 150, rotation = newAngle})
     portrait.alpha = 1
     landscape.alpha = 0
   end

end
```

Save and run.

Hmm, not quite what we want yet, is it? The problem is that since
we are looking at two objects, the change in the event.delta is only
updating for the last rotation. There are several ways this could
be corrected. We can keep track of how many orientation
changes have occurred and pass that to our rotation. We could
use just one text object, changing the text on each rotation. Or we
could rotate both objects each time, so that they are both always
in sync. In practice, the last option is easiest for this project:

```
local function onOrientationChange (event)
   if (event.type =="landscapeRight" or event.type ==
"landscapeLeft") then
     local newAngle = landscape.rotation - event.delta
     transition.to( landscape, {time= 150, rotation = newAngle})
     transition.to( portrait, {rotation = newAngle})
     portrait.alpha = 0
     landscape.alpha = 1
   else
     local newAngle = portrait.rotation - event.delta
     transition.to( portrait, {time= 150, rotation = newAngle})
     transition.to( landscape, {rotation = newAngle})
```

```
      portrait.alpha = 1
      landscape.alpha = 0
   end
end
```

And there we have a functional app that will detect orientation change!

Here is the full program just in case you missed something:

```
--Declare two text objects, set one to white and make one not
visible
local portrait = display.newText("Portrait", display.contentWidth/2,
display.contentHeight/2, native.systemFont, 24)

local landscape = display.newText("Landscape",
display.contentWidth/2, display.contentHeight/2,
native.systemFont, 24)

portrait:setFillColor(1, 1, 1)
portrait.alpha = 1

landscape:setFillColor(1, 1, 1)
landscape.alpha = 0

local function onOrientationChange (event)
```

```
    if (event.type =="landscapeRight" or event.type ==
"landscapeLeft") then
        local newAngle = landscape.rotation - event.delta
        transition.to( landscape, {time= 150, rotation = newAngle})
        transition.to( portrait, {rotation = newAngle})
        portrait.alpha = 0
        landscape.alpha = 1
    else
        local newAngle = portrait.rotation - event.delta
        transition.to( portrait, {time= 150, rotation = newAngle})
        transition.to( landscape, {rotation = newAngle})
        portrait.alpha = 1
        landscape.alpha = 0
    end

end

Runtime:addEventListener( "orientation", onOrientationChange )
```

Summary

In chapter 3, we learned about Boolean expressions, loops, and decisions, examined how to do animation with a loop and the better way of using 'transition.to'. Then we looked at using the alpha to hide or fade objects on the screen. Finally, we examined how to detect a device orientation change and used the rotation property to change the rotation of an object.

Programming Vocabulary

Boolean Expression
Decision Statement
Loop
Syntax

Questions

1. What app orientations are allowed for a smartphone? For a tablet?
2. What does alpha control?
3. What are three types of loops?
4. How would you make an object look faded?
5. Define Boolean expression.
6. What type of event is an orientation change?
7. Define an infinite loop.
8. Given that you need to sum the numbers 1 through 100, write a loop to complete the operation.
9. List two of the operations that can be accomplished with transition.to.
10. What is the difference between using 'else' and 'elseif' when using an if...then statement.

Assignments

1. Using a function, modify the project 3.1 Alpha Fun, so that the square is randomly repositioned to a new location and moves toward the center on each relaunch of the app.

2. Adjust project 3.2 to use only one text object instead of two, making the appropriate changes to the function.

3. Load 3 different buttons with different colors. Using alpha and orientation change reorganize the buttons when the simulator's orientation is changed by setting the alpha of each button to zero, then use a transition.to to move the button to its new location, fading it in as it moves.

Boolean Practice Answers

Below are the answers to the Boolean Practice

1. False
2. False
3. True
4. True
5. False
6. True
7. True
8. False
9. True
10. True

Chapter 4 Working with Data

Learning Objectives
In chapter 4 we will begin working with various types of data:

- How to enter data using textfield and textbox
- Using the String API
- Using the Math API

Most apps work with data. Sometimes the user enters the data through their simulated keyboard, other times it is through a picker wheel or drop-down lists. In this chapter, we will focus on working with textfields and textboxes.

TextField and TextBox
A TextField and TextBox are a part of the native user interface for Apple iOS and Android devices. What does this mean? The TextField and TextBox are all a part of the individual operating systems of the different mobile devices and not a part of the OpenGL canvas that Solar2D uses.

Okay, and what does THAT mean?
The TextField and Textbox are handled very differently by Apple and Android. They are 'native' tools. Everything else that we do in a mobile app is moving graphics around on the screen. But TextFields and TextBoxes receive user input from the built-in keyboard. That means they are different. They are referred to as 'native' to the user interface. Since they are native, they have a few different rules that we have to consider when using them.

Now, let's look at the difference between a TextField and a TextBox. The TextField is used for a single line of text input. As it is not part of the OpenGL canvas, it does not play well with Solar2D's display object hierarchy. What does that mean for you as a developer? Basically, while you can change a TextField's location, it will always appear above (or in front of) all other objects on the screen.

The rules are the same for a TextBox. A TextBox is used for multiple lines of text input. It will always appear above (or in front of) all other objects on the screen.

The mistake that I see many students make initially when making a TextField or TextBox is that they do not make it large enough and it cuts off the text that is entered by the user.

The API for creating a TextField is:

native.newTextField(*left, top, length, height [, handler function]*)

For creating a TextBox, the API is:

native.newTextBox(*left, top, length, height [, handler function]*)

You also have control as to the type of keyboard that will be called when the user begins to enter data:

- "default" - the default keyboard of general text, numbers, and punctuation
- "number" – a numeric keyboard
- "phone" – a keypad layout for phone numbers
- "url"   - a keyboard for entering website URLs
- "email" - a keyboard for entering email addresses

The String API

In this next project we will be working a great deal with strings. Strings are created using a matching set of single or double quotes. Anything that is typed into a TextField or TextBox is considered a string, even if it is a number. Fortunately, we have a lot of great tools that make working with strings easy.

The string API includes:

- string.byte() – returns the string ASCII code for the string character specified.
- string.char() – returns the character for the given ASCII code.
- string.find() – returns the start and end locations for a matched string within a string.
- string.format() – returns a formatted string based on the supplied arguments.
- string.gmatch() – when used in a loop, returns the next pattern match from the string.
- string.gsub() – searches and replaces all occurrences of the supplied pattern within a string.
- string.len() – returns the length of the supplied string.
- string.lower() – changes uppercase characters into lowercase characters.
- string.match() – returns a substring matching a supplied pattern.
- string.rep() – returns a string that includes *n* concatenated copies of the original string.
- string.reverse() – returns the reverse of the supplied string.
- string.sub() – returns a substring based upon character location.
- string.upper() – changes lowercase characters into uppercase characters.

If you want to make two strings into one string, you are performing what is referred to as concatenation. Concatenation is accomplished by using two dots '..' between the objects to be concatenated.

For example, if I want to concatenate the words "My" and "house" into a single string, I would use the code:

```
local newString = "My" .. "house"
```

The only problem is that if I display that as text or print it to the terminal window, I get

Myhouse

No space. If you want spaces included, you have to add them yourself.

Concatenation also works with variables or a mixture of variables and strings. Thus, if I wanted to create a string, I could:

```
local string1 = "My"
local string2 = "house"
local newString = string1 .. " ".. string2
```

would result in the string "My House"

The Math API

You might be wondering that since we discussed the string API, what about the math API? The math API is extensive and we already used one of its components in the last chapter when we generated a random number to move the text on the screen. Here is a full list of the available APIs in math. Each starts with the keyword math. In all examples x and y are a number:

- math.abs(x) – returns the absolute value of x.

- math.acos(x) – returns the arc cosine of x in radians (a number between 0 and pi). x must be between -1 and 1.
- math.asin(x) - returns the arc sine of x in radians (a number between $-pi/2$ and $pi/2$). x must be between -1 and 1.
- math.atan(x) - returns the arc tangent of x in radians (a number between $-pi/2$ and $pi/2$).
- math.atan2(y, x) - returns the arc tangent of y/x (in radians). Useful when converting rectangular coordinates to polar coordinates.
- math.ceil(x) – returns the smallest integer larger than or equal to x.
- math.cos(x) – returns the cosine of x in the range of -1 to 1.
- math.cosh(x) – returns the hyperbolic cosine of x.
- math.deg(x) – converts a radian value (x) to degrees.
- math.exp(x) – returns the value of e^x.
- math.floor(x) – returns the largest integer smaller than or equal to x.
- math.fmod(x, y) – returns the remainder of dividing x by y, rounding the quotient towards zero.
- math.frexp(x) – returns the split of x into a normalized fraction and an exponent.
- math.huge - returns a value larger than or equal to any other numerical value (basically an infinite number, but computers don't handle infinite very well, so a really, really big number).
- math.inf - same as math.huge, returns a value larger than or equal to any other numerical value.
- math.ldexp(m, e) – returns m* 2^e.
- math.log(x) – returns the natural logarithm of x.
- math.log10(x) – returns the base-10 logarithm of x.
- math.max(x, ...) – returns the largest value from the supplied arguments.

- <u>math.min(x, ...)</u> – returns the smallest value from the supplied arguments.
- <u>math.modf(x)</u> – returns the integer part of x and the fractional part of x.
- <u>math.pi</u> – returns pi.
- <u>math.pow(x, y)</u> – returns x^y.
- <u>math.rad(x)</u> – converts radians to an angle in degrees.
- <u>math.random([x][, y])</u> – returns a pseudo-random number. If x is not provided, then a number between 0 and 1 is generated. If x is provided, then a number between 1 and x. If x and y are provided, then a number between x and y is generated.
- <u>math.randomseed(x)</u> – sets x as the seed number for the pseudo-random number generator. If the same x is always used, the sequence of random numbers will be the same.
- <u>math.round(x)</u> – returns the x rounded to the nearest integer.
- <u>math.sin(x)</u> - returns the sine of x in the range of -1 to 1.
- <u>math.sinh(x)</u> - returns the hyperbolic sine of x.
- <u>math.sqrt(x)</u> – returns the square root of x.
- <u>math.tan(x)</u> - returns the tangent of x.
- <u>math.tanh(x)</u> – returns the hyperbolic tangent of x.

One last thing before we start our project. We need to set up our app so that if the user taps outside of TextFields, the keyboard will be dismissed. To handle this operation, I am going to use a background image that is 2360-by-1640. By using this size, I know that we will handle everything on my test device, an iPad Air 2022.

Project 4.0: What's Your Age?
For this project, we are going to build a fun little app that will ask for the user's name and birth date. Then we will do a few fun things to their name and compute how old they are in minutes and seconds. You will need two graphics for this project: the

background image previously mentioned and a "Submit" button to start the calculations for age. I am targeting this for newer devices such as the iPad Air.

To get started, create a new project and copy the background image and a submit button in the folder, The first code we will add to our main.lua app is set up the variables to make our future calculations easier.

main.lua

```
local daysInYear = 365.2425  -- # days based on gregorian cal
local weeksInYear = daysInYear / 7
local daysInMonth = daysInYear / 12  --average # days a month
```

```
local weeksInMonth = daysInMonth / 7 -- # of weeks in a month
local secInMin = 60    -- # of seconds in a minute
local secInHour = 60 * secInMin   -- # of seconds in a hour
local secInDay = 24 * secInHour   -- # of seconds in a day
local secInWeek = 7 * secInDay    -- # of seconds in a week
local secInMonth = daysInMonth *secInDay  -- ave # of
sec/month
local secInYear = daysInYear *secInDay   --# seconds in a year
local todaysDate = os.date("*t")

--print (todaysDate.year, todaysDate.month, todaysDate.day)
```

Notice the last two lines of the code above. os.date is part of the API and returns the today's date (or whatever date the phone is set to). Using the "*t" parameter tells os.date to return the current date and time as numbers: 2013, 02, 14, 12, 00, 00 would be the year 2013, second month, 14th day, 12th hour, 00 minutes, 00 seconds. You can see in the print statement that is commented out how to retrieve the specific information.

Next, we will load the background and store it as the variable background. By loading as the first object, we are making sure it is 'behind' everything else that is loaded onto the screen. After loading the background, we will load the submit button.

```
-- load background to be used for dismissing keyboard
local background = display.newImage("bkgrd.png", 0, 0)
local submit = display.newImage("submit.png")
submit.x = display.contentWidth/2
submit.y = display.contentHeight-100
```

Now we will display instructions to the user and add the TextFields.

```
-- Get the user's name and birthdate
local nameInstructions = display.newText("Enter your name", 10,
50, native.systemFont, 24 )

local usersName = native.newTextField(10, 100, 350, 50)
usersName.inputType = "default"

local bdayInstructions = display.newText("Enter your birthdate
(mm/dd/yyyy)", 10, 160, native.systemFont, 24)

local bday = native.newTextField(10, 200, 350, 50)
bday.inputType = "default"
```

We must declare the type of keyboard that will be shown for each
TextField. The next step is to set up the keyboard dismissal. This
is accomplished by setting a tap event for the background that will
call the function keyboardListener. The keyboardListener function
removes the use of the keyboard by setting its focus to nil.

```
local function keyboardListener (event)
        native.setKeyboardFocus(nil)
end

background:addEventListener("tap", keyboardListener)
submit:addEventListener("tap", calculateAge)
```

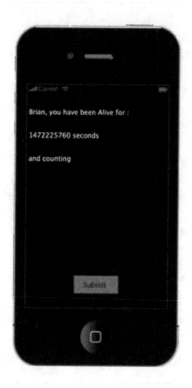

Now we are ready to add the function that will be called by our submit button. The calculateAge function is going to make heavy use of some of the String API functions that we have previously reviewed. I am adding this function **above** the background:addEventListener line and **below** keyboardListener function's end statement.

The first step in our function is to remove from the bday variable the year, month, and day of the user's birthday. At this time, we are going to assume that the information was entered in the correct form. To get the birth year, we will use two string functions: string.len and string.sub. It is possible to do it with just string.sub, but then we would miss out on all the fun of using both! String.len will return the length or number of characters contained in the birthday string. Notice that I am passing the parameter of bday.text. Anytime you are using a TextField or TextBox, you must use .text to work with what was stored in the variable.

```
local function calculateAge()
        -- Get the birth year, month, and day
        local bdayLen = string.len(bday.text)
```

Now that we have the number of characters that are stored, we can use .sub to extract a portion of the string. String.sub accepts a variable or string as the first parameter, the first letter position we want to extract as the second parameter, and the last letter position to be extracted as the final parameter.

```
local birthYear = string.sub(bday.text, bdayLen-3, bdayLen)
local birthMonth = string.sub(bday.text, 1,2)
local birthDay = string.sub(bday.text, 4, 5)
- print(birthYear, birthMonth, birthDay)
```

Next, I would like to clear the screen of the previous text and TextFields. To do this, I am going to use a method called removeSelf(). RemoveSelf does just like it sounds like it would do, it completely removes the object from the screen. Actually, it removes the object completely from memory. Poof! It no longer exists, nor can it be referenced again in the app! If I wanted the TextFields or text again, I would have to start from scratch and create them again.

```
bday:removeSelf()
usersName:removeSelf()
nameInstructions:removeSelf()
bdayInstructions:removeSelf()
```

Time to calculate some time! There are SO many ways that this could be done. I decided to go with a very straightforward approach. I calculated how many seconds since the date 1/1/1 for both the current date and the given birth date. After we have those two rather large numbers, we can subtract the birth date second count from today's date second count, giving us the approximate number of seconds the person has been alive (give or take a few hours).

```
        -- How many seconds from 1/1/1 to today
        local totalSecToday = (todaysDate.year * secInYear) +
(todaysDate.month * secInMonth) + (todaysDate.day * secInDay)

        --How many seconds from year 0 to birthdate
        local totalSecBday = (birthYear * secInYear) + (birthMonth
* secInMonth) + (birthDay * secInDay)

        local totalSecAlive = totalSecToday - totalSecBday

        local secAliveText = display.newText(usersName.text..",
you have been Alive for :", 10, 100, native.systemFont, 30)

        local secAlive = display.newText(totalSecAlive.." seconds",
10, 200, native.systemFont, 30)

        local secAliveText2 = display.newText("and counting", 10,
300, native.systemFont, 30)
end
```

Finally, we can use a few display.newText lines to show the user's name, and how long they have been alive.

Summary

Once again we have covered a great deal of material very quickly! I recommend that you spend a little time with the string and math API functions. They are very powerful and when combined with loops and if-then, you can do a lot of very powerful calculations!

Programming Vocabulary
Concatenation
Strings

Questions
1. Define concatenation.
2. Using the math API, how can you find the value of PI?
3. What is the difference between a textfield and a textbox?
4. Which keyboard should be used to enter a phone number? for a URL?
5. How can the keyboard be dismissed?
6. How do you concatenate two strings?
7. Name one of the required things you must have to deploy to an Apple device.
8. Which property contains what a user typed in a textfield?
9. To reverse a string, use which string API commands?
10. Can a textfield hide passwords entered into an app?

Assignments
1. Revise Project 4.0 to also show how many days and months the person has been alive.

2. Create an app that shows how long it will be until the user's next birthday.

3. Create an app that asks for the user's name then shows the user's name with the letters in reverse order.
4. Create an app that asks for the user's name and then displays the name down the side of the screen, one letter at a time.

5. Challenge: Using if-then statements, check to make sure that the user entered the birth date information correctly.

Chapter 5 Working with Graphics

Learning Objectives

One of the things that many people find appealing about Solar2D is how easy it is to create and load graphics into the mobile environment. In this chapter we are going to:

- Create vector-based graphics
- Load bitmap graphics
- An introduction to sprite sheets
- Review associated graphic properties
- Identify App Store Icon requirements
- Explore additional animation methods

We all know it is the driving force of why smart phones are popular; the ability to create interactive graphics. In this chapter, we are going to look at how to draw basic graphic shapes with vector graphics and how to work with bitmap graphics created in other software such as Photoshop or GIMP. We will also examine how to use sprite sheets in Solar2D and how to create animation frame by frame.

Vector Graphics

A vector graphic is a geometrical primitive (such as a line, curve, circle, or rectangle) that is based on a mathematical equation. Vector graphics are the smallest files and the fastest images to display (as far as drawing to the screen) and are able to be resized or scaled infinitely since the shape is based upon a math equation instead of a bitmap image comprised of pixels.

There are four basic vector graphic API commands:

- display.newCircle(xCenter, yCenter, radius) – creates a circle at xCenter, yCenter with the given radius.
- display.newLine(x1, y1, x2, y2) – draws a line from the first point to the second point. You can append line segments with the :append method.
- display.newRect(x, y, width, height) – creates a rectangle placing it at the location given for the center x, y. Width and height parameters are absolute pixel lengths (i.e. they set the height and width off of the top, left corner location)
- display.RoundedRect(left, top, width, height, cornerRadius) – like the newRect except with rounded corners. CornerRadius sets the quarter radius of each corner.

Vector-based objects, with the special exception of newLine, all have a default reference point at their respective center. They all have the following properties or methods that can be set:
- object.strokeWidth - Sets the width of the line in pixels
- object:setStrokeColor(r, g, b [,a]) - Sets the color of a line object based upon r, g, b (and optionally alpha) values between 0 and 1
- object:setFillColor(r, g, b[, a]) - Sets the fill color for vector objects based upon r, g, b (and optionally alpha) between 0 and 1
- display.setDefault(r, g, b) – Allows you to change the default color (white) to another fill color.

display.newLine has a property all it's own:
- object:append() - Appends one or more line segments to an existing display.newLine object

Now that you have seen the commands, let's put them into use.

Project 5.0: Vector Shapes
For our first graphics project, we are going to create each of the vector shapes, and then use the methods and objects available to

manipulate them in the display environment. To get started, create a new blank project and name it VectorShapes.

As you think about the coordinates on the mobile device, remember that the left, top corner is coordinate 0, 0. Anything above or to the left of the top left corner (i.e., off of the screen) would be a negative coordinate. By using negative coordinates or coordinates that are greater than the resolution of the device, we can slide items onto the screen from the sides. You can think of the drawing space on a mobile device as a flipped Cartesian coordinate system:

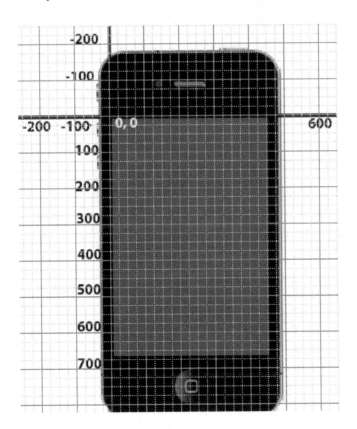

We will start by finding the center of the display and storing it in the variables w and h. Then we will create a star shape using a line segment and appending the additional lines to the initial segment. After we draw the star, we will set the stroke color to white and the stroke width to 3 pixels.

main.lua

```
-- Store the center of display for later use
local w = display.contentWidth/2
local h = display.contentHeight/2

-- Star shape: need an initial segment to start
-- newline accepts the start x, y and end x, y of line
local star = display.newLine( 0,-110, 27,-35 )


-- further segments can be added later
star:append( 105,-35, 43,16, 65,90, 0,45, -65,90, -43,15, -105,-35, -27,-35, 0,-110 )
star:setStrokeColor( 1, 1, 1, 1 )
star.strokeWidth = 3
```

As you might have noticed, a portion of the star is off the screen (the negative numbers), but we will bring it into view shortly. Next, we will add a rectangle and a circle to the display.

```
local rectangle = display.newRect( 100, 100, 50, 50)
rectangle.strokeWidth = 5
rectangle:setFillColor( 1, 0, 0)
rectangle:setStrokeColor(0, 0, 1)


local circle = display.newCircle(display.contentWidth/2,
display.contentHeight/2, 15)
circle.strokeWidth = 2
circle:setFillColor(0, 1, 0)
circle:setStrokeColor(1,1,1)
```

To create a vector rectangle object we use **newRect(left, top, width, height)** – the left, top corner of the rectangle is at 100 down and 100 pixels over from the top left corner of the device display. The rectangle has a width of 50 pixels and a height of 50 pixels (so it is a square). We set the fill color of the rectangle to red, its line stroke (outline) color to blue, and the pixel width of the rectangle outline to 5 pixels.

The circle – newCircle(x Center, y Center, radius) – is located in the center of the screen with a radius of 15 pixels, a stroke width of 2, a fill color of green, and a stroke color of white.

Now that we have these three objects added to our display, we will move them using the transition.to command to the center of the screen.

```
transition.to(star, {x=w, y=h, time=1500})

transition.to(rectangle, {x=w, y=h, time = 1500})
```

Notice two things:
First, the objects stack in the order that they were loaded: with the star in the background, the rectangle in the middle, and the circle on top.
Second, the star is not 'centered' like the rectangle and circle. This is because the star's location is based on the first line that was drawn, not the center of the collection of lines. For our star, this has the effect of everything being lined up for the object's x parameter, but the y parameter is off.

To correct this problem, we can either move the object by subtracting 110 pixels from the y parameter or use the .anchorY parameter. Changing anchorY changes the reference point for the y of the object so that all movement and rotation are now based upon the new value instead of the original y value for the first line segment. By default, the anchor point for any object is the center of the object. However, as this object is composed of multiple line segments, it is necessary to reset the anchor to the center of the object.

The anchorX and anchorY parameters range from 0 to 1, with 0 being the left (x), or top (y), and 1 being the right (x), bottom (y). By default, both anchorX and anchorY are set at .50 (the center of the object). But before we can set the star's anchor, we must tell Solar2D that it is okay to change the anchor on a line object.

```
star.anchorSegments = true
star.anchorY = .5
```

We will place these commands before the transition.to commands and run your app to see the difference. Being able to change the x and y reference points on an object can be very handy if you need to rotate the object on an edge or corner instead of on the center of the object.

Let's make one more change before we move on. We used the rotation parameter previously when we were working on device orientation. Add a rotation of 360 degrees to the transition.to commands so that your final code looks like:

```
-- Vector graphics example
local w = display.contentWidth/2
local h = display.contentHeight/2

-- need initial segment to start
local star = display.newLine( 0,-110, 27,-35 )
star:append( 105,-35, 43,16, 65,90, 0,45, -65,90, -43,15, -105,-35, -
```

```
27,-35, 0,-110 )
star:setStrokeColor( 1, 1, 1, 1 )
star.strokeWidth = 3
star.anchorSegments = true
star.anchorY = .5

local rectangle = display.newRect( 100, 100, 50, 50)
rectangle.strokeWidth = 5
rectangle:setFillColor( 1, 0, 0)
rectangle:setStrokeColor(0, 0, 1)

local circle = display.newCircle(w, h, 15)
circle.strokeWidth = 2
circle:setFillColor(0, 1, 0)
circle:setStrokeColor(1,1,1)

transition.to(star, {x=w, y=h, time=1500, rotation=360})
transition.to(rectangle, {x=w, y=h, time = 1500, rotation = 360})
```

While vector graphics are very fast (processor-wise), they are
time-consuming to code and somewhat limited in features and
complexity. Let's be honest with ourselves, can you see yourself
creating a complex landscape or background with vector
graphics? Sure, it has been done (I am thinking of several classic
arcades and early home console games from the 70s and 80s
such as Lunar Lander or Star Fox), but today's smartphone users
expect a little more! Fortunately, Solar2D has taken care of this
issue with bitmaps!

Bitmap Graphics

A bitmap graphic is created by using a series of colored pixels to
form complex (or simple) images. They are stored in external files
in various formats, the most common of which are JPEG, GIF, and
PNG. Any photo that you take with your smartphone or digital
camera is an example of a bitmap graphic. Generally, they are

saved as either jpg or png.   PNG is the recommended bitmap format for maximum compatibility across multiple mobile device platforms.

We have been using display.newImage() for a couple of chapters to load our bitmap graphic content into our app. There are a couple of considerations to keep in mind on your graphics:

- Make sure you use "Save for Web" when exporting your images. This will ensure that the image does not contain an embedded ICC profile and is an appropriate file size for a mobile device.

- To help conserve memory (always a problem when you start working on image-intensive apps!) make sure that your image is between 72 dots per inch (DPI) and 170.   72 is the default for Photoshop when you start a new image.

- There may be gamma and color differences between the system you develop the graphics on and the devices you plan to export.   Make sure your art person has calibrated their display to your export device, or that great yellow texture might not be as appealing on the device.

- Maximum image resolution supported is 4096 x 4096. For the broadest compatibility, keep the resolution at or below 2048 x 2048.

The full command list for display.newImage() command is:

object = display.newImage([parentGroup,] filename [, baseDirectory] [, left, top] [,isFullResolution])

We will discuss parentGroup and baseDirectory in chapter 7. You should already be familiar with left and top (sets the images left and top corner). That leaves us with **isFullResolution**.

The **isFullResolution** is a Boolean parameter that overrides autoscaling (I will discuss why this is a bad idea in Chapter 6) and forces the image to be shown at its full resolution. By default, this parameter is false.

Icons

While we are on the topic of resolution, if you are leveraging your resources so that you can deploy to multiple platforms (that's what first attracted me to Solar2D), then you will need icons for all the required sizes by the various vendors. It is recommended that you begin all of your graphics for the largest size and then scale them down as appropriate. At the minimum, you need to be concerned with:

Android	Apple
108 x 108px	58 x 58px
162 x 162px	76 x 76px
216 x 216px	80 x 80px
324 x 324px	87 x 87px
432 x 432px	114 x 114px
	120 x 120px
	152 x 152px
	167 x 167px
	180 x 180px

Don't forget you will need a 1024x1024px of the icon for the iTunes store. To make life easy on yourself, start with the 1024x1024 resolution of your icon, then resize the image to the required, smaller, sizes.

Build.Settings and Config.lua

To handle all of the many different available devices, Solar2D has two files that help instruct the SDK on how to handle various device builds or configurations that might occur when you deploy your app to many different types of devices.

build.settings

Solar2D allows you control over the build of your app through the build.settings file. build.settings uses Lua syntax to specify the default settings for your app. The build.settings file is used to set the application orientation options and auto-rotation behavior. It may also contain platform-specific parameters. The build.settings file automatically is created in the same folder as your main.lua file.

Sample build.settings:

```
settings =
{
   orientation =
   {
      default = "portrait",
      supported =
      {
         "portrait", "portraitUpsideDown", "landscapeRight",
"landscapeLeft"
      }
   },
}
```

In this sample build.settings file, we configure the default orientation to portrait and support auto-rotation to all four orientations. This only impacts iOS devices. Android devices will automatically open to the orientation of the device unless only one orientation is specified.

The build.settings is capable of a few other advanced configuration settings which we will discuss at a later time.

config.lua

As we have previously discussed, not all mobile devices have the same resolution. The working screen resolution for early iPhones and iPods is 320 x 480. With config.lua, you can allow your app to do dynamic content scaling or load different resolutions of images so that your app looks and runs great on any device, even those with a higher screen resolution. The config.lua file is included in the same folder as your main.lua.

Dynamic Content Scaling

To use dynamic content scaling, open the config.lua file in your project folder with your editor. You will set the width and height in pixels of your original target device, and then set your auto-scaling. Auto-scaling has four predefined settings:
- "none" – turns off dynamic content scaling
- "letterbox" – scales the content up as evenly as possible while still maintaining all of the content on the screen.
- "zoomEven" – preserves aspect ratio while filling the screen uniformly. If the new device has a different aspect ratio, some of the content might be placed off-screen.
- "zoomStretch" – scales all content to fill the screen, but doesn't worry about stretching some of the content vertically or horizontally. All content will remain on the screen.

Sample config.lua file:

```
application =
{
        content =
        {
```

```
            width = 320,
            height = 480,
            scale = "letterbox"
      },
}
```

Dynamic Image Resolution

To take full advantage of the higher resolution of newer devices, you will need multiple versions of your graphics. Apple defined a naming convention for developers transitioning to the higher resolution (starting with the iPhone 4) by adding "@2" and "@3" suffixes to their filenames.

Solar2D uses a more general method for defining alternative images that allows you, the developer, to select your image naming patterns. The Solar2D system also does not require you to know the exact resolution of your target device.

To define your image naming convention and the corresponding image resolutions, you will need to create a table named imageSuffix in your config.lua file:

```
application ={
   content = {
   imageSuffix = {
        ["@2"] = 2,
        ["@3"] = 3
            },
        },
      }
```

With this example configuration in our config.lua file, we have specified that images with a @2 suffix will be 2 times the base resolution and @3 will be 3 times the base resolution.

To load your images, use
display.newImageRect(*filename, base width, base height*)
and Solar2D will choose the closest matching suffix, as defined by your scale.

Scaling

Once your image is loaded, you have three ways of adjusting the scale of an object: yScale and xScale, the scale method, and using the scale method with xScale and yScale. You can use the object property xScale and yScale, which scales the object based on the object's reference point. For most objects, this is the center of the object. Use the scale(sx, sy) method to set the xScale and yScale properties. Each time you modify the scale using the scale method, the object is multiplied times the values xScale and yScale. If xScale and yScale have not been set, they default to the value of 1.

Example:

```
myImage.xScale = .5
myImage.yScale = .5

myImage:scale(.5, .5)
```

This short piece of code would result in an image that was displayed at ¼ its original size after the code was completed. Why, you might ask? When you call the scale method, it will multiply the set scale by any previous scale that has been set. So we get the result of .5 x .5 = .25. This is an important item to remember if you use the scaling methods.

Masking

Masking allows you to hide a portion of your screen by placing one graphic in front of another. Masking is a very powerful tool and can be used to create spectacular effects in your apps.

A mask is always associated with another object, whether it is another graphic, text, or a display group (which will be discussed in detail in Chapter 7). Masks can also be nested.

To create your own mask, you will need to create a bitmap image that will cover a portion of the object to be masked. You can think of it like a ballroom mask. If you desire to hide a portion of your face, you need to decide what portions will be visible and what will be hidden.

When you are creating your mask image, dark areas will cover or hide the covered object, and white areas will be clear or not hidden. Load the mask using:

```
local mask = graphics.newMask(filename)
```

To apply the mask to an image:

```
image:setMask (mask)
```

graphics.newMask converts the image to a gray scale with the black values acting as masks, and the white values becoming transparent. Anything outside the mask is filled with black pixels (thus masking the rest of the screen). A few notes on masking:

- The mask image width and height must be a multiple of 4.
- The mask image must have a black border around the mask that is at least 3 pixels.

Masking does not impact the touch and tap events of an image. In other words, if you mask something, touch and tap events can still occur even if the object is hidden.

To set a mask to an object, you use the setMask() method:
object:setMask(mask object)

You can also rotate, scale, and set the x and y of the mask with the appropriate parameter:

object.maskRotation
object.maskScaleX
object.maskScaleY
object.maskX
object.maskY

Project 5.1: Masks
This is a little app to give you a quick idea of how masks work. I have created two images, the first a simple graphic with black and white bars, the second with the text "Solar2D Rocks."

Solar 2D Rocks!

First, in the build.settings file, we will set the default orientation of the app to landscape right.

build.settings

```
settings = {
        orientation =
        {
                default = "landscapeRight",
        },
}
```

We are going to load the "Solar2D Rocks" image and apply the bars as a mask, which will cause some of the characters to look faded.

main.lua

```
local solar= display.newImage("solar.png",
(display.contentWidth/2)-200, (display.contentHeight/2)-150 )

local mask = graphics.newMask("mask.png")
solar:setMask(mask)
```

And now we have a simple mask applied to our image!

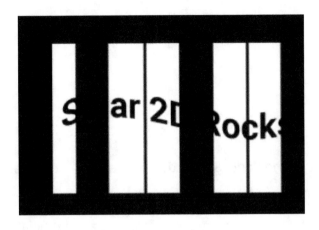

Sprite Sheets

Sprite sheets are commonly used for games and animation. They are a series of 2D images saved in a single PNG image file (which is called a sprite sheet). This allows for a more effective and efficient use of memory. Individually, each of these images might use 5 or 10k of memory. While not a problem for just a few images, it quickly adds up if we have a significant number. By placing them all in one image file, we use much less device memory, which helps game and app performance. We can also take advantage of their placement on the sheet to simulate movement by displaying the images in the same location one after another.

Solar2D provides support for two types of sprite sheets: uniform frames and non-uniform frames. Uniform frames are 2D images that are all the same size throughout the sprite sheet. The image below is an example of a uniform frame sprite sheet provided in the Jungle Scene sample project that ships with Solar2D.

Jungle Scene Sprite Sheet - demonstrating uniform frames

As you can see, each image is uniform in size and positioning, providing an animation sequence of the character running.

The second type of sprite sheet, a non-uniform frame, contains multiple images that are of varying height and width. A non-uniform frame sprite sheet stores the location and size of each frame in an external data file (called a sprite data sheet) so that Solar2D is able to properly load each of the frames. Below is an example of a non-uniform sprite sheet.

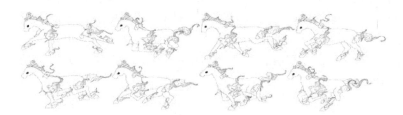

Horse Animation Sprite Sheet - demonstrating non-uniform frame sizes

To assist with your sprite sheet creation, there are many great tools available such as Texture Packer and Zwoptex (Mac only). If you would like to learn more about the process of creation of sprite sheets, I recommend Andreas Loew (developer of Texture Packer), who has created a great video on the subject: http://www.codeandweb.com/what-is-a-sprite-sheet. Since how to create the sprite sheet is outside the scope of this book, we are going to focus on using a few already-made sprite sheets.

Sprites are incredibly useful and powerful for game creation. We will examine how to create a game that makes use of sprite sheets in a later chapter. For now, we will take what we have learned about sprite sheets to create a simple project.

Project 5.2: Sprites

For this project, we are going to create a simple app that displays a sprite. The sprite is stored in GreenDinoSheet.png with the parameters for each sprite stored in GreenDinoSheet.lua (our sprite data sheet). The green dino sprites include a walk, a look, a roar, and a run sequence. The green dino sprites are from Reiner's Tile sets (http://www.reinerstilesets.de). I used SpriteHelper to create the sprite sheet from BMP files and to create the animation sequences.

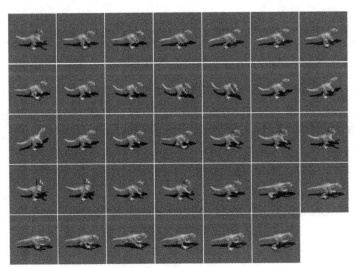

Uniform space and size sprite sheet

Adding a sprite to your app is fairly simple once you have the sprite sheet.

You will first need to load the sprite sheet into memory. To do this, we need to tell Solar2D how the sprite sheet is laid out. We can do this by hand by giving all the dimensions, which would look something like:

```
local options = {
        width = 128,
        height = 128,
        numFrames = 87
        }
```

Or we can take advantage of the fact that we used a program like SpriteHelper to create our sprite sheet. SpriteHelper (as well as other sprite sheet tools) allows for the creation of a lua file that will pass all of the parameters of our sprite sheet. To take advantage of the external lua file, we first have to load it into memory:

```
local GreenDinoSheetData = require("GreenDinoSheet")
```

The keyword "require" tells Solar2D that this is an external program file with functions and information that will be used in the app. There is no need to include the .lua file extension. Solar2D understands that this will be a .lua file. Now all we need to do is load the data from the sprite data file:

```
local options = GreenDinoSheetData.getSpriteSheetData()
```

The command GreenDinoSheetData.getSpriteSheetData() is a function call. By putting GreenDinoSheetData first, Solar2D understands that this function will be located in the GreenDinoSheet.lua file that we required. The function name is getSpriteSheetData. By assigning it to the variable options, we are telling Solar2D to store all of the data that is in the getSpriteSheetData function in the options.

Those two lines of code do all of the heavy lifting for us, and we are now ready to load graphics on the screen:

```
local sheet1 = graphics.newImageSheet("GreenDinoSheet.png",
options)

local  GreenDino = display.newImage(sheet1, 2)
GreenDino.x = display.contentWidth/2
GreenDino.y = display.contentHeight/2
```

We are using a new command here: graphics.newImageSheet. We are assigning the sprite sheet to the variable sheet1, passing it the name of the sprite sheet and the options variable. Solar2D now knows all about the sprite sheet: that each of the images is 128 x 128, that there are 87 of them, and how to access each one by number. The first image in the file is image 1, the second is 2, etc.

Thus, if I want to display an image from the sprite sheet on the screen, I can use display.newImage and pass it sheet1 and the image number I want to load onto the screen (just like I did above).

Try it out. Also, change the number 2 above to any number between 1 and 87 to see different images.

I know, you want to see animation! Where is the rampaging dinosaur!?! Let's work on that next.

Project 5.3 Sprite Animation

SpriteHelper (and most other sprite sheet tools) has another neat feature that lets me create animation sequences from the sprite sheet, just like the GreenDinoSheet.lua file, these sequences allow me to easily animate my dinosaur. In this project, we are going to make the dinosaur appear to walk around on the screen.

If you open the Walking.lua file you will find the following information:

Walking.lua

```
function getAnimationSequences()
        local sequences = {
                        name = "Walking",
                        frames = {80,81,82,83,84,85,86,87},
                        time = 800,
                        loopCount = 10,
        }
        return sequences
end
```

SpriteHelper again did most of the hard work for me. It provides Solar2D with the basic information for a walking sequence and even names it Walking. The walking images in the sprite sheet are images 80 through 87. It also provides a basic timing loop for how quickly to play the images to make it look more 'realistic'.

Let's take advantage of this information to create a simple animation. To begin with, we will load the external lua files that contain our data. As you can see, we are including WalkingData to load the file and Walk to load the specific walk sequence.

main.lua

```
local GreenDinoSheetData = require("GreenDinoSheet")
```

```
local WalkingData = require("Walking")
local options = GreenDinoSheetData.getSpriteSheetData()
local Walk = WalkingData.getAnimationSequences()
```

Next, we will load the sprite sheet with the graphics.newImageSheet command. Then we will load the animation sequence with the command display.newSprite. It is possible to group your animation sequence into one file, but for simplicity, I broke it into multiple animation sequences.

```
local sheet1 = graphics.newImageSheet("GreenDinoSheet.png",
options)
local dinoWalk = display.newSprite(sheet1, Walk)
```

Now we will place the dinoWalk animation on the screen and tell it to play (which will start the animation).

```
dinoWalk.x = 64
dinoWalk.y= display.contentHeight/2

dinoWalk:play()
```

Hmm, needs one more thing, don't you think? Wouldn't it be nice if the dino actually walked?

```
transition.to(dinoWalk, {x=display.contentWidth, time = 10000})
```

Here is a list of the various sprite commands and what they do:

- graphics.newImageSheet(*image, layout*) – creates the sprite sheet given the image file and the layout of the sprites in the image file.
- display.newSprite(*imagesheet, animation sequence*) – create a sprite that can be played.

109

Sprite Control Methods
- animation:play() – starts the animation created with the display.newSprite command.
- animation:pause() – pauses an animation that is playing.
- animation:setFrame(*frame*) – sets the start frame of the animation.
- animation:setSequence(*sequence*) – changes to a different sequence if you have multiple sequences loaded.

Sprite Properties
- object.frame - returns the current frame of the animation.
- object.isPlaying – returns true if the animation is currently playing.
- object.numFrames – returns the number of frames in the current animation sequence.
- object.sequence – returns the name of the currently playing animation sequence.
- object.timeScale – will return or set the scale to be applied to the animation time. Can be used to speed-up or slow down an animation by a multiple of the value given. Minimum of 0.05, maximum of 20.0.

Sprite Event Listeners
Sprite event listeners are an easy way to check on the status of your sprite. Using an event listener, you can cause your animation to move to the next animation or determine when it has finished the current animation sequence. We will discuss event phases more in chapter 9, but here is what you can listen for with sprites:
- began – the sprite has started playing.
- ended – the sprite has finished playing.
- bounce – the sprite bounded from forward to backward while playing (bounce is also a play setting).

- loop – the sprite has looped to the beginning of its sequence.
- next – the sprite has moved on to the next sequence.

Other Uses of Image/Sprite Sheets

If you have thought about it, Image sheets have far more uses than just loading graphics. For example, if you need to include a special-looking font or characters in your app, this is an easy way to import and use the graphics to get a very special look and feel. If you have ever tried to create your own font, you will appreciate this use.

Note: If you use SpriteHelper for a similar project, I had to modify all of the animation files, removing the title of the animation from within the file. If you make the file look similar to what is above, yours should work.

Summary

This chapter included a number of essential elements for creating and using graphics in a Solar2D project. At this point you should feel comfortable creating a vector-based graphic, loading a bitmap image, importing sprites, using a mask, scaling, and handling multiple resolutions. In our next chapter, we will jump into the world of handling the user interface.

Questions

1. Which type of graphic uses less memory and is infinitely scalable?
2. Can vector graphics be moved once they are placed on the display?
3. What are the four icon sizes for an iOS app?
4. What are the three icon sizes for Android apps?
5. What is the maximum size of a bitmap image in Solar2D?

6. Describe the function of a mask.
7. To animate a sprite, what information must you have?
8. Name one use of the config.lua file.
9. Name one use of the build.settings file.
10. What is the naming convention for bitmap graphics that are at different resolutions?

Assignments

1) Create your own stacked set of vector based graphics. Using the new line, create a pentagon and an octagon shape.

2) Using vector shapes, simulate various special effects such as an arrow, laser, or bubbles.

3) Using the sprite sheet of green dino, create a short dramatization. Included in the green dino sheet are animation sequences for look, roar, run, and walk.

4) Create an app using the green dino that walks to a tap location on the screen.

5) Create your own sprite sheet and build an app to show off your creation.

Chapter 6: Creating the User Experience

Learning Objectives

In this chapter we will be learning about creating a good user experience. This includes learning:

- How to hide and show the status bar
- How to load custom fonts
- How to group objects
- How to create and use external modules
- How to use composer API to create additional views for the user

The User Experience

One of the goals of creating a good mobile application or game is to create an enjoyable user experience. The user should be able to easily navigate and find the resources that they are looking for in your app. They should not need to navigate through multiple screens to accomplish the goal of your apps. Requiring the user to navigate through more than two screens (sometimes also referred to as views) is a sign of a poor user interface.

Creating a good interface is the first step toward creating a good user experience. People who are serious about creating successful apps consider multiple design configurations and even the look of the icon. I recently read where a very successful small company that makes mobile games designed over 30 icons for their game and then play-tested their design and icons to ensure that they had the best possible design that their target audience would find appealing.

A few things to consider when developing your app include:

- Group objects that perform similar functions or are a part of the same function. Placing a rectangle around the functions can help inform your user that they are part of the same functionality.
- Use color to inform your users of functionality. Using red to signify stop and green to go is very helpful to those who will use your app.
- Use a minimum of 11pt font for readability.
- Be careful with your selection of a font type. Some fonts are built into the mobile device, while others will be replaced with default fonts.
- Utilize buttons to make actions and navigation options clear to those who will use your app.

Hiding the Status Bar

Hiding the status bar for an app is a common practice. However, you shouldn't hide the status bar just because you can. Many times the status bar on the smartphone or tablet provides important information to the user. If your application's performance or look and feel is not impacted by the status bar, then you should leave it visible. If, however, the status bar detracts or distracts from the app, then it can be hidden with the command:

```
display.setStatusBar(display.HiddenStatusBar)
```

As a general rule, for most general purpose and information based apps, the status bar should remain visible. For game or graphic-intensive apps, the status bar should be hidden.

The other options besides display.HiddenStatusBar are:

- <u>display.DefaultStatusBar</u> – returns status bar to normal or default setting
- <u>display.TranslucentStatusBar</u> – sets the status bar to translucent
- <u>display.DarkStatusBar</u> – sets the status bar to dark.

If you need to know the height of the status bar for calculating the placement of objects in your app, the command **display.statusBarHeight** returns the height in pixels.

Custom Fonts

When working with multiple types of devices running on different operating systems, it can be very difficult to know if a particular font is available on the system. For most applications, using the default font will be sufficient. However, there are times when the judicious use of custom fonts can be a great way to improve your app. You can find many free fonts at http://www.1001freefonts.com/ or http://www.dafont.com/. Be sure to check the readme.txt file included with the font if you will be using your app for commercial purposes (i.e. you plan to make money with it in any way).

Custom fonts can be easily incorporated into applications as long as they are registered in the build.settings file.

```
settings =
{
    iphone =
    {
        plist =
        {
            UIAppFonts =
            {
                fontFileName
                }
            }
```

```
        }
}
```

For Android, simply including the font in the application folder is sufficient. You must also have the exact font name (not just the name of the file containing the font) for the display.newText API call.

Project 6.0 Custom Fonts

Our goal for this project is to load a custom font and display it on the screen. To accomplish this we are going to learn a few more commands and procedures. The method of using custom fonts on an Apple and Android device varies slightly, but I will show you a great workaround that will make it easy!

First, we will need to configure the build.settings file:

build.settings

```
settings =
{
  iphone =
        {
                plist =
                {
                        UIAppFonts = {"Baroque Script.ttf"}
                },
        },
}
```

If the BaroqueScript.ttf file is located in the same folder as the main.lua and build.settings file, it will be loaded for use.

Next, we will determine what the font is named inside the font file. The internal name can vary widely, so it is a good idea to perform this procedure anytime you are using a custom font. **If you are running on the Solar2D Simulator, you will need to make sure the font is installed before you run the simulator.** If you don't install it first, it will not show up on the list. This app will go through and show the fonts that are currently loaded in the system memory. If your font isn't installed, it won't show up.

The first thing we will do is load the native fonts into a variable called 'font'.

```
local fonts = native.getFontNames()
```

Next, we will display the font names that are available using a 'for do' command. This command allows us to look at information that is installed in an array or table (which we will discuss more in Chapter 10). For now, what you need to understand is that the command will step through all of the fonts that are loaded in and display them to the terminal window.

```
-- Display each font name in the terminal console
for i, fontname in ipairs(fonts) do
     print( "fontname = " .. tostring( fontname ) )
end
```

At the end of the list you should see the font that you loaded in the build.settings file.

```
Corona Simulator Output
fontname = Myriad Web Pro
fontname = Cambria
fontname = Cambria Math
fontname = MS Reference Sans Serif
fontname = OCR-A II
fontname = OCR B MT
fontname = QuickType II Condensed
fontname = QuickType II Mono
fontname = QuickType II Pi
fontname = QuickType II
fontname = DejaVu Sans Condensed
fontname = Gentium Basic
fontname = DejaVu Serif
fontname = Liberation Sans Narrow
fontname = Gentium Book Basic
fontname = DejaVu Serif Condensed
fontname = DejaVu Sans Mono
fontname = DejaVu Sans
fontname = DejaVu Sans Light
fontname = OpenSymbol
fontname = Andale Sans for VST
fontname = Thorndale for VST
fontname = Calibri Light
fontname = Baroque Script
```

As you can see in the image above, "Baroque Script" is at the bottom of my list. Now comes the fun part. Since Android and Apple handle loading fonts differently, I can GREATLY simplify my life by just changing the filename in the folder to match the name of the font that is listed above!

The next step then is to change the filename to "Baroque Script.ttf" in my project folder. After changing the file name, you will also need to modify it in your build.settings file:

build.settings

```
settings =
{
  iphone =
        {
                plist =
                {
                        UIAppFonts = { "Baroque Script.ttf" }
                },
        },
}
```

Note that you may need to reinstall the font to your Windows or Macintosh since the file name has changed to system to continue testing in your Solar2D Simulator.

One last line to add is the display.newText that shows the font in use:

```
display.newText("Hello World",10, 10, "Baroque Script", 24)
```

You can add up to 100 fonts in this way. Just place a comma between each font in the build.settings file.

Groups

Group objects will quickly become one of your favorite commands for working with multiple display objects. Group allows you to place multiple objects into the same group and be able to apply effects to all of the objects at the same time. This is very handy when working with multiple views and needing to move, fade, or hide a large number of objects quickly. By making a display object a member of a group, you can apply a change to the entire group with just one command.

Think of groups as a basket. Everything that is placed in that basket is moved at the same time, rotated at the same time, can have the color changed at the same time, and can be hidden at the same time.

There are just four commands for working with a group:
- display.newGroup() – creates a new group
- group.numChildren – returns the number of display objects in a group
- group:insert(object) – inserts a new object into a group

119

- group:remove(index or object) – removes an object from a group

Project 6.1: Group Movement

In this project we are going to load three images (a couple of button images), add them to a group, and use transition.to to move the group down the screen with one command.

main.lua

```
local b1 = display.newImage("Button1.png",10, 10)
local b2 = display.newImage("Button2.png", 100, 50)
local b3 = display.newImage("Button3.png", 200, 100)

local group1 = display.newGroup()
      group1:insert(b1)
      group1:insert(b2)
      group1:insert(b3)
transition.to(group1, {y=300, time=2000})
```

Objects can still be acted upon individually, but I'm sure that you can see how this can be used to easily create the appearance of multiple screens or views of an app without the need to do all that extra programming. An object can only be a member of one group at a time. If you insert it into a second group, it is removed from the first group.

Modules and Packages

As you gain experience creating apps, you will find that certain functions and code segments are used all the time. Fortunately, Lua allows us to create modules that can be loaded and reused in our apps quickly and easily. The use of additional Lua files is best shown when you begin to use the Composer API.

120

Composer

Composer supplies built-in scene (also referred to as views or screens) creation and management. This means that you can create multiple views or screens and be able to easily load and unload them as you need. Composer includes easy transition methods between individual scenes. The scene object is an event listener that responds to specific events, simplifying scene management for your applications.

Project 6.2 A Simple Story

For this first project using composer, we are going to create a simple project that uses 3 Lua files for different views or screens. We will have a main.lua, mom.lua, and dad.lua.

To get started, we will first write our main.lua file. Remember to place all of your Lua files and graphics in the same folder. We only need two commands to get everything started using Composer. The first is to load composer into memory using the require "composer" command.
Second, we will use composer to transition to the mom.lua file using a fade transition effect that will take 400 milliseconds to perform.

main.lua

```
local composer = require "composer"

-- Load the first scene to be shown
composer.gotoScene( "mom",{effect= "fade", time = 400} )
```

The gotoScene command API is:

composer.gotoScene(*sceneName* [, *options*])

where sceneName is the name of the lua file to be loaded and run. Options include the transition effect to be used and how long the transition should take to perform.

Transition effects include: fade, zoomOutIn, zoomOutInFade, zoomInOut, zoomInOutFade, flip, flipFadeOutIn, zoomOutInRotate, zoomOutInFadeRotate, zoomInOutRotate, zoomInOutFadeRotate, fromRight (over original scene), fromLeft (over original scene), fromTop (over original scene), fromBottom (over original scene), slideLeft (pushes original scene), slideRight (pushes original scene), slideDown (pushes original scene), slideUp (pushes original scene), and crossfade.

You can also pass additional parameters as part of the transition; a nice way to pass variables that might be used in the next segment of your program! Now that we have called mom.lua from main.lua, we should probably say hi! We will start the mom.lua file with a comment to help us remember which file we are working in and load the composer api into memory (this will need to be done for each scene or file that uses composer).

Next, we will create a variable called scene to hold all of the information about this scene. Finally, we will create a display group as discussed earlier in the chapter to make viewing the scene information easier.

mom.lua

```
-----------------------------------------------------
-- mom.lua
-----------------------------------------------------
local composer = require "composer"
local scene = composer.newScene()
```

After we set up our variables, we will set up the scene like we would normally if we were just working with only a main.lua file with a few minor variations. Composer is incredibly efficient in making sure that the scene can be pre-loaded, shown multiple times in a sequence, hidden when the user leaves the scene, or disposed of to free memory.

To take advantage of this efficiency, we will need to use a few special functions to manage the loading and unloading of the scene. The first is the **create** function. This function preloads all of the information before showing the scene. This can make for very efficient memory usage. **Create** will only execute if it isn't already loaded into memory. If the scene has already been visited, it will not execute.

Thus, as we are designing our scene, we need to keep in mind that it might be loaded and hidden from view several times. This is where our display group becomes very useful. By adding all of our display objects to a display group, we are able to hide or show all of them at once by changing the alpha. To begin with, we will just load the images and text and then set up an event listener should the background be tapped.

```
-----------------------------------------------------
-- BEGINNING OF YOUR SCENE
-----------------------------------------------------

--Called if the scene hasn't been previously seen
function scene:create ( event )
```

123

```
local MomGroup = self.view

bgImage = display.newImage("bg.jpg", 0, 0)
MomGroup:insert(bgImage)

hiMomText = display.newText("Hi Mom!!",0 ,0, nil, 36)
hiMomText.x = display.contentWidth/2
hiMomText.y = display.contentHeight/2
MomGroup:insert( hiMomText )
end
```

The scene:create function will handle loading our graphics and text to the screen. Next, we will create a little function that when the user touches the background, we can fade to the dad.lua file over 400 milliseconds.

```
function onBackgroundTouch()
    composer.gotoScene("dad", "fade", 400)
end
```

Now we need to handle the situation of the user coming back to this scene after it has been hidden from view. Using the scene:**show** function, we will initialize an event listener to handle the background touch (which will call the fade to dad routine).

```
function scene:show(event)
        bgImage:addEventListener("touch", onBackgroundTouch)
end
```

We need to remove the event listener when composer determines we are leaving this scene. This is handled by the scene:**hide** function:

```
function scene:hide(event)
```

```
    bgImage:removeEventListener("touch", onBackgroundTouch)
end
```

All that is left is to set our event listeners and give a final required command when using the composer API: return scene. The return scene communicates back to the main.lua file that everything has been loaded so that composer can continue running properly.

```
-- "create" is called when the scene is FIRST called
scene:addEventListener( "create", scene )

-- "show" event is dispatched when scene transition has finished
scene:addEventListener( "show", scene )
-- "hide" event is dispatched before next scene's transition begins
scene:addEventListener( "hide", scene )

return scene
```

Now that we have mom.lua taken care of, we will do the same thing with dad.lua with the exception that dad.lua will pass control back to mom.lua should the background be tapped.

dad.lua

```
-----------------------------------------------------
-- dad.lua
-----------------------------------------------------
local composer = require( "composer" )
local scene = composer.newScene()
-----------------------------------------------------
-- BEGINNING OF YOUR SCENE
-----------------------------------------------------
--Called if the scene hasn't been previously seen
 function scene:create( event )

   local DadGroup = self.view

   backgroundImage = display.newImage("bg2.jpg", 0, 0)
   DadGroup:insert(backgroundImage)

   hiDadText = display.newText("Hi Dad!",0 ,0, nil, 36)
   hiDadText.x = display.contentWidth/2
   hiDadText.y =  display.contentHeight/2
   DadGroup:insert(hiDadText)

end

local function onBackgroundTouch()
   composer.gotoScene( "mom", {effect = "zoomInOut", time = 800
} )
end

function scene:show(event)
   backgroundImage:addEventListener("touch",
onBackgroundTouch)
end

function scene:hide(event)
   backgroundImage:removeEventListener("touch",
onBackgroundTouch)
```

```
end
-- "create" is called when the scene is FIRST called
scene:addEventListener( "create", scene )

-- "show" event is dispatched when scene transition has finished
scene:addEventListener( "show", scene )
-- "hide" event is dispatched before next scene's transition begins
scene:addEventListener( "hide", scene )

return scene
```

A few notes on troubleshooting when using external files.
Often when you begin to try to find your error when working with
external files, you will see the first file listed as causing the first
error (i.e. main.lua) and it will list the line number that makes the
call to the next scene. Ignore this error and continue reading
through the error log. The compiler is actually listing the stack of
calls until it gets to the root error. So when you see "main:14" as
the error source and main.lua line 14 is calling the next lua file,
ignore it and continue to the next line. Dig deep enough and you
will find the source of all the errors.

There are a few commands that I didn't use that would have
provided better memory management if this were a much larger
program. Using the various purge commands of the API (listed
below), you can remove the previous scene from memory.

The composer API includes:

- composer.getScene() – returns the scene object. Can be
  used to call a function in a specific scene.

- composer.getSceneName() –returns the current scene
  name

- composer.getVariable() – returns the value of a variable
  set with composer.setVariable().

- composer.gotoScene() – for transitioning to a new scene. Causes exitScene to be called.

- composer.hideOverlay() – hides the current overlay scene

- composer.isDebug - outputs debugging information to the Solar2D Terminal

- composer.loadScene() – used to preload a specified scene without causing a scene transition

- composer.newScene() – creates a new scene object

- composer.recycleOnLowMemory – If a low memory warning is issued by the operating system, composer will recycle the least recent scene. To disable this feature, set the property to false.

- composer.recycleOnSceneChange – automatically removes previous scene from memory after the scene change. Default is false.

- composer.removeHidden() – removes all scenes except the current scene

- composer.removeScene() – purges the specified and unloads the scenes module

- composer.setVariable() – sets a variable that can be passed to subsequent scenes

- composer.showOverlay() – loads a scene above the current scene, leaving the current scene intact.

- composer.stage – returns a reference to the top-level composer display group.

Project 6.3: Creating a Splash Screen

Typically, one of the first things requested by my students is how to add a splash screen to their app. We all know that a good splash screen is critical to any app. It introduces the app to the user, informs them of who created the app, and gives the hardware a few moments to load any external resources that might be needed.

There are many ways we can add a splash screen. We could create a function in our main.lua to show and dismiss a splash screen. We can use composer to handle our splash screen. We could even create the splash screen as an external library that handles animations and preloading of assets. As this is a rather simple project, let's keep the splash screen simple as well, going with the first option of adding the splash screen as a function in our main.lua.

There are also many ways we can develop our splash screen. Usually, it will be a PNG file developed by the artists on your team, but there is nothing keeping you from building a simple screen using text objects and background.

Starting with The default Lua file, I have created a function called splash(). The splash function creates a display group to simplify the management of all of the elements that are a part of the splash screen.

main.lua

```
-- Project: Splash Screen

local function splash()
    -- Create a group to make dismissing the splash screen easy
    splashGroup = display.newGroup()

        -- Create a background with a vector rectangle.  Must be a
global variable since it is called outside of the function
        bg = display.newRect(splashGroup, 0, 0, 320, 480)
        bg:setFillColor( 10, 10, 200)

        -- Add text object of app title
        local splashText = display.newText(splashGroup, "Hi\n
Dad!", 100, 150,native.systemFont, 40 )
        splashText.rotation=-30

        -- Tell the user how to proceed
        local proceedText = display.newText(splashGroup, "Tap
To Give A Shout Out", display.contentWidth/2-100,
display.contentHeight-100, nil, 20)

end
```

Using a vector rectangle with a blue fill, the background is added to the splashGroup and also used as our button below. Since it is used outside of the local function, bg (our background image) must be declared as a global variable.

The splashText is also added to the splashGroup. This text object uses a \n to force a new line in the display and is then rotated -30 degrees because I liked it better that way.

We will add the proceedText to let the user know what is expected of them, which is always a good user interface consideration.

Next, we add a function to be called when the user gives a 'shout out' to Dad and a second function to handle when the background is tapped. I chose to fade the splashGroup out over three seconds before calling the main function.

```
function hiDad()
        textObj = display.newText("Can I have $10?", 50,
display.contentHeight/2, native.systemFont, 24)
        textObj:setFillColor(1, 1, 1)
end

local function bgButton(event)
        -- handle dismissing the splash screen when it is tapped
by fading out the splashGroup
        transition.to(splashGroup, {alpha = 0, time = 3000})

        -- pass control to the main function
        main()
end
```

In main I have placed some of the code from our previous project. Prior to this call, I added a removeSelf for the splashGroup to remove it from memory. This is always a good practice and will help keep the overhead of your larger projects more manageable.

Finally, we call splash() to get the whole ball rolling and add the event listener for the user to tap the background for the dismissal of the splash screen. Remember, if code is placed in a function, it is not processed until it is called, but it must be made available (or declared) before the call.

```
function main()
    -- remove splashGroup from memory
        splashGroup:removeSelf()
    hiDad()
end
```

```
--call the splash screen and add event listener for background
splash()

bg:addEventListener("tap", bgButton)
```

Of course we could also use the composer API for creating a good splash screen (and we will in later projects), but it is always a good idea to see multiple methods for completing the same task.

Summary

This chapter included a number of essential elements for making a good user experience in your app. We have examined the user experience, how to load custom fonts, how to use groups, the composer API for creating different views, and how to add a splash screen.

Questions

1. What is a group and why are they useful?
2. True or False: A custom font does not have to be included in the app folder.

Assignments

1. Create a project using 2 different fonts.

2. Create a splash screen for one of your previous projects that uses a display group to show and then hide the splash screen.

3. Using Project 6.2 as a starting point, add a splash screen using the composer API.

4. Using Project 6.2 as a starting point, add a splash screen using the composer API and use 2 different custom fonts for the mom.lua and dad.lua scenes.

132

Chapter 7 Working with Media

Learning Objectives

Sound, music, photos, and movies make up a very important part of the mobile device culture. In this chapter we are going to look at using, playing, and recording all four of these types of media. Specifically, we will learn to:

- the difference between loading and streaming audio
- load and play sound effects
- load and play long sound files such as music files
- use the built-in camera on a device
- play movies in your app

Audio

Sound effects and audio responses are a critical part of any user interface. Sound and music can turn a boring humdrum game or movie into a riveting adventure if done correctly!

We will be using the new Solar2D Audio system for all of our projects. The audio system gives us access to advanced OpenAL features. Solar2D currently supports up to 32 distinct audio channels.

Sound File Types

As one of the major reasons why people adopt Solar2D is the ability to build for multiple platforms, we must keep in mind which sound file types are available for use with both platforms. The supported sound file types are:

iOS: .mp3, .caf, .aac, and .wav (16-bit uncompressed)
Android: .mp3, .ogg, and .wav (16-bit uncompressed)

OS X (Mac): .mp3, .ogg, .caf, .aac, and .wav (16-bit uncompressed)
Windows Desktop: .mp3, .ogg, .aac, and .wav (16-bit uncompressed)

To keep your life simple, plan to use .mp3 and 16-bit uncompressed .wav file formats for all your sound needs. .caf, .aac, and .ogg are great formats but are not accepted by all platforms. So unless you are building for a specific platform and have a special need for one of these file formats, I recommend using mp3 and wav.

For best performance on mobile devices with .mp3, use mono instead of stereo. It makes the file size significantly smaller and will improve your app's performance.

Timing Is Everything

The audio system in Solar2D is a best-effort system. It will attempt to play the sound when the request is made. However, if there is a delay (such as a problem with streaming a sound or processor demand), then it will play the sound(s) as soon as it can. This could create a problem in some games or apps, so you should keep it in mind when planning your audio. In my experience, I have found that preloading sound effects makes the sound system very responsive. Since streaming sound must be decompressed at the time of play, it is not quite as responsive if you have a lot happening within the app.

Streams and Sounds

There are two ways to load sounds for your app. The first way is to use the audio.loadSound(filename) which loads and pre-processes the entire sound file into memory. The sound file can then be called upon at any time. All of the processing is done on the front end so app performance is not impacted and it can be played on demand:

```
local explosionSound = audio.loadSound( "explosion.wav")
```

The sound can be played as many times as needed using the audio.play() command, with each sound going to a new channel (if needed). For example, if I had a game that had 4 things blow up in a row and each required the sound to be played for explosions, I could issue the commands:

```
audio.play(explosionSound)
audio.play(explosionSound)
audio.play(explosionSound)
audio.play(explosionSound)
```

and each would be played in its own channel. There is no need for the sound to be loaded multiple times; the explosion sound will play multiple times. The nice thing about using the audio system in this fashion is that Solar2D will manage your audio channels for you, releasing previously used channels for future use when the current sound effect is finished.

The second method to load sounds into your app is with audio.loadStream(). loadStream will load and process small chunks of the sound file as needed. loadStream is best used in situations where possible latency (small slowdowns in app performance) will not have a critical impact upon the usability of the app. Streaming does not use as much memory, so it is considered the best choice for large sound files such as background music.

Unlike loadSound, loadStream can only play one channel at a time. If you needed the same sound file to stream on multiple channels, you would need to load it to two different variables:

```
local backgroundMusic1 = audio.loadStream( "myMusic.mp3")
local backgroundMusic2 = audio.loadStream( "myMusic.mp3")
```

This shouldn't create memory problems since loadStream works with small chunks of memory. However, it could have a

135

performance impact since the sound files are processed in real-time.

Basic Audio Controls

The basic audio controls provide the foundation of working with sound files, allowing the loading, playing, and stopping of sound files. The basic properties are:

- audio.loadSound(*filename*) – Loads the entire sound file into memory.
- audio.loadStream(*filename*) – Opens a file to read as a stream.
- audio.play(*audioHandle, {[channel=c] [, loops=1] [duration =d] [, fadein=f] [, onComplete=o] }*) – begins the play of the previously loaded audio loop (either via loadSound or loadStream). All additional parameters are optional. Channel will assign the audio playback to a specific channel (auto-selected if omitted); loops set the number of times the playback will loop (default 0); duration will stop playback at a specific time, whether the audio file is finished playing or not, in milliseconds; fadein controls – time to increase the playback to full volume in milliseconds; onComplete passes an event parameter back to the calling procedure on the completion of the playback. Options to be returned include: channel, handle (audio variable), or completed (true if normal completion, false if audio was stopped).
- audio.pause([*audioHandle*]) - pauses playback on specified channel or all channels if no parameters are included.
- audio.resume([*audioHandle*]) – resumes playback on specified channel or all channels if no parameters are included.
- audio.stop(([*audioHandle*]) - stops playback on specified channel or all channels if no parameters are included.

136

- audio.stopWithDelay(duration [, { *audioHandle* }]) - stops playback on specified channel or all channels if no parameters are included after the given number of milliseconds.
- audio.rewind(*[audioHandle] [, { channel=c }]*) – rewinds the specified audio to its beginning position. For files loaded with audio.loadSound, you may only rewind based upon channel, not handle (since multiple instances of the audio handle could be playing). audio.loadStream can be called by handle or channel, but may not update until after the current buffer finishes playing. To rewind 'instantly', stop the stream, rewind, and then play.
- audio.seek(*time* [, *audioHandle*] [, *{channel = c}*]) – Seeks to a time position in the audio file. If no handle or channel is specified, all audio will seek to the specified time, which is provided in milliseconds.
- audio.dispose(*audioHandle*) – release memory that was associated with the handle. The audio should not be active when it is freed.

Duration Audio Controls
- audio.fade([{ [channel = c] [, time=t] [, volume=v] }]) – fades a playing sound in the specified time to the specified volume. If channel is not specified, all channels fade. If time is omitted, the default fade time is 1000 milliseconds. Volume may range from 0.0 to 1.0. If omitted, the default value is 0.0.
- audio.fadeOut([{ [channel = c] [, time=t] }]) – stops the playing sound in a specified amount of time and fades to a minimum volume. At the end of the time, the audio will stop and release the channel. To fadeout all channels, specify 0. Time default is 1000 milliseconds.
- audio.getDuration(*audioHandle*) – returns the total time in milliseconds of the audio. If the length cannot be determined, -1 is returned.

137

Volume Controls

- audio.setVolume(volume[, { [channel = c] }]) – sets the volume of a specified channel or the master volume if no channel is specified. Volume may range from 0.0 to 1.0
- audio.setMaxVolume(volume[, { [channel = c] }]) – sets the maximum volume for all channels.
- audio.setMinVolume(volume[, { [channel = c] }]) - sets the minimum volume for all channels.
- audio.getVolume([{ [channel = c] }]) – returns the volume of the channel of master volume if no channel is specified.
- audio.getMaxVolume({ channel = c}) - returns the maximum volume of a channel. Returns average maximum volume if no channel is specified.
- audio.getMinVolume({ channel = c}) - returns the minimum volume of a channel. Returns average minimum volume if no channel is specified.

Audio Channels

Solar2D uses a channel system to keep track of various sounds that are playing within your app. At this time there are 32 channels available for audio playback.

- audio.findFreeChannel([startChannel]) - returns the channel number of an available channel or 0 if no channels are available.
- audio.freeChannels – returns the number of channels that are available.
- audio.isChannelActive(channel) – returns true if the channel is playing or paused.
- audio.isChannelPaused(channel) – returns true if the channel is paused.
- audio.isChannelPlaying(channel) – returns true if the channel is playing.
- audio.reserveChannels(channels) – reserves a certain number of channels so they will not be automatically

assigned to play calls. Typically used to reserve lower number channels for background music, voice-over, or specific sounds. 0 will unreserve all channels. A number between 1 and 32 set aside the specified number of channels.

- <u>audio.reservedChannels</u> – returns the number of reserved channels
- <u>audio.totalChannels</u> – returns the total number of channels (currently 32).
- <u>audio.unreservedFreeChannels</u> – returns the number of channels available for playback, excluding reserved channels.
- <u>audio.unreservedUsedChannels</u> – returns the number of channels in use excluding reserved channels.
- <u>audio.usedChannels</u> – returns the number of channels in use including reserved channels.

Project 7.0: Beatbox

Our project will be to create a beatbox app to play percussion sounds. For this project you will need to copy the wav and mp3 files (graciously provided for our learning pleasure by Shaun Reed of http://www.constantseas.com) as well as the ui.lua file from the resources into your project folder (which I named BeatBox). Go ahead and create a new project from the Solar2D Console.

config.lua

```lua
-- config.lua for project: BeatBox
application =
{
        content =
        {
                width = 320,
                height = 480,
                scale = "letterbox",|
                fps = 60,
                antialias = false,
                xAlign = "center",
                yAlign = "center"
        }
}
```

In our config.lua file we have set the default width to 320 pixels, height to 480 pixels with letterbox scaling. The default frames per second will be 30, anti-aliasing is off, and xalign and yalign are set to their default center alignment should scaling be necessary.

build.settings

```lua
-- build.settings for project: BeatBox
settings =
{
        orientation =
        {
                default ="landscapeRight",
                supported =
                {
                        "landscapeLeft"
                },
        },
}
```

The build.settings file is being used to tell the compiler that this app should be run in landscape mode, with a default to landscapeRight. Portrait is not supported for this app.

In our main.lua file, I am introducing a new command: system.activate("multitouch"). system.activate("multitouch") is a required command for any app that will be accepting multiple, simultaneous touches.

main.lua

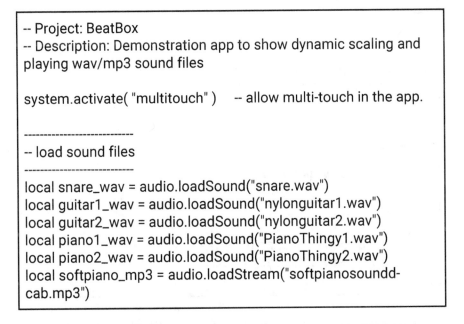

```
-- Project: BeatBox
-- Description: Demonstration app to show dynamic scaling and
playing wav/mp3 sound files

system.activate( "multitouch" )    -- allow multi-touch in the app.


---------------------------
-- load sound files
---------------------------
local snare_wav = audio.loadSound("snare.wav")
local guitar1_wav = audio.loadSound("nylonguitar1.wav")
local guitar2_wav = audio.loadSound("nylonguitar2.wav")
local piano1_wav = audio.loadSound("PianoThingy1.wav")
local piano2_wav = audio.loadSound("PianoThingy2.wav")
local softpiano_mp3 = audio.loadStream("softpianosoundd-
cab.mp3")
```

After setting our system for multi-touch, we set up variables to load each of the sound files into. In the last line, softpiano_mp3, we are using streaming instead of load to save memory on our device.

```
----------------
-- Button Press events
----------------
```

```
local playButton1 = function (event)
        audio.play(snare_wav)
end


local playButton2 = function (event)
        audio.play(guitar1_wav)
end


local playButton3 = function (event)
        audio.play(guitar2_wav)
end


local playButton4 = function (event)
        audio.play(piano1_wav)
end


local playButton5 = function (event)
        audio.play(piano2_wav)
end


local playButton6 = function (event)
        audio.play(softpiano_mp3)
end
```

Next we create the button press events. To simplify button creation, I set a variable, w, to hold the value of the display width divided by 5 with an additional 25 pixels removed to center a 50px graphic. This allowed me to evenly space the buttons across the bottom of the device, no matter the number of pixels I was working with, making dynamic scaling much easier.

```
--Create Buttons
local w = (display.contentWidth/5) - 25
local snareButton = display.newImage( "Button1.png", w,
display.contentHeight-100)

local guitar1Button = display.newImage( "Button2.png", w*2,
display.contentHeight-100)

local guitar2Button = display.newImage( "Button3.png", w*3,
display.contentHeight-100)

local piano1Button = display.newImage( "Button4.png", w*4,
display.contentHeight-100)

local piano2Button = display.newImage( "Button5.png", w*5,
display.contentHeight-100)

local mp3Button = display.newImage( "Button6.png",
display.contentWidth/2 -25, display.contentHeight/2)

snareButton:addEventListener("tap", playButton1)
guitar1Button:addEventListener("tap", playButton2)
guitar2Button:addEventListener("tap", playButton3)
piano1Button:addEventListener("tap", playButton4)
piano2Button:addEventListener("tap", playButton5)
mp3Button:addEventListener("tap", playButton6)
```

You will notice that the simulator does not support multi-touch
events (anyone have two mice?). To fully appreciate your
composing abilities, you will have to publish the app to your test
device.

Where did I put that file?

As we prepare to discuss recording and accessing external files
such as media files and photos, let us take a moment to discuss
the directories on your mobile device. Both iOS and Android
create a 'sandbox' around your app so that it is unable to impact

other apps that are running on the mobile device. Each app has access to three folders: the Resource directory, Documents directory, and Temporary directory. To access any of these folders you must place the keyword system in front of it. Let us look at each of these types of folders:

- system.ResourceDirectory – is the folder or directory where your assets are stored. Do not change anything in this folder while the app is running. It could invalidate the app and the OS will consider the app malware and refuse to launch. The Resource Directory is assumed (i.e., the default folder) when loading assets for your app, so you don't have to specify it when loading an image or sound file.
- system.DocumentsDirectory – should be used for files that need to persist between sessions. When used in the simulator, the user's documents folder is used.
- system.TemporaryDirectory – Just as the name says, is temporary. Only use for in-app, temporary data. No guarantee that the file will be there the next time the app is used.

When you are programming and need to know where a file is stored on the phone, you can use the command: system.pathForFile(*filename [, baseDirectory]*) to find the absolute path to access files. This command will return nil if file does not exist.

Movies

Yes, you can play video through Solar2D. When you call for video playback the media player interface takes over. If showControls is true, the user can pause, start, stop, and seek in the video. It is a good idea to use a listener to notify your app when the video has ended (i.e. give it a function to be called when the user is done playing the video). iOS supported formats include .mov, .mp4, .m4v, and .3gp using H264 compression at 640x480 at 30fps and MPEG-4 Part 2 video.

144

At the time of this writing,, playback is not supported on the Windows version of the Solar2D Simulator.

media.playVideo(path [,baseSource], showControls, listener) – plays the video in a device-specific popup video media player.

Playing a movie might look something like this:

```
local function doneWithVideo()
    print ("Video finished playing")
end

media.playVideo("catplayspiano.mov", true, doneWithVideo)
```

Camera

The final piece of the media tools is the camera. The API call opens a platform-specific interface to the device camera or photo library. The required listener handles the image, whether from the camera or library. Since there is not a real camera in the simulator, it will instead open a finder window to allow you to select an image file to substitute for the camera image.

media.show(imageSource, listener) –. *imageSource* can be: media.PhotoLibrary, media.Camera, media.SavedPhotosAlbum.

Project 7.1 X-Ray Camera

That's right, you read the title of this project correctly, and we are going to turn the camera on your smartphone into an X-Ray Camera! This is so much better than those X-ray glasses that we (okay, I) paid too much for as a child from the back of comic books!

This app falls under the 'joke app' category. For this app, we will really take someone's picture; do a bit of processing with a mask, then display the skeleton.

Christina Cheek of Art & Design Studios has graciously allowed the use of an illustrated skeleton for our project.

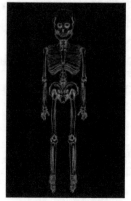

Image: Christina Cheek

Before we dive into the code, a reminder: The camera API is not available through the Windows simulator. You will be able to select an existing image for testing in the Solar2D Simulator.

Our config file is standard for most projects.

config.lua

```
application =
{
        content =
        {
                width = 320,
                height = 480,
                scale = "letterbox",
                fps = 60,
                antialias = false,
                xalign = "center",
                yalign = "center"
        }
}
```

Next, we will setup the build settings. My target device is an iPhone, but I have included icon settings for an iPad.

build.settings

```
-- build.settings for project: Ch11 X Ray Camera
settings =
{
        androidPermissions =
        {
                "android.permission.CAMERA"
        },
        iphone =
        {
                plist =
                {
        CFBundleIconFile = "icon.png",
        CFBundleIconFiles = {
          "icon.png",
          "icon@2x.png",
        },
                },
        },
        orientation =
        {
                default ="portrait",
                content = "portrait",
                supported =
                {
                        "portrait"
                },
        },
}
```

On to our main file. We will hide the status bar and check to see if the app is running on a device that supports this operation (at this

147

time, an iPhone or Macintosh running the Solar2D simulator). If the device is not supported, display an appropriate message.

main.lua

```
local proceedButton
display.setStatusBar(display.HiddenStatusBar)
local isXcodeSimulator = "iPhone Simulator" ==
system.getInfo("model")

if(isAndroid or isXcodeSimulator) then
        local alert = native.showAlert( "Information", "Camera API
not available on Android or iOS Simulator.", { "OK"})
end
```

Load a background and set the color to red. Display a text message to tap the screen to begin.

```
local bkgd = display.newRect( 0, 0, display.contentWidth,
display.contentHeight )
bkgd:setFillColor( .5, 0, 0 )

local text = display.newText( "Tap anywhere to launch Camera", 0,
0, nil, 16 )
text:setFillColor( 1, 1, 1 )
text.x = 0.5 * display.contentWidth
text.y = 0.5 * display.contentHeight
```

Next, create the 'processing' function that will be called from a button press event. The processing function will hide the process button, load a scan bar, and transition the scan bar from the top of the screen to the bottom over the course of 2 seconds.

```
local processing = function (event)
        proceedButton.alpha = 0
        local scanbar = display.newImageRect("scan.png", 320,
50)
```

```
        scanbar.x = display.contentWidth/2
        scanbar.y=0
        transition.to(scanbar, {y=display.contentHeight, time=
2000})
```

As the scan bar slides down the screen, we face out the photo
image and fade in the skeleton.

```
        local skeleton = display.newImageRect ("invertskele.png",
302, 480)
        skeleton.alpha = 0
        skeleton.x = display.contentWidth/2
        skeleton.y = display.contentHeight/2
        transition.to(image,{alpha = 0, time = 4000})
        transition.to(skeleton, {alpha=1, time = 5000})
end
```

The sessionComplete function handles the display of the image.
After assigning the results from the event (handled after this
function), print is used to pass basic information to the terminal to
help with troubleshooting. If an image is loaded, it is centered.
Finally, this function calls the function above, processing, from a
button that is displayed over the top of the image.

```
local sessionComplete = function(event)
        image = event.target

        print( "Camera ", ( image and "returned an image" ) or
"session was canceled" )
        print( "event name: " .. event.name )
        print( "target: " .. tostring( image ) )


        if image then
                -- center image on screen
                image.x = display.contentWidth/2
```

```
                image.y = display.contentHeight/2
                local w = image.width
                local h = image.height
            print( "w,h = ".. w ..","  .. h )

            proceedButton= display.newImage("button.png")
                proceedButton.x = 160
                proceedButton.y = 340
                proceedButton:addEventListener("tap", processing)
        bkgd:setFillColor(0,0,0)
                bkgd:removeSelf()
            text:removeSelf()
    end
end
```

And here is where the magic happens: media.show calls the
camera, and then passes the resulting image to sessionComplete
when the user taps the opening screen. Finally, an event listener
is used for the background (bkgd) image tap that calls the camera
routine.

```
local listener = function( event )
        media.show( media.Camera, sessionComplete )
        return true
end
bkgd:addEventListener( "tap", listener )
```

Note that we haven't saved the image. It is only maintained in
memory until the app is closed. We will discuss saving
information to the local device in a later chapter.

Recording Audio

It is possible to record audio using the Solar2D interface. While
different platforms support different formats, both Apple and

Android support the raw audio file format. The recording commands are:

- media.newRecording([*path*]) − Creates the object for audio recording. If the path is omitted, the recorded audio will not be saved.

- object:startRecording() − starts audio recording and cancels any audio playback.

- object:isRecording() − returns true if audio recording is in progress.

- object:stopRecording() − stops audio recording.

- object:setSampleRate(r) − sets the sampling rate. Valid rates are: 8000, 11025, 16000, 22050, and 44100. Note: Windows simulator with a sample rate of 44100Hz may create an aif file that is corrupt and not playable. setSampleRate must be called before the startTuner.

- object:getSampleRate() − returns the current audio recording sample rate.

- object:startTuner( ) − Turns on audio tuning feature. Should be started before startRecording is called.

- object:stopTuner() − stops the tuner.

- object:getTunerFrequency() − returns the last calculated frequency in Hz.

- object:getTunerVolume() − returns the mean squared normalized sample value of the current audio buffer (i.e., a value between -1 & 1).

Summary

As you can see, the media capabilities of Solar2D are quite extensive. In this chapter, we reviewed using the audio API, and the media API. With the media API, we are able to record audio, take pictures, and show movies.

Assignments

1) Add a restart button so that the x-ray app does not need to be restarted every time.

2) Add additional graphics to be seen once the image is 'processed'.

3) Create your own mp4 or mov player using the media.playVideo API.

4) Modify the audio player by adding fade-in/out controls.

5) Add audio to the x-ray app so that you can add a short message about the photo that was taken.

6) Create an app that makes a sound or plays music after a specific length of time. Great for people like me who lose track of time when they are doing something they enjoy!

Chapter 8: A Little Phun with Physics

Learning Objectives

The physics in Solar2D is just plain fun (or phun). In this chapter, we will examine the basics of using physics in Solar2D. This includes:

- Setting gravity
- Types of bodies
- Detecting collisions
- Working with joints

Turn on Physics

The physics implementation in Solar2D is built upon the popular Box2D. The great people at Solar2D Labs have simplified the implementation so that you can quickly and easily add physics to your environment. With just a few lines of code you can add gravity, detect collisions between objects, and use joints to connect objects.

Remember, physics comes at a cost. The number of calculations required by Solar2D to run your app will dramatically increase. To turn on physics place the commands

```
require("physics")
physics.start(true)
```

at the beginning of your main.lua file. The (true) parameter in the physics.start command is to prevent the bodies that gravity is affecting from going to 'sleep'. In other words, if a body isn't involved in a collision, it will go to 'sleep', which reduces the overhead on the processor, but in some cases, if the bodies are asleep, they will stop responding to changes in the physics environment.

If it isn't important that all bodies stay awake, you can use the 'false' parameter and save on processor demand.

Scaling

To create accurate pixel-to-meter ratios, you may need to adjust the scaling of the physics engine. This is only done once before any bodies are added. Scaling can be changed with the command

```
physics.setScale(n)
```

where n should be the width in pixels of the sprite divided by the real-world width. So if an object is 50 pixels on the screen and is 2 meters in the real world, n should be set to 25 = (50/2). By default, the scale is set to 30 pixels per meter which is optimal to represent 0.1m to 10m objects to correspond to bodies between 3 and 300 pixels in size. This is an appropriate setting for iPhones through 3GS. For iPhone 4, iPad, and Android devices, you may need to increase this value.

Scaling is based on original content dimensions. So if you are using the scaling features discussed in previous chapters, you may need to tweak the setScale value to give you more realistic responses.
The setScale property has no impact on onscreen objects scaling. It only impacts how the physics engine performs calculations.

Bodies

A body is any object that has been changed so that it can simulate a physical object. To make an object a body you use the command

```
physics.addBody(object, [bodyType,] {density=d, friction=f,
bounce = b [, radius =r or shape=s]})
```

154

When you convert a display object into a physics object (a body), the physics engine's rules take over. The physics engine will assume the reference point of the object is the center of the object, no matter where it was set as a display object. Scaling and rotating the object can still be done, but the physics engine will continue to treat the object as it was before the scaling or rotation. So if you are going to scale or rotate, make sure that you do it before you convert it into a physics object. In my experience this means getting any resizing/scaling done before you do your addBody, otherwise, it might have some strange results.

Body Types

Body type is an optional string parameter with the possible values of "static", "dynamic", and "kinematic". The default type is "dynamic".

- **Static** bodies do not move and do not interact with other objects. Typically the ground and walls will be set to static.
- **Dynamic** bodies are affected by collisions with other objects and gravity.
- **Kinematic** objects are affected by forces but not by gravity. Draggable objects are set to "kinematic" during the drag event (see Chapter 9 for an example).

Density, Friction, and Bounce

Physical bodies have three main properties; density, friction, and bounce.

Density is multiplied by the area of the body's shape to determine its mass. The basis of this calculation is that 1.0 is equivalent to water. If a material has less mass than water, such as wood (or a duck or very small rocks - plus 5 points for those who get the reference), the density should be less than 1.0. Heavier materials such as stone or metal will have a density greater than 1.0. But

155

don't feel constrained by these guidelines. It's your app and the material can have the density that you feel makes your game flow correctly.

Friction can be any non-negative number. A value of 0 means no friction. A 1.0 is high friction. The default is 0.3. Friction is applied as the body moves through the environment.

Bounce is used to calculate how much of an object's velocity is returned after a collision occurs. A value greater than 0.3 can be considered bouncy. A value of 1.0 would mean that an object keeps all of its velocity; nothing is lost from the collision. A value greater than 1.0 will cause the object to gain velocity after the collision. The default value is 0.2.

Body Shapes

If no shape or radius information is supplied, then the body boundaries will snap to the rectangular boundaries of the display object. While this is fine for a box, the ground, or a platform, it can create strange occurrences if the physics body is a diagonal line shape. In this case, a diagonal line shape will have a bounding box that is a rectangle of the full area between the corners of the object.

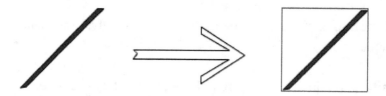

Using the default body shape rectangle can simplify calculations, but it can also create strange collisions if you have a circle or complex shape. If a radius is provided, then the body boundaries will be circular, centered in the middle of the object used to create the physics body. If a shape is supplied, then the body boundaries will follow the polygon provided by the shape. The maximum number of sides per shape is 8 and all angles must be convex (angles have to bulge or curve out, not in; or no innie belly buttons; only outies).

When working with complex shapes, you can use polygon bodies to define the shape. If you want to save a great deal of time, I recommend Physics Editor (https://www.codeandweb.com/physicseditor) or the new graphics.newOutline() command. If you want to do it yourself, then you can set the shape of the object using coordinates. Coordinate sets must be defined in clockwise order with no concave areas:

```
local line = display.newLine(0, 0, 30, 30)
local lineShape = {0, 0, 30, 30}
physics.addBody(line, {density = 2, friction =0.3, bounce=0.3,
shape = lineShape})
```

You can also set the body to be a circle instead of a rectangle, and you can set the radius of the object to better handle collisions:

physics.addBody(object, [bodyType,] { density=d, friction=f, bounce=b, radius=r})

Body Properties
There are many body properties available to assist your virtual environment to operate correctly. These are all .properties to simplify interacting with them in your app:
- body.isAwake –Boolean. Will fetch the current state of the body or force the body to wake or go to sleep by passing a

Boolean. By default, bodies will go to sleep if nothing happens for several seconds until a collision occurs.

- body.isBodyActive – Boolean. Sets or returns the current body. Inactive bodies are not destroyed, but they no longer interact with other bodies.
- body.isBullet – Boolean. Sets whether the body should be treated as a "bullet". Bullets perform continuous collision detection rather than checking on environment (or world) updates. This is processor expensive but will keep bullets from passing through solid barriers.
- body.isSensor – Boolean. Sets whether the body should be treated as a sensor. Sensors allow other bodies to pass through them, but fire a collision event. Other bodies will not bounce off of a sensor. Sensors do not have to be visible to interact with other bodies.
- body.isSleepingAllowed – Boolean. Sets whether a body is allowed to sleep. The default is true.
- body.isFixedRotation – Boolean. Sets whether a body can rotate. The default is false (i.e. can rotate). Useful for platforms that should not rotate when another object collides or lands on it.
- body.angularVelocity – Number. The value of rotational velocity in degrees per second.
- body.linearDamping – Number. Determines how much a body's linear motion should be dampened. Default is zero.
- body.angularDamping – Number. Determines how much a body's rotation should be dampened. Default is zero.
- body.bodyType – "static", "dynamic", "kinematic". Static bodies do not move and are not affected by other forces (for example: the ground). Dynamic (default) bodies are affected by gravity and collisions. Kinematic bodies are affected by forces other than gravity. Used for drag.

Body Methods

Body methods allow a force to be applied to a body causing it to move or rotate. As with all methods, a ":" is used to separate the object (body) from the method.

- body:setLinearVelocity(x, y) – passes the x and y velocity in pixels per second.
- body:getLinearVelocity – returns the x and y values in pixels per second of the body's velocity. The normal standard command would be: vx, vy = myBody:getLinearVelocity()
- body:applyForce(x, y, body.x, body.y) – applies a linear force or velocity (x, y) to a point in the body. If you apply the force off-center, it will cause the body to spin. Note that the body's density will affect the force required to move the object.
- body:applyTorque(n) – set the applied rotational force. Rotation occurs around its center of mass.
- body:applyLinearImpulse(x, y, body.x, body.y) – A single pulse of force (instead of the constant force of applyForce) applied to the object.
- body:applyAngularImpulse(n) – Similar to applyTorque, but is a single pulse of force applied to the object.

Gravity

Gravity is very easy to simulate with Solar2D. You can set gravity for a variety of different effects based on the x or y direction. A positive value will cause bodies to fall toward the bottom of the screen, while a negative number will cause them to rise toward the top of the screen. If there are no ground or wall bodies (bodies set to static as their type), the bodies being affected by gravity will eventually leave the screen. The default gravity setting is (0, 9.8) which will simulate Earth's gravity, pulling bodies downwards on the y-axis.

Gravity is set using

physics.setGravity(x, y)

To get the current value of gravity, you can use

gx, gy = physics.getGravity()

159

Ground and Boundaries

If you are going to keep things from moving off the screen due to physics, you will need to set boundaries. This is done by loading an image and placing it at your boundary. Then when you add the body to physics, set it as a static type.

Your boundary can be anything from a line to a complex sprite environment.

local ground = display.newImage("ground.png", 0,320)
physics.addBody(ground, "static")

Project 8.0: Playing with Gravity

This is a small little project to demonstrate how gravity can be adjusted and manipulated within your app. I am planning this app for a tablet to give a little more maneuvering room.
We will begin by turning on physics and setting gravity to zero. Then create a border area so that our body (a crate from the sample projects) doesn't fall off the screen. Make sure you use a rectangle for the boundary. Problems can arise if you just use a line. My target for this project is a tablet device.

```
-- Project: Ch8PlayingWithGravity
local physics = require("physics")
physics.start(true)

-- set initial value for gravity
physics.setGravity(0,-0.1)

-- initialize gx and gy to store gravity changes
gx = 0
gy = -0.1

-- A couple of variables to make locating the sides easier
```

```
local xCenter = display.contentCenterX
local yCenter = 768/2

-- create border area so object doesn't fall off screen
 local ground = display.newRect(xCenter, 768, 768, 10)
ground:setFillColor(1,1,1,1)
local leftSide = display.newRect(5,yCenter, 10, 768)
leftSide:setFillColor(1,1,1,1)

local rightSide = display.newRect(763,yCenter,10,768)
rightSide:setFillColor(1,1,1,1)

local top= display.newRect(xCenter,0,768,10)
top:setFillColor(1,1,1,1)

 -- add border to physics as a static object (unaffected by gravity)
physics.addBody(ground, "static")
physics.addBody(leftSide, "static")
physics.addBody(rightSide, "static")
physics.addBody(top, "static")
```

Next we load an image to be thrown around by the gravity fluctuation.

```
-- load the crate and add it as a physics body
local crate = display.newImage("crateB.png" )
crate.x = 389
crate.y= 389
physics.addBody(crate, {density=1.0, friction =0.3, bounce =  0.2})
```

By creating a local text object, we can see the current value of gravity. First, we create the text objects and load the buttons. Notice that I used the same button image, just rotated it according to the direction that it needs to face.

```
local gravityX = display.newText("0.0", 490, 875,
native.systemFont, 36)
local gravityY = display.newText("0.0", 195, 875,
native.systemFont, 36 )

-- load arrow buttons and position buttons
local upButton = display.newImage("arrowButton.png", 200, 800)
upButton.rotation = -90

local downButton = display.newImage("arrowButton.png", 200,
950)
downButton.rotation=90

local leftButton = display.newImage("arrowButton.png", 400, 875)
leftButton.rotation=180

local rightButton = display.newImage("arrowButton.png", 600,
875)
```

Using a function, we will update the text object holding the values of vertical and horizontal gravity. Due to the precision of the gravity variable, it is necessary to show just the first 4 digits of the variable. To accomplish this, we will use the string sub method; a string method that returns the specific character range you wish to show.

```
-- Update the displayed value of gravity
local function updateGravity()
    gx, gy = physics.getGravity()
    gravityX.text = gx
    gravityX.text = (gravityX.text:sub(1,4))
    gravityY.text  = gy
    gravityY.text = (gravityY.text:sub(1,4))
end
```

Next, we will create a function for each button to handle adjusting the gravity. After adjusting gravity, the text update function is called to update the displayed gravity values.

```
-- adjust the gravity for each button event
local function upButtonEvent (event)
        physics.setGravity(gx,gy-0.1)
        updateGravity()
end
local function downButtonEvent (event)
        physics.setGravity(gx,gy+0.1)
        updateGravity()
end
local function leftButtonEvent (event)
        physics.setGravity(gx-0.1,gy)
        updateGravity()
end
local function rightButtonEvent (event)
        physics.setGravity(gx+0.1,gy)
        updateGravity()
end
```

And finally, we add our event listeners.

```
-- add event listeners for each button
upButton:addEventListener("tap", upButtonEvent)
downButton:addEventListener("tap", downButtonEvent)
leftButton:addEventListener("tap", leftButtonEvent)
rightButton:addEventListener("tap", rightButtonEvent)
```

As a final note, this project has been supplemented and turned into a game available on the iTunes app store and Google app store.

Collision Detection

If you want to build a game, I am sure you have been wondering, "How do I know when one body hits another?" Three collision events are available through the Solar2D event listener. The first type is for general collision events and is named "collision". A collision has two phases, "began" and "ended", which represent the initial contact and when the contact has ended. These can be used for normal two-body collisions and body-sensor collisions.

The second type of collision event is a "preCollision". This event fires before the objects begin to interact. This type of collision can be very noisy and may send several events prior to actual contact. You should only use pre-collision if it is essential to your game logic. Make sure your listener is a local event rather than a global one to reduce the overhead and to reduce the number of pre-collision events.

The final type of collision event is a "postCollision". This event type fires after the objects have interacted. Within this event, the collision force is reported and can be used to determine the magnitude of the collision, if needed for your game. The force is returned at the property event.force in a post-collision event. Like pre-collision, post-collision can be a noisy event generator. It is best to keep the event local and screen out small post-collision forces to maintain your game performance.

Sensors

Sensors are very handy tools in game apps. When another physics body collides with a body that has been turned into a sensor, it fires a collision event. Sensors do not have to be visible and can be any physics body. The difference between a sensor and another body is that a sensor will allow the colliding body to pass through, whereas a normal body-body collision will cause a physics reaction, such as bounce, friction, etc.

Sensors are very handy when you need something to begin happening when the player comes within range. It can greatly reduce processing if an animation or other sequence is paused until the player reaches a certain point in the game.

Joints

Joints allow you to join bodies to create complex game objects. To create a joint, you first create the bodies that will be joined. After creating the bodies, you select the type of joint needed to create the effect you desire for your app. The available types of joints include:
- Pivot joint
- Distance joint
- Piston joint
- Friction joint
- Weld joint
- Wheel joint
- Pulley joint
- Touch joint

Pivot Joint

A pivot joint is used to join two bodies that overlap at a point. It can be used in many ways including a ragdoll figure for the head and neck as well as appendages. The initial command to create a pivot joint requires the joint type, the two bodies to be joined, and an anchor point.

myNewJoint = physics.newJoint("pivot", bodyA, bodyB, 200,300)

Each pivot joint has several properties to specify the limitations and actions of the joint:

- .isMotorEnabled(Boolean) – allows the pivot point to act as if it had a motor attached. Usually used to simulate a spinning object such as a wheel.
- .motorSpeed(number)- get/sets the linear speed of the motor in pixels per second
- .motorTorque() – returns the torque of the joint motor
- .maxMotorTorque(number) – sets the torque of the joint motor
- .isLimitEnabled(Boolean) –get/set whether the joint is limited in motion
- :setRotationLimits(lowerLimit, upperLimit) – sets the rotation limit in degrees from zero.
- :getRotationLimits() – returns the rotation limits in the format lowerLimit, upperLimit = myNewJoint:getRotationLimits()
- .jointAngle() – returns the current angle of the joint in degrees.
- .jointSpeed()- returns the speed of the joint in degrees per second.

Distance Joint

Adding a distance joint to your app creates a join between two bodies that are at a fixed distance. The distance should be greater than zero (otherwise, you should use a pivot joint).

myNewJoint = physics.newJoint("distance", bodyA, bodyB, bodyA.x, bodyA.y, bodyB.x, bodyB.y)

The bodyA.x and .y and the bodyB.x and .y are the anchor points for each body. Additional parameters include:

- .length(number) – sets the distance between the anchor points
- .frequency(number) –sets the mass-spring damping frequency in hertz
- .dampingRatio(number) – sets the damping ratio. Range is 0 (no damping) to 1(critical damping).

166

Piston Joint

The piston joint creates a join between two bodies on a single axis of motion, just like you would expect from a piston or a spring. When creating your bodies for a piston joint, one of them should be dynamic.

myNewJoint = physics.newJoint("piston", bodyA, bodyB, bodyA.x, bodyA.y, axisDistanceX, axisDistanceY)

Unique properties of the piston joint are:

- .jointTranslation() – returns the linear translation of the joint in pixels.
- .jointSpeed() – returns the speed of the joint in degrees per second.

Piston joints may also use the parameters discussed under the pivot joint.

Friction Joint

A friction joint is a joint that resists motion, or is 'sticky'.

myJoint = physics.newJoint("friction", bodyA, bodyB, 200,300)

Its properties are:

- .maxForce(number) – sets the maximum force that can be exerted on the joint.
- .maxTorque(number) – sets the maximum torque that can be applied to the joint.

Weld Joint

Just as the name implies, the weld joint 'welds' two bodies together at a point. It does not allow for movement or rotation.

myJoint = physics.newJoint("weld", bodyA, bodyB, 200,300)

Wheel Joint

A wheel joint combines a piston and pivot joint, acting like a wheel that is mounted on a shock absorber of a car. It makes use of the piston and pivot joint properties.

myJoint = physics.newJoint("wheel", bodyA, bodyB, bodyA.x, bodyA.y, axisDistanceX,axisDistanceY)

Pulley Joint

A pulley joint attaches two bodies with an imaginary line or rope that remains a constant length. If one body is pulled down, the other will move up.

It is more complicated than other joints since it must specify a joint anchor point within each body and a stationary anchor point for the 'rope' to hang from. There is a ratio property associated so that a block and tackle can be simulated (i.e. one side of the rope moves more quickly than the other). By default, the ratio is set to 1.0, simulating a simple pulley.

myJoint = physics.newJoint("pulley", bodyA, bodyB, anchorA_x, anchorA_y, anchorB_x,anchorB_y, bodyA.x, bodyA.y, bodyB.x, bodyB.y, ratio)

Read-only properties of the pulley joint include:

- .length1() – returns the distance between the 1st joint and the stationary pulley anchor point.
- .length2() – returns the distance between the 2nd joint and the stationary pulley anchor point.
- .ratio() – returns the ratio of the pulley joint

Touch Joint

A touch point creates a temporary elastic joint between a body and your finger. The body will attempt to follow the touch until stopped by other solid objects. If the body that is following the touch collides with another body, a collision event will occur. A body will also rotate based upon gravity when it is 'picked up by an end'.

To move an object by its center point (keeping it from being affected by gravity):

touchJoint = physics.newJoint("touch", crate, crate.x, crate.y)

To move an object based upon where it was touched:

touchJoint = physics.newJoint("touch", crate, event.x, event.y)

Properties of touch joint include:
- .maxForce(number) –get/set the speed of the joint. Default is 1000 for the rapid dragging effect.
- .frequency(number) – get/set the frequency of the elastic joint in hertz.
- .dampingRatio(number) – get/set the damping ratio from 0 (no damping) to 1 (critical damping).

Common Methods and Properties for Joints
These properties and methods are available to all joints:
- .getAnchorA() – returns the x, y coordinates of the joints anchor points for bodyA. Values returned are in the local coordinates of the body, so a value of 0, 0 would be the center of the object.
- .getAnchorB() – see .getAnchorA()
- :getReactionForce() – returns the reaction force at the joint anchor for the second body.
- .reactionTorque()- returns the reaction torque at the joint anchor for the second body.
- :removeSelf() – destroys an existing joint and detaches the two bodies.

Now that we have seen the API for physics, let's put some of these into action.

Project 8.1 Sample Physics Projects

One of the most confusing projects for many people getting started with physics programming is how to use the various joints. To help solve that problem, I am providing a couple of short programs that will demonstrate some of the joints and how it can be used.

8.1A: Touch Joint

In my opinion, one of the most misunderstood joints is the touch joint. The touch joint creates a link between the user's touch and the object that they are touching, allowing the user to drag the object around the screen, yet the object still interacts with the physics environment with collisions. The touch joint creates an elastic connection between the touch and the object touch. The object will attempt to follow the user's touch, but will still be impacted by gravity or other on-screen physics objects.

main.lua

```
display.setStatusBar(display.HiddenStatusBar)
local  physics = require("physics")
physics.start()
```

After hiding our status bar and starting physics, the first step is to create a function to handle the movement of the user's finger on the screen, which will drag the box around the screen.

The dragBody function is fairly standard and you will see it several more times as we work our way through more advanced projects. A dragBody function will generally have three (3) event phases that need to be handled: began, moved, and ended. These directly correspond with the start of the touch event, the user

170

moving/dragging their finger on the screen, and the user releasing or lifting their finger from the screen.

After the creation of the function, we are going to create three (3) variables: body, phase, and stage. Body refers to what the user is going to drag (the crate or box in this case). Phase will store the current phase of the event: began, moved, or ended. The stage variable makes sure that the only thing we are moving is the box.

```
-- handling touch joint events
local function dragBody( event )
    local body = event.target
    local phase = event.phase
    local stage = display.getCurrentStage()
```

We are now ready to handle the 'began' stage. This is when the user has initially touched the crate and is ready to start moving it. In this stage we set the focus of the environment to the box and create the touch joint between the user's touch and the place they tapped on the box. You could give the x and y location as the center of the object, but I thought it would be more interesting for you to see what happens when the user touches a corner of the box and starts to drag it around the screen.

```
if "began" == phase then
    stage:setFocus( body, event.id )
    body.isFocus = true

    -- Create a temporary touch joint and store it in the object
    body.tempJoint = physics.newJoint( "touch", body, event.x,
event.y
```

Next, we will handle the 'moved' phase. The only thing that needs to be done in the move phase is to tell the box to try to follow where the touch is currently located (i.e. where the user moved their finger to). This is done with the setTarget method by passing the current location of the touch event.

```
elseif body.isFocus then
    if "moved" == phase then
        -- Update the joint to track the touch
        body.tempJoint:setTarget( event.x, event.y )
```

The final part of the dragBody function is to handle the release of the object. This occurs when the user stops touching the screen. First, the stage is returned to normal (i.e. the box is no longer the focus). After resetting the focus, we remove the touch joint so that it will no longer be active. Finally, we do a return true, to make sure that the app doesn't continue to try to continuously perform touch events while we are handling the initial event.

```
elseif "ended" == phase or "cancelled" == phase then
        stage:setFocus( body, nil )
        body.isFocus = false

        -- Remove the joint when the touch ends
        body.tempJoint:removeSelf()

    end
end
-- Stop further propagation of touch event
return true
end
```

Now the basic program: A little text to tell us what is happening, loading the box and ground, adding them to the physics engine, and setting up the event listener for the touch joint event, which is initialized by a touch event (remember, a touch event is when the user continues to touch the screen, whereas a tap event is a quick touch and release).

```
local mytext = display.newText("Touch Joint",0 ,0, nil, 36)

local box = display.newImage("crate.png",
display.contentWidth/2, 0)
local ground = display.newImage("ground.png", 0,
display.contentHeight - 50)

physics.addBody(ground, "static")
physics.addBody(box, "dynamic", {density= 1, friction =0.3,
bounce = 0.5 })

box:addEventListener("touch", dragBody)
```

8.1B: Pulley Joint

Compared to the touch joint, the pulley joint is fairly straightforward, though it has a great deal of built-in power and flexibility. With the pulley joint, you can simulate a two-pulley system that can handle ratios, thus allowing you to simulate block and tackle configurations.

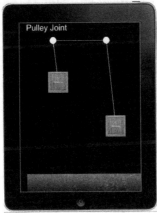

For our example, I am going to use both pulleys and show how it can be used to simulate simple pulley systems. As before, we

173

start by hiding the status bar, enabling physics, displaying some text as to what the app will demonstrate, and loading two crates and the ground. Then two circles are created to represent the pulleys and a connecting line is drawn from the center of the boxes to the pulleys. We move the two lines to the back so that they are not in front of the boxes and add the boxes to the physics engine. I set box2 to be slightly denser than box1 so that we can see the pulleys in action.

main.lua

```
display.setStatusBar(display.HiddenStatusBar)
local  physics = require("physics")
physics.start()

local mytext = display.newText("Pulley Joint",0 ,0, nil, 24)

local box1 = display.newImage("crate.png",
display.contentWidth*0.25, 200)
local box2 = display.newImage("crate.png",
display.contentWidth*0.75, 200)
local ground = display.newImage("ground.png", 0,
display.contentHeight-50)

local pulley1 = display.newCircle(display.contentWidth*0.25, 50,
10)
local pulley2 = display.newCircle(display.contentWidth*0.75, 50,
10)
line1 = display.newLine(box1.x, box1.y, pulley1.x, pulley1.y)
line2 = display.newLine(box2.x, box2.y, pulley2.x, pulley2.y)
line3 = display.newLine(pulley1.x, pulley1.y, pulley2.x, pulley2.y)

line1:toBack()
line2:toBack()

physics.addBody(ground, "static")
physics.addBody(box1, "dynamic", {density= 1, friction =0.3,
bounce = 0.5 })
```

```
physics.addBody(box2, "dynamic", {density=1.01, friction = 0.3,
bounce = 0.5 })
```

To create the pulley, we just need to specify the two objects that
will be on each end of the pulley (box1 & box 2), the pulleys x & y
location, the two boxes starting location, and the ratio between the
boxes. The default ratio is 1 or equal.

```
-- physics.newJoint("pulley", bodyA, bodyB, anchorA_x, anchorA_y,
anchorB_x,anchorB_y, bodyA.x, bodyA.y, bodyB.x, bodyB.y, 1.0 )

local myJoint = physics.newJoint("pulley", box1, box2, pulley1.x,
pulley1.y, pulley2.x, pulley2.y, box1.x, box1.y, box2.x, box2.y, 1)
```

To make the app more visually appealing, I update the lines every
time the frame updates. Typically most apps run at 30 frames per
second. Thus the lines are being re-drawn each time the app
starts a new frame.

The RunTime:addEventListener ("enterFrame", listener) is a handy
command to remember for your graphic-intensive apps; rather
than being time-sensitive, the graphics can be updated each time
the screen is updated.

```
local function lineUpdate()
    line1:removeSelf()
    line2:removeSelf()
    line1 = display.newLine(pulley1.x, pulley1.y, box1.x, box1.y)
    line2 = display.newLine(box2.x, box2.y, pulley2.x, pulley2.y)
    line1:toBack()
    line2:toBack()
end

Runtime:addEventListener("enterFrame", lineUpdate)
```

Project 8.2: Wrecking Ball

This project will demonstrate the use of pivot joints and the impact of density and force upon objects.

We will use four graphic objects for this project: the crane arm, the line (3 copies of it), a ball, and a crate (2 copies). As you might expect, we will begin the project by turning on physics and setting the gravity. I have told the physics engine to not allow items to go to sleep. Usually, I avoid this setting; but for everything to react properly, I found it necessary to turn this on. I set the gravity at (0, 9.8) which should simulate Earth's gravity for the project.

```
local physics = require("physics")
physics.start(true)
physics.setGravity(0, 9.8)

-- create the ground
 local ground = display.newRect(0, 438,  900, 438)
ground:setFillColor(1,1,1,1)
```

After creating the ground, we load the crane arm, line, wrecking ball, and crates. I found that I needed to scale the crane arm up to look right for the app. The lines were placed slightly overlapping so that the pivot joints could be created easily.

```
-- load the crane, line, ball and crate
local crane = display.newImage("crane arm.png", 10, 70)
crane.rotation = 90
crane:scale(2,2)

local line1 = display.newImage("line.png", 170, 20)
local line2 =display.newImage("line.png", 170, 110)
local line3 = display.newImage("line.png", 170, 205)

local ball = display.newImage("wrecking ball.png",110, 280)

local crate1= display.newImage("crateB.png", 300, 300)
local crate2 = display.newImage("crateB.png", 300, 225)
```

Next, add each item as a physics body. The ground and crane will
not move and should not be affected by gravity, so we set them as
static. The lines should have no bounce or friction, and a higher
density than water. The wrecking ball is a 'heavy' item and needs
to be heavier than the crates. I went with 10, which might be a
little low, but as you will see when it comes time to apply force to
the ball, we have to keep the density reasonable. Finally, I set both
crates to a density of 5, keeping the default bounce and friction.

```
-- make all of the objects into physics bodies
physics.addBody(ground, "static")
physics.addBody(crane, "static")
physics.addBody(line1, {density = 2, friction =0, bounce=0 })
physics.addBody(line2, {density = 2, friction =0, bounce=0 })
physics.addBody(line3, {density = 2, friction =0, bounce=0 })
physics.addBody(ball, {density = 10, friction = 0.7, bounce =0.2})
physics.addBody(crate1, {density=5})
physics.addBody(crate2, {density=5})
```

Creating the pivot joints is very straightforward. Create a joint for
each connection. Select a point where the two items overlap for
the final values.

177

Finally, we apply a linear impulse to the wrecking ball's center of mass to get the ball moving. As you can see, I had to use a fairly high value to get the swing to look the way I wanted.

```
local joint1 = physics.newJoint("pivot", crane, line1, 170, 22)
local joint2 = physics.newJoint("pivot", line1, line2, 170,112)
local joint3 = physics.newJoint("pivot", line2, line3, 170, 206)
local joint4 = physics.newJoint("pivot", line3, ball, 170,280)
ball:applyLinearImpulse(3000, 200, ball.x, ball.y)
```

Trouble Shooting Physics

If you are getting unexpected actions or reactions from your objects, try using the physics.setDrawMode() for troubleshooting help. The setDrawMode property has three settings:
- **debug** – shows the collision engine outlines of bodies only
- **hybrid** – overlays collision outlines over the bodies
- **normal** – default with no collision outlines

physics.setDrawMode("debug")

Summary

Let's face it; there are a lot of possibilities when you add physics to the app environment. I'm sure you have many ideas on how you would like to implement some of these tools. In this chapter we looked at how to create a physics-based environment, adding bodies to the environment, applying force to a body, enabling gravity, detecting collisions, and working with joints. In our next chapter, we will use some of these tools to create a game.

Assignments

1) Modify Project 8.0: Playing with Gravity to provide object density, friction, and bounce information. Add additional

buttons to reset gravity to zero. Adjust the crate density to see the impact on how much gravity is required to move the object.

2) Create a Rube Goldberg Machine that uses the various physics joints and forces to accomplish a very simple action.

3) Modify the density, friction, and bounce of the crates in project 8.2. What impact does changing these parameters have?

4) Add walls inside the gravity area of project 8.0. Modify the bounce settings. Attempt to navigate the box around the new wall. Add a sensor area that will tell you that you have "won" when you move the box to that area.

5) Create 3 simple box bodies and apply force, linear velocity, and linear impulse to each body respectively, and observe the results.

Chapter 9 Mobile Game Design

Learning Objectives

One of the most exciting areas of mobile devices is being able to develop and play games. The concepts behind mobile game development are appropriate for an entire book or series of books. Consider this chapter a very brief introduction to some of the basic programming considerations. In this chapter, we will learn:

- How to use timers
- Handling drag events
- Using frame base animation
- How to make a game

Timers

Timers are one of the key components of game development. Typically within a game, you will need to perform an action every so many seconds or milliseconds. By using the timer API you can call a function to control the functions of your game or app. The primary use of the timer API is timer.performWithDelay.

timer.performWithDelay(*delay*, *listener* [, *iterations*])- provides listener after a period of delay. The listener call cannot contain parameters in the actual function call. Passing parameters within the function call (the *listener*) of a timer.performWithDelay causes the function to be called immediately, thus rendering the delay ineffective. The *delay* is in milliseconds. *Iterations* is 1 by default; passing a 0 will create an infinite loop (until canceled).

Example:

timer.performWithDelay(400, gameLoop, 0) -- will call the function *gameLoop* every 400 milliseconds until canceled.

Timer includes the additional methods of:

- <u>timer.cancel(*timerId*)</u> –cancels the timer operation.
- <u>timer.pause(*timerId*)</u> – pauses the timer operation.
- <u>timer.resume(*timerId*)</u> – resumes a paused timer operation.

More on Touch/Multi-touch

Typically in most games you will have multiple touch events occurring at the same time. To handle those events, you will need to use multi-touch. To respond to a touch or multi-touch event, an event listener (i.e. a function) must be registered for the object (i.e. button) that the user is touching. Touch events have several phases (which can be found in the event.phase parameter that is passed to the event listener). The phases include:

- **began** – occurs when the user first touches the object
- **moved** - occurs if the user moves their finger as they are touching the object
- **ended** & **cancelled** – occurs when the user lifts their finger or the touch is otherwise canceled.

While it is not necessary to check for the event phase in many event listener situations, it can be very useful in many applications. For example, can the user drag items around on the screen in your game? Can they hold (i.e. mash) a button for continuous running or jumping? If so, then you will need to setup a multi-touch event to handle those situations.

Multi-touch can be activated with the command:

system.activate("multitouch ")

When multi-touch is enabled, multiple touches to the same object are handled as a single touch event. We will use multi-touch in our game example later in this chapter for moving the spaceship.

setFocus

setFocus is used to make a display object the target for all future touch events. Generally setFocus is used for objects that change appearance or location after they are touched. It can be used in conjunction with multi-touch. To restore normal focus, pass nil in place of the obj. An example of using setFocus would be dragging an object on the screen. We will use setFocus later in the chapter for our spaceship movement.

*stageObject:***setFocus(***obj***)**

'enterFrame' Animation

In chapter 3 we examined creating animation effects using the transition.to command. Now we are ready for a method of animation that works a little differently. If you are creating animations or need to call a function at the beginning of each frame (a normal situation in game development), the enterFrame event is just what you need. The frame interval of your application can be set in the config.lua file at either 30 or 60 frames per second.

For better battery performance on mobile devices, 30 frames per second is recommended. Remember, just because a device can support a faster frame rate, doesn't mean it should.

Project 9.0: enterFrame Animation

To show how you can use an enterFrame event, I have modified the animation project from Chapter 3. Using the same graphics as before, we will use the enterFrame event and a function to move the square to the center of the screen.

First, we will need a **config.lua** file:

```
application =
{
        content =
        {
                width = 640,
                height = 960,
                scale = "letterbox",
                fps = 60,
                antialias = false,
                xalign = "center",
                yalign = "center"
        }
}
```

I used a typical resolution for most games. Note that the fps
(frames per second) is set to 30.

main.lua

```
local center = display.newImage("Ch3Center.png")
local square = display.newImage("Ch3Square.png")

center.x = display.contentWidth/2
center.y= display.contentHeight/2

square.x = math.random( display.contentWidth )
square.y = math.random( display.contentHeight )

local function move()
  if (square.x > center.x) then
    square.x = square.x -1
  elseif (square.x < center.x)then
    square.x = square.x +1
  end

  if (square.y > center.y) then
    square.y = square.y -1
```

```
   elseif (square.y < center.y)then
      square.y = square.y +1
   end
end


Runtime:addEventListener("enterFrame", move)
```

There are only three modifications from our original program in chapter 3:

- The movement of the square is now a function called move
- Removed the while...Do loop from the function
- Added the event listener for enterFrame, which calls the move function

When you try this app, you will find that the square will slowly move toward the center of the screen. It is moving at the rate of 30 pixels per second: 1 pixel per frame.

Note: The fps in config.lua has only two possible settings: 30 and 60. 60 is the default.

Game Development

The field of game development, particularly mobile game development, is one of the fastest-growing industries in the world. One of the reasons I first became interested in Solar2D was in large part due to how easily you could make an app or game with the same SDK. It is always nice to be able to leverage what you have learned in making business or personal apps for the creation of games.

I originally created this project with one of my mobile programming classes with the beta of the Solar2D Game

Development (now included in the standard release of Solar2D). The students put so much time and energy into this project; I knew we had something fun, at least from a development standpoint. Several students in that class went on to modify or expand the game for their final project.

Note that this is a proof-of-concept project. It is not intended to be ready for release to an app store.

Design Inspiration

Star Explorer is inspired partially by my misspent youth, spending all the money that I earned on arcade games. After many years playing Asteroids, Galaga, Defender, and other popular games of the late 70's and early 80's, how could I not create my own asteroid shooting game?

The goal for the proof of concept is simple:
- Create a game that has a starship.
- Starship must shoot the moving asteroids.
- Move the ship by dragging it.
- Fire by tapping on the ship.
- If an asteroid hits the ship, one life is lost.

We will start with 3 lives and keep track of the score for the player as well. I am beginning this project targeting it for the iPhone.

As for assets, we will need a ship, an asteroid, a graphic for firing, a starry background, and some sound effects.

To keep everything simple for this game, we will use just one programming file (main.lua). To begin with, we will hide the status bar, enable multi-touch, and start the physics engine. As we are in space, gravity will be set at 0, 0. I am going to allow the engine the ability to put the bodies that gravity is affecting to sleep in order to reduce the overhead on the processor.

main.lua

```
-- Hide status bar
display.setStatusBar(display.HiddenStatusBar)
system.activate("multitouch")


-- Setup and start physics
local physics = require("physics")
physics.start()
physics.setGravity(0,0)
```

This is a good place to initialize any variables that will be needed by the game. I usually encourage my students to find a nice big dry-erase board and begin writing down what will be tracked in their game. This is an important step that too many beginning game developers gloss over, assuming they can add the variables as they need. Following that method often leads to the repetition of variables and very long debugging sessions.

In considering our variables, try to think through the game process. The obvious variables that we will need are: background, ship, shots fired, asteroids, lives, and score. As we begin to think about the game mechanics, a few more variables need to be considered:

- How many shots have been fired? This will help us remove shots that did not collide with anything. We don't want to track shots that are off the screen forever.
- How long ago was the shot fired, or better, what is the maximum age I want for each shot? If it exceeds that limit, it should be removed.
- How many asteroids have been created?
- Asteroids and shots will have to be tracked in an array, due to the number in play. This will simplify checking the age of the shots and if the object has moved off the screen. Don't get too hung up on arrays at this point; we will discuss them in greater detail in Chapter 10. Think of them as being able to store multiple values in one variable.
- How fast do we want the game to add new asteroids?
- Are we 'dead'? Multiple collisions can create problems with handling the proper number of lives left.

With these concepts in mind, we can begin initializing our variables. To simplify keeping track of the graphics and sound files for this project, I placed all of my graphics files in a folder named images and my sound files in a folder named sounds.

```
-- Initialize variables
local background = display.newImage ("images/bg1.png", true)
background.x = display.contentWidth /2
background.y = display.contentHeight /2
local lives = 3
local score = 0
local numShot = 0
```

```
local shotTable ={}
local asteroidsTable = {}
local numAsteroids = 0
local maxShotAge = 1000
local tick = 400 -- time between game loops in milliseconds
local died=false
local explosion = audio.loadSound("sounds/explosion.wav")
local fire = audio.loadSound("sounds/fire.wav")
```

Now let's set up the Lives and Score text on the display. We will
do this with functions so that they can be easily called at the
appropriate time during the game. By using functions to set the
lives and score text, they can be shown when we are ready to
display them.

```
-- Display lives and score
local function newText()
    textLives = display.newText("Lives: "..lives, 10, 30, nil, 12)
    textScore = display.newText("Score: "..score, 10, 10, nil, 12)
    textLives:setFillColor(1, 1, 1)
    textScore:setFillColor(1, 1, 1)
end

local function updateText()
    textLives.text = "Lives: "..lives
    textScore.text = "Score: "..score
end
```

Dragging Objects

Let's go ahead and add in the routine for moving our starship.
This is an event initiated by a touch on the ship. A touch is
different from a tap in that the user continues to touch the ship. It
tracks the body's original position, the change to a new position,
and changing the body to a kinematic body type so that it can be
moved. The touch event has 3 phases: began, moved, and ended.

When the ship movement first starts from a touch event, it becomes the focus (t.isFocus) for future ship-touch actions.

```
-- basic dragging physics
local function startDrag( event )
        local t = event.target

        local phase = event.phase
        if "began" == phase then
                display.getCurrentStage():setFocus(t)
                t.isFocus = true

                --Store initial position
                t.x0 = event.x - t.x
                t.y0 = event.y - t.y

        -- make the body type 'kinematic' to avoid gravity problems
                event.target.bodyType = "kinematic"

                -- stop current motion
                event.target:setLinearVelocity( 0,0)
                event.target.angularVelocity = 0

        elseif t.isFocus then
                if "moved" == phase then
                        t.x = event.x - t.x0
                        t.y = event.y - t.y0
                elseif "ended" == phase or "cancelled" == phase
then
                        display.getCurrentStage():setFocus(nil)
                        t.isFocus = false

                        -- switch body type back to "dynamic"
                        if (not event.target.isPlatform) then
                                event.target.bodyType = "dynamic"
                        end
                end
        end
        return true
```

```
end
```

Next we will load the ship. I set the density, bounce to the default values. For this version of the game these values do not matter, but I might use them in a future version. In the final line of code in this section, we give the starfighter a myName value. The myName is used later in collision detection so that we know that the starfighter was involved in the collision and can respond appropriately. The last line of this function will keep the ship from rotating after it gets hit by an asteroid. This will ensure the ship is always pointing up or forward.

```
local function spawnShip()
        starfighter = display.newImage("images/starfighter1.png")
        starfighter.x = display.contentWidth/2
        starfighter.y = display.contentHeight - 50
        physics.addBody (starfighter, {density=1.0, bounce=1.0})
        starfighter.myName="starfighter"
        starfighter.isFixedRotation = true
end
```

Time to load the asteroid body. Each asteroid is set with a low density (1.0), no friction (we are in space after all), and a rather high bounce rate for better collisions with other asteroids.

There are a couple of things that have to be considered; mainly, where will the asteroid be coming from and moving toward on the screen. To give the game more of a 'moving through space' feel, I decided that asteroids could not appear from the bottom of the screen; only from the sides or top.

We will need to keep track of how many asteroids are created so that they can be properly removed later in the game. This is a simple method of garbage collection to keep memory leaks from occurring during the game.

Each asteroid is loaded into our array of asteroids (stored in asteroidsTable). After they are loaded into the array, I used a random number generator to determine which direction the asteroid would load from: left, top, or right.

```
local function loadAsteroid()
   numAsteroids= numAsteroids +1
   asteroidsTable[numAsteroids] =
display.newImage("images/asteroids1-1a.png")

physics.addBody(asteroidsTable[numAsteroids],{density=1,frictio
n=0.4,bounce=1})
   local whereFrom = math.random(3)
   asteroidsTable[numAsteroids].myName="asteroid"
```

If the asteroid was entering from the left, a random location on the left side was generated, with the bottom 25% 'off limits' for a starting point. After setting its start point, I needed to determine where it was going. Using transition.to, I generated a random location on the opposite side of the screen and set a random amount of time for the asteroid to move across the screen. This gives us random fast-moving and slow-moving asteroids, hopefully making the game more challenging and fun.

The process is then repeated for asteroids entering from the top or the right side.

```
    if(whereFrom==1) then
        asteroidsTable[numAsteroids].x = -50
        asteroidsTable[numAsteroids].y = (math.random(
display.contentHeight *.75))

        transition.to(asteroidsTable[numAsteroids], {x=
(display.contentWidth +100), y=(math.random(
display.contentHeight)), time =(math.random( 5000, 10000))})

    elseif(whereFrom==2) then
        asteroidsTable[numAsteroids].x = (math.random(
display.contentWidth))

        asteroidsTable[numAsteroids].y = -30

        transition.to(asteroidsTable[numAsteroids], {x=
(math.random(display.contentWidth)), y=(display.contentHeight +
100), time =(math.random(5000, 10000))})
    elseif(whereFrom==3) then
        asteroidsTable[numAsteroids].x = display.contentWidth+50
        asteroidsTable[numAsteroids].y = (math.random(
display.contentHeight *.75))

        transition.to(asteroidsTable[numAsteroids], {x= -100,
y=(math.random(display.contentHeight)), time
=(math.random(5000, 10000))})

    end
end
```

Collision Detection

On to collision detection! Obviously, this is a fairly important
routine, so let's break it down. In the first if...then statement, we
are looking at the names of the objects that were involved in the
collision. If the starfighter was either one of the objects, then we
check to see if this is the first collision to occur on this starfighter
life (it is possible that two collisions occur simultaneously, which

causes a double reduction in lives). If this is the first collision (i.e. died == false), then we set died equal to true so that no more collisions are registered until we can handle everything that goes with a starfighter collision.

```
local function onCollision(event)
    if(event.object1.myName =="starfighter" or
event.object2.myName == "starfighter") then
        if(died == false) then
            died = true
```

Next, we check to see how many lives are left. If the value is 1, then the game is over and an encouraging message is displayed to the player. Otherwise, an explosion sound is played, the starfighter is set to an alpha of 0, lives are reduced by 1, a cleanup routine is called and a routine to re-initialize the starfighter is called with a 2-second delay.

```
    if(lives ==1) then
        audio.play(explosion)
        event.object1:removeSelf()
        event.object2:removeSelf()
        lives=lives -1
        local lose = display.newText("You Have Failed.", 30, 150,
nil, 36)
        lose:setFillColor(1, 1, 1)
    else
        audio.play(explosion)
        starfighter.alpha =0
        lives=lives-1
        cleanup()
        timer.performWithDelay(2000,weDied,1)
    end
  end
end
```

The second type of collision that is checked for is the collision of an asteroid and a shot fired. Any other type of collision is ignored.

During an asteroid and a shot collision, the explosion sound is played, the objects are removed and set to a nil value and the score is incremented by 100.

```
  if((event.object1.myName=="asteroid" and
event.object2.myName=="shot") or
(event.object1.myName=="shot" and
event.object2.myName=="asteroid")) then
      audio.play (explosion)
      event.object1:removeSelf()
      event.object1.myName=nil
      event.object2:removeSelf()
      event.object2.myName=nil
      score=score+100
  end

end
```

The weDied function moves the starfighter back to its starting position and fades in the ship over 2 seconds. The routine also resets the died variable to false, allowing collisions to occur.

```
function weDied()
      -- fade in the new starfighter
      starfighter.x=display.contentWidth/2
      starfighter.y=display.contentHeight -50
      transition.to(starfighter, {alpha=1, timer=2000})
      died=false
  end
```

Take Your Best Shot
The fireshot function creates and tracks each of the shots fired by the ship. The shot will originate just above the ship, lined up with the current x value of the ship's center. Each shot is set as a bullet, forcing the physics engine to check continuously for collision. An age property is used to determine when the shot was fired.

195

```
local function fireshot(event)
        numShot = numShot+1
        shotTable[numShot] =
display.newImage("images/shot.png")
        physics.addBody(shotTable[numShot], {density=1,
friction=0})
        shotTable[numShot].isbullet = true
        shotTable[numShot].x=starfighter.x
        shotTable[numShot].y=starfighter.y -60
        transition.to(shotTable[numShot], {y=-80, time=700})
        audio.play(fire)
        shotTable[numShot].myName="shot"
        shotTable[numShot].age=0
end
```

Reducing Overhead

The cleanup function removes all asteroids and shots fired from
memory each time the player dies. This reduces overhead and
frees memory for the next round of play.

```
function cleanup()
        for i=1,table.getn(asteroidsTable) do
                if(asteroidsTable[i].myName~= nil) then
                        asteroidsTable[i]:removeSelf()
                        asteroidsTable[i].myName=nil
                end
        end
        for i=1,table.getn(shotTable) do
                if(shotTable[i].myName~= nil) then
                        shotTable[i]:removeSelf()
                        shotTable[i].myName=nil
                end
        end
end
```

Game Loop

The gameLoop function is the heart of the game. It is called every 400 milliseconds by a timer. It is responsible for updating the Text, loading new Asteroids, and removing old shots fired from memory and the screen so that they don't have to be continually processed.

```
local function gameLoop()
        updateText()
        loadAsteroid()
        --remove old shots fired so they don't stack
        for i = 1, table.getn(shotTable) do
                if (shotTable[i].myName ~= nil and
shotTable[i].age < maxShotAge) then
                        shotTable[i].age = shotTable[i].age + tick
                elseif (shotTable[i].myName ~= nil) then
                        shotTable[i]:removeSelf()
                        shotTable[i].myName=nil
                end
        end
end
```

That takes care of our functions for the game. Remember, functions are not processed until they are called, so to start the game, we need to spawn our first ship, have the text displayed initially, and set up our event listeners and a timer. The timer is set to call gameLoop every 400ms (or whatever the tick is set at). To slow or speed up the game, just adjust the tick.

```
--Start the game
spawnShip()
newText()

starfighter:addEventListener("touch", startDrag)
starfighter:addEventListener("tap", fireshot)
```

```
Runtime:addEventListener("collision", onCollision)

timer.performWithDelay(tick, gameLoop,0)
```

Time to play test!
Yes, there are a lot of things that could be done differently (and
with greater memory efficiency), but this project serves as a proof
of the game concept. Once you have the concept working
correctly, then it is time to make improvements!

Summary

Now you have created your first game for a mobile device! We are
far from done with this project for it to be ready for the store. We
have discussed how to do animation with enterFrame events,
using multi-touch, and working with timers. In our next chapter,
we will delve more deeply into using arrays (also referred to as
tables in Lua).

Assignments

1) Modify the project so that the ship rotates in the center of the
   screen instead of using drag to move the ship.

2) Add additional objects to the space game. It doesn't have to
   be just asteroids that are being shot.

3) Add additional sound effects for different types of collisions.

4) Background music would be nice! Add a streaming mp3
   music track.

Chapter 10: Tables and Arrays

Learning Objectives

In this chapter we are going to begin working with Tables. Tables have become a critical part of mobile application development, with Apple having spent enormous amount of effort in the creation and refinement of tables for the iPhone and iPad. Tables are one of the simplest ways to store large quantities of data.

In our examination of tables we will:
- Clarify the term table and array
- Examine the tools available for tables
- Create a simple table

Tables vs. Tables vs. Arrays

The term table has many different meanings in programming. It can be used to refer to an array (which is the common usage in Lua), a grid layout (like a spreadsheet), or a table view (popularized by Apple for developing data intensive applications) - sometimes also referred to as a list view. For the purposes of this chapter (and all chapters in this book), I will use the term table view to refer to the table view/list view associated with app development that has been used by Apple and can be reproduced widgets (Chapter 11). If I am referring to an array table (a term commonly used in Lua), I will specify it as an array or a Lua array table. The only time I will use the term "table" without qualification will be in reference to the table API, which we will discuss later in the chapter.

I should note that Solar2D does have a table command and a table widget in the API. The table command refers to the Lua array table. This should not be confused with the table widget (which we will discuss in Chapter 11) that emulates a table or list view.

Confused? I was initially as well! For now, we are just going to focus on Lua array tables and the table API. We will save table or list views for Chapter 11.

Introducing Arrays

When teaching programming, one of the dividing lines between the novice programmer and the intermediate programmer is the understanding of the concept of arrays. If you can get this concept, you will be set for a whole new world of programming concepts and items that you can create.

I have always found it easiest to conceptualize an array by picturing a single column in a spreadsheet. If I wanted to create an array of the first names of students in my class, it might look something like:

myStudents =

Joe
Jean
Fred
Cindy
Mary

In this example, I have 5 students. All of the students are stored in one variable: myStudents. Because they are all stored as one variable, I am able to work with them easily as a group of records.

Each part or row of the array is referred to as an element. Thus "Joe" is the value of the first element of the array.

To create an array in Lua, you use curly brackets in the variable declaration:

local myStudents = {}

You can also declare the contents of the array:

local myStudents = {"Joe", "Jean", "Fred", "Cindy", "Mary"}

Note: If you want Solar2D to treat the names as strings, they must be in quotations else they will be treated like variables.

Now I can easily access each of the students using a for...do loop:

```
local myStudents = {"Joe", "Jean", "Fred", "Cindy", "Mary"}

for count1 = 1, 5 do
        print (myStudents[count1])
end


Terminal Output:
Joe
Jean
Fred
Cindy
Mary
```

Table API
We have several very useful commands that can be used through the table API:

- table.concat(*array [, string, number1, number2]*) – concatenates the elements of an array to form a string. Optionally, you can pass a string to be inserted between the values (such as ", "). Number1 and number2 refer to the index of the elements to be concatenated. Number1 must be less than number2. If omitted, number1 will be the first element in the table and number2 will be the last element.
- table.copy(*array*) – creates a copy of a table. Multiple tables can be included in the copy.

- table.indexOf(*array, element*) – returns the index number of the element of a table. In other words, it will search the array for the supplied element and return the index number of that element.

- table.insert(*array, [position,] value*) - inserts the provided value into a table. If a position is supplied, the value is inserted before the element currently in that position.

- table.maxn(*array*) – returns the largest positive index number of a table (i.e. the last positive index number).

- table.remove(*array [, position]*) – removes the table element in the supplied position. If a position is not provided, then the last element in the array is removed.

- table.sort(*array [, comparison]*) – sorts the table element into a given order, updating the table to the new sorted order. By default < (less than or alphabetical order) is used. If a comparison is supplied, it must be a function that receives two table elements.

Let's examine the usage of each of these API commands:

Concatenation:

When concatenating an array, you are creating a string using the elements within the array:

```
local myStudents = {"Joe", "Jean", "Fred", "Cindy", "Mary"}
print (table.concat(myStudents, ","))


Terminal Output:
Joe, Jean, Fred, Cindy, Mary
```

Copy:

Copy returns a duplicate of the table or tables passed to it. It can be used to join additional arrays:

```
local myStudents = {"Joe", "Jean", "Fred", "Cindy", "Mary"}
local myStudentsScores = { 98, 87, 68, 100, 89}
local newArray = table.copy(myStudents)
print(table.concat(newArray, ", "))
```

Terminal Output:
Joe, Jean, Fred, Cindy, Mary

```
local newArray2 = table.copy(myStudents, myStudentsScores)
print (table.concat(newArray2, ", "))
```

Terminal Output:
Joe, Jean, Fred, Cindy, Mary, 98, 87, 68, 100, 89

indexOf:

The indexOf API command returns the index of a supplied element that is in the array. If the element is not present in the array, nil will be returned.

```
local myStudents = {"Joe", "Jean", "Fred", "Cindy", "Mary"}
print (myStudents, "Jean")
```

Terminal Output:
2

insert:

Inserts a new element into an array. If a position is not provided as an argument, the new element will be added as the last element of the array. If a position is provided, the new element will be inserted before the element previously at that index (i.e. what was the second element becomes the third element).

```
local myStudents = {"Joe", "Jean", "Fred", "Cindy", "Mary"}
```

```
table.insert(myStudents, 2, "Jeff")
print(table.concat(myStudents, ", ")
```

Terminal Output:
Joe, Jeff, Jean, Fred, Cindy, Mary

Maxn:

By using the table.maxn() API, it isn't necessary that I know how many elements are in the array:

```
local myStudents = {"Joe", "Jean", "Fred", "Cindy", "Mary"}
for count1 = 1, table.maxn(myStudents) do
        print (myStudents[count1])
end
```

Terminal Output:
Joe
Jean
Fred
Cindy
Mary

In this example, table.maxn(myStudents) returns the number of elements in the array, making it much easier to work with tables of an unknown size. This can only be used in cases where the index is numerical. A non-numerical index will return nil causing an error.

Note: In some languages, the index of the first element in an array is element 0. In Lua, the index of the first element is 1.

Remove:

The remove API deletes from the array the element at the provided index position. If no index position is provided, the last element will be deleted from the array.

```
local myStudents = {"Joe", "Jeff", "Jean", "Fred", "Cindy", "Mary"}
table.remove(myStudents, 2)
print(table.concat(myStudents, ", ")


Terminal Output:
Joe, Jean, Fred, Cindy, Mary
```

Sort:

The sort API command sorts the table into alphabetical or numerical order if an operand is not provided. If a different sort order is needed, you will need to supply a function that will return true or false if the sort condition is not met. For example, if you wanted to sort an array in reverse-alphabetical order (i.e. >), then you would need a code such as:

```
local myStudents = {"Joe", "Jean", "Fred", "Cindy", "Mary"}

local function compare(a, b)
   return a > b
end

table.sort(myStudents, compare)

print(table.concat(myStudents, ", ")

Terminal Output:
Mary, Joe, Jean, Fred, Cindy
```

Sort will pass the elements two at a time for our compare function to determine if the first element is greater than the second element. Thus, in the first instance, Joe and Jean will be passed. Since "Joe" is greater than "Jean" (at least alphabetically), the compare function will return the value TRUE, which tells the sort API it doesn't need to do anything. In the case of Joe and Mary, it will return FALSE, causing the sort API to place "Mary" before "Joe".

Flexibility of Lua Array Tables

Lua Array tables are very flexible in the content that they can contain. They are commonly used to handle events and a return from a function. In most programming languages, arrays must be of a specific data type such as integer, string, floating decimal, Boolean, etc. In Lua, we have more flexibility. Lua array tables can be heterogeneous. They can contain any type of data except nil.

Once you have declared a Lua array table, you can also use it to represent records or objects with field names as we did in the last chapter when we created our asteroids and shots fired. The process is simple. Once you have created your array, you can create your own field names as needed by placing a period after the variable name, just like you would access a property for the variable such as the x or y location:

```
local myArray = {}
myArray.id = 1
myArray.myName = "Array 1"
myArray.x = 10
myArray.y = 50
```

You can also use a Lua array table to describe an object. For instance, if I am creating an RPG (Role Playing Game), I might create a player object such as:

```
local player1 = {}
player1.location = level
player1.class = "fighter"
player1.name = "Conan"
player1.weapon = "sword"
player1.health = 10
player1.image = display.newImage("player1.png")
```

Lua array tables are very flexible and can help organize your app data in many useful ways. All of this information is now associated with the variable player1 and can be accessed through its properties. Note that you can associate images, sounds, or even functions to an element of an array table.

The 4th dimension and beyond

That takes care of a single or one-dimensional array, but what about multi-dimensional arrays? Yes, it is possible (and often necessary) to create arrays that are 2, 3, 4, or more dimensions! To keep it simple, we are just going to look at 2-dimensional arrays. The same concepts apply if you find yourself needing to build more complex arrays.

To create multi-dimensional array tables, you can assign an array table within an array table. To simplify working with multi-dimensional tables, I recommend that you always use a numeric index:

Project 10.1 Multi-dimensional Array

```
local myArray ={}
```

```
myArray[1]={"Joe", "Jean", "Fred", "Cindy"} -- first name
myArray[2] = {"Smith", "Smith", "Smith", "Smith"} – last name
myArray[3]={"142 Main", "163 South St."} -- address
myArray[4]={} -- city
myArray[5] = {} -- state
myArray[6] = {} – zip code

for i = 1, 6 do
        for j = 1,4 do
                print (myArray[i][j])
        end
end
```

This creates a 2-dimensional array:

myArray =

Joe	Smith	142 Main			
Jean	Smith	163 South St.			
Fred	Smith				
Cindy	Smith				

Note: How you choose to conceptualize the array is a matter of personal preference. In the first visual, I used a column to represent a 1-dimensional array. In this visual, I have instead used the first dimension to represent a row, with the second dimension representing the columns.

Just like before, we have complete flexibility in what we can store within the Lua array table. One warning: be very careful when storing certain information in any type of variable. Numbers such as telephone numbers, social security, driver's licenses, etc. should be treated as strings and not as numbers. In other words, storing 321-555-4651 is very different than "321-555-4651". The first number will be treated as a number and calculated resulting in -4,885. The second, since it is enclosed in quotes will be treated as a string and retain its original meaning.

To cycle through a more complex array such as what we have in our example, you will need to use a nested loop:

```
for i = 1, 6 do
        for j = 1,4 do
                print ( myArray[i] [j] )
        end
end
```

To access each dimension of an array, use a bracket for the index number. For example: If I have the command print(myArray[1][2]) the result will be Jean; the 1st column, 2nd row. As you can see, I did not fully populate the array. When the app runs, the empty elements will be returned as nil.

Now that we have been exposed to Lua array tables, let's see it in action for a simple game.

Project 10.2 Conway's Game of Life

John Conway's Game of Life is a classic example of cellular automation (as in cells in the body, not cell phones). Devised in 1970, it is a zero-player game; it shows a theory for the evolution of life based on a few simple rules. It requires no input from the player, but will do nicely to demonstrate how array tables can be used in a game.

First, the rules (modified from Wikipedia: http://en.wikipedia.org/wiki/Conway%27s_Game_of_Life):

The universe of the Game of Life is an infinite two-dimensional grid of square *cells*, each of which is in one of two possible states, *alive* or *dead*. Every cell interacts with its eight *neighbors*, which are the cells that are horizontally, vertically, or diagonally adjacent. At each step in time, the following transitions occur:

1. Any live cell with fewer than two live neighbors dies as if caused by under-population.
2. Any live cell with two or three live neighbors lives on to the next generation.
3. Any live cell with more than three live neighbors dies, as if by overcrowding.
4. Any dead cell with exactly three live neighbors becomes a live cell, as if by reproduction.

The initial pattern constitutes the *seed* of the system. The first generation is created by applying the above rules to every cell in the seed—births, and deaths occur simultaneously, and the discrete moment at which this happens is sometimes called a *tick* (in other words, each generation is a pure function of the preceding one). The rules continue to be applied repeatedly to create further generations.

The following code is based on a sample code and has been modified to work in the Solar2D SDK environment.

To get started, we will set up our environment. The variable m is used to specify the number of rows and columns in the "universe." The game will go through 10 iterations (num_iterations). We will create the array tables for storing the life process. To make it more visually appealing, we will use graphics to represent the life process.

main.lua

```
------
-- Conway's Game of Life in Solar2D
-- Chapter 10.2
-- Demonstration of multi-dimensional Arrays
-----


local m = 8        -- number rows / columns
local num_iterations = 10
local myCell = {}
local cell = {}
local iteration = 0
```

Next we will create the function setup. Setup will create our initial universe based upon m (which is currently set to 8, thus an 8 by 8 array). I am loading an image to all cells as part of the initialization to represent the base or no-life environment.
The images are both 32x32 pixel, so placement can be easily accomplished with just a bit of math. We'll start our 'life' at cells on the 3rd row in columns 2 through 6.

```
local function setup()
  for i = 1, m do
    cell[i] = {}
    myCell[i] ={}
```

```
      for j = 1, m do
        cell[i][j] = 0
        myCell[i][j] = display.newImage("base.png")
        myCell[i][j].x =(i * 32)
        myCell[i][j].y=  (j * 32)+20
      end
    end

    cell[3][2] = 1
    cell[3][3] = 1
    cell[3][4] = 1
    cell[3][5] = 1
    cell[3][6] = 1

end
```

The Evolve function is the heart of the program. It receives the cell array and steps through it with a for...do loop, first making a copy (cell2) then checking to see if life continues, grows, or dies based upon the count of surrounding life. After all the calculations are completed, the cell array is returned with its new values.
Notice that life is represented as a value of 1 and no life is represented by 0 through the entire process.

```
local function Evolve( cell )
  local m = #cell
  local cell2 = {}
  for i = 1, m do
    cell2[i] = {}

    for j = 1, m do
      cell2[i][j] = cell[i][j]
    end
  end

  for i = 1, m do

    for j = 1, m do
```

```
        local count
        if cell2[i][j] == 0 then count = 0 else count = -1 end

        for x = -1, 1 do

            for y = -1, 1 do
                if i+x >= 1 and i+x <= m and j+y >= 1 and j+y <= m and
cell2[i+x][j+y] == 1 then count = count + 1 end
                end
            end
            if count < 2 or count > 3 then cell[i][j] = 0 end
            if count == 3 then cell[i][j] = 1 end
        end
    end
    return cell
end
```

The updates function is called every one and a half seconds to update the life universe. It is a simple for...do routine to display either life or no life on the board. Once the board has been updated, the cell array is updated by passing cell to the Evolve function above.

```
local function updates()
    for i = 1, m do
        for j = 1, m do
            if cell[i][j] == 1 then
                myCell[i][j] = display.newImage("life.png")
                myCell[i][j].x =(i * 32)
                myCell[i][j].y=  (j * 32)+20
            else
                myCell[i][j] = display.newImage("base.png")
                myCell[i][j].x =(i * 32)
                myCell[i][j].y=  (j * 32)+20
            end
        end
    end
    cell = Evolve( cell )
```

```
    iteration = iteration + 1
    print(iteration)


end
```

Now we can launch the program by calling the initial setup function and then setting a timer.performWithDelay to update the screen every 1 ½ seconds for the number of iterations called for at the beginning of the program.

```
setup()

timer.performWithDelay(1500, updates, num_iterations)
```

Hopefully seeing Conway's Game of Life will trigger some of your own ideas on game or app development.

Summary

You now have a taste of working with arrays. Congratulations! This concept is what is generally considered to separate the beginner from the intermediate programmer! It will take some time to become comfortable working with arrays, but you are now well on your way! Now that we have the fundamentals of programming and app development, we can jump into some of the interesting tools available for creating interesting apps on smartphones and tablets in our next chapter.

Assignments

1. Create a simple array showing exam scores for a class of 6 students: 85, 67, 92, 42, 99, 77. Using table.insert, add an additional score of 96.

2. Building on assignment 1, sort the array in ascending order.

3. Building on assignment 1, remove the 3rd element.

4. Create a lamp object that has the following properties:

   Color: blue status: off   bulb: 60W   power: battery
   Then write a function to change the lamp status to on if it is off,
   or off if it is on.

5. Create a two-dimensional array that shows 5 students' names
   in the first column and their current class grade (in percent) in
   the second column.

6. Challenge: Building on assignment 5, add the following
   features:
   Search for student by name and change their grade.
   Add a new student
   Remove a current student.

Chapter 11: Going Native - Working with Widgets

Learning Objectives

Time to jump into tools that will make your apps user interface appear native. These tools or widgets allow us to add picker wheels, buttons, scroll bars, and sliders with ease. We will also examine tools for creating mock-ups. Specifically, we will learn:

- Examine various mock-ups or pre-design tools
- How to use widgets in app development
- How to use widget themes
- Review the use of the different types of widgets
- How to properly remove a widget

Mock-ups and pre-design tools

Think back to one of the classic Disney films you saw as a child. Whether it was Snow White, Sleeping Beauty, or one of the many other Disney classics, you were watching a film that had been carefully planned and designed. Walt Disney was known for his long storyboarding sessions to carefully communicate the flow and design of the entire movie. This attention to detail is what separates the professional from the amateur. When designing apps or games, while it is sometimes still called storyboarding, the process of pre-planning your project is also called a mock-up, flow, or conceptualization of the project.

On one project that I was working on several years ago, we were to develop an app for the iPad. The problem was, that the iPad wasn't even released. Yes, that's right, we were developing an app for a product that hadn't even been released. To help all of us, the artists, clients, and programmers, have a better concept of what we were developing, one of the team leaders created 5 wooden versions of the "iPad" so that everyone on the project could get a feel for the device. This proved to be a very useful mockup, and the wooden mockups were much prized and sought after at the end of the project.

Whether working by yourself or on a team, being able to conceptualize the project and try different configurations will save you a great deal of time. When working on a team or for a client, the ability to show the concept and possible screen flow or arrangement of objects in the app saves misunderstandings and can greatly improve.

When creating such projects, it is critical to show the screen flow as different parts of the app are used. Showing what screen will become active is critical for understanding the complexity and flow of the project. It can also help you to avoid dead ends or overly complicated designs.

While creating a mock-up or pre-design of an app can be done with a pencil and paper, many developers prefer to use tools that speed up the design process even more. In Chapter 20 I have included several mockup tools that are popular with mobile developers. The majority of these tools take advantage of the pre-built widgets that are available in iOS and Android devices. So let's talk about widgets!

Widgets

Widgets provide user-interface tools that are standard features when programming in the native development environment for iOS and Android. With widgets, you can create apps that include native features such as a picker wheel or slider, but take a fraction of the time to develop.

Be aware that widgets have gone through several stages in Solar2D. We are now on Widgets 2.0 (as of this writing), which are much more sophisticated and consistent in their usage compared to the first version.

To use a widget in your app, you must load the widget library prior to using any objects:

```
local widget = require( "widget" )
```

The appearance of the widgets is controlled by image sheet objects. You can find sample image sheets that you can customize (or just use in your apps) in the Solar2DSDK > SampleCode > Interface > WidgetDemo > assets folder.

Some of the widgets that you can use in your app include:

- **Buttons** - the widget.newButton provides a button that supports onPress, onRelease, and onEvent events.
- **Picker Wheel** – The picker wheel widget allows the user to rotate a dial to select their response for the application using tables to store each column of data.
- **Progress Bar** – The progress bar can be used to show startup, download, upload, or any number of situations where a progress bar is needed.
- **Scroll View** - The scroll view widget allows you to create scrolling content areas. If you want a scroll view that does not extend the full height of the screen, you will need to create a bitmap mask that is the width and height of the scroll view that you desire for your app.
- **Segmented Control** – The segmented control allows you to set up multiple buttons where only one can be selected at a time.

- **Slider** - The widget.newSlider allows you to create a slider object that can be adjusted in width.
- **Spinner** – The spinner widget is a useful tool for showing background processing or loading so that users know that the app is functioning and to be patient.
- **Stepper** – The stepper widget is used to increase or decrease (increment or decrement) a value. You have control over how much the value is changed.
- **Switch** – The switch widget is a very flexible tool. It is used to show a binary situation (on/off, true/false, 1/0), but can do this as a radio button, checkbox, or on/off switch depending on your needs.
- **Tab Bar** – The tab bar allows you to create a customizable tab bar. Tabs are auto-positioned based on the number of buttons.
- **Table View** - The table view widget allows you to create scrolling lists. With this widget you can control the rendering of the individual rows.

You should not consider a widget a typical display object. While they can be included in groups, they must be inserted by their view property:

```
myGroup:insert(myWidget.view)
```

Making Your Widgets Look Good

If you would like to use a theme that either makes your widgets look like native Apple iOS or Android widgets, you can use the widget.setTheme() API command. This should be called immediately after the loading of the widget API (i.e. right after you have the command line *local widget = require ("widget").*

The theme files are Lua files with tables that correspond to each of the widgets. The easiest way to get started creating your own custom theme is to edit the existing widget themes. You can find a sample of the theme files in the widget demo sample file under the Solar2D Folder.

To set a specific theme for the widgets that are either iOS or Android themed, you simply include the line:

```
– for iOS:
widget.setTheme("widget_theme_ios7" )

– for Android (choose one):
widget.setTheme"widget_theme_android_holo_dark")
widget.setTheme"widget_theme_android_holo_light")
```

widget.newButton

The first widget will be a popular addition to your apps. The button widget adds some nice features that make it easy to use within your apps instead of having to create your own button each time. There will be times when you will want to use your own customized button, but for most instances, being able to use the widget button will be your first choice.

The widget.newButton provides a button that supports onPress, onRelease, and onEvent. The button widget is very powerful and flexible with many options.

Button Parameters:

- id – an optional string that can be used to identify the button (default is "widget_button").
- left, top – initial coordinates of buttons left, top corner (default is 0, 0).
- width, height – allows adjusting the button's width and height. It should be set to the size of your button image or if using the 9-piece button, it will scale.
- label – text that will appear on the button.

- labelAlign – text alignment of button label. Valid options are "left", "right", and "center" (default is "center").
- labelColor – RGBA (red, green, blue, alpha) table showing default and over-color states of the label text.
- labelXOffset, labelYOffset – adjust the x & y axes of the label text
- font – allows changing the button label font (default is native.systemFont)
- fontSize – the label font size in pixels (default is 14).
- emboss - will allow the text to appear embossed if set to true (default is true).
- onPress – callback function for when the button is tapped.
- onRelease – optional callback function that is called when the user ends the tap/press of the button.
- onEvent – optional function and should only be used if none of the other above events are used. The callback function will need to test for event.phase.
- isEnabled – optional. If false, the button will not respond to touch events (default is true).
- x, y - center coordinates of the button.

Methods

- setLabel(*string*) – Changes the button's label text.
- getLabel() – returns the button's current label text.
- setEnabled() – set to false to disable the button.

The button image can be implemented in one of three ways:

Button from an image file (i.e. loading a button.png):

- defaultFile, overFile – image files to represent different states of the button. If no image is specified and there is no theme, the button will default to a rounded rectangle.
- baseDir – base directory for custom images (default = system.ResourceDirectory – the project folder).

Button – 2 frame image sheet:

- <u>sheet</u> – the image sheet containing the images for your button.
- <u>defaultFrame</u> – frame number containing the default image of the button.
- <u>overFrame</u> – frame number containing the pressed (over) image of the button.

Button – 9 slice image sheet:

- <u>sheet</u> – the image sheet containing the images for your button.
- <u>topLeftFrame, topLeftFrameOver</u> – default and pressed frame numbers for the top left slice of the button.
- <u>middleLeftFrame, middleLeftFrameOver</u> – default and pressed frame numbers for the middle left slice of the button.
- <u>bottomLeftFrame, bottomLeftFrameOver</u> - default and pressed frame numbers for the bottom left slice of the button.
- <u>topRightFrame, topRightFrameOver</u> - default and pressed frame numbers for the top right slice of the button.
- <u>middleRightFrame, middleRightFrameOver</u> - default and pressed frame numbers for the middle right slice of the button.
- <u>bottomRightFrame, bottomRightFrameOver</u> - default and pressed frame numbers for the bottom right slice of the button.
- <u>topMiddleFrame, topMiddleFrameOver</u> - default and pressed frame numbers for the top middle slice of the button.
- <u>middleFrame, middleFrameOver</u> - default and pressed frame numbers for the middle slice of the button.
- <u>bottomMiddleFrame, bottomMiddleFrameOver</u> - default and pressed frame numbers for the bottom middle slice of the button.

Project 11.0 widget.newButton Example

```
local widget = require( "widget" )

-- Function to handle button events
local function handleButtonEvent( event )
  local phase = event.phase

  if "ended" == phase then
    print( "You pressed and released a button!" )
  end
end

-- Create the button
local myButton = widget.newButton
{
  left = 100,
  top = 200,
  width = 150,
  height = 50,
  defaultFile = "default.png",
  overFile = "over.png",
  id = "button_1",
  label = "Button",
```

```
    onEvent = handleButtonEvent,
}
```

widget.newPickerWheel

The picker wheel widget allows the user to rotate a dial to select their response for the application. This widget has a great deal of flexibility, and with that comes a great number of parameters. The picker wheel only accepts one argument, which is an array table that can contain the following parameters:

Parameters:

- id – string to identify the picker wheel (default is "widget_PickerWheel").
- left, top – top, left corner of the widget.
- font – font used when rendering column rows (default is native.systemFontBold).
- fontSize – size in pixels of the font used for rendering the text (default is 22).
- fotnColor – RGBA table for the text color of each column (default is black).
- columnColor – RGBA table for column background color (default is white).
- columns – table array that will hold the arrays representing the individual columns of your picker wheel.

Methods:

- getValues() – returns the selected values from the picker wheel.

Column Properties:

- width – sets the column to a custom width (default is all columns are equal width).

- startIndex – sets the column at a specific row.
- align – sets the text to left, right, or center alignment (default is center).
- labels – stored in a table, sets the label for each row.
- Methods:S

- picker:getValues() – returns a table holding the value/index of the rows that are currently selected.

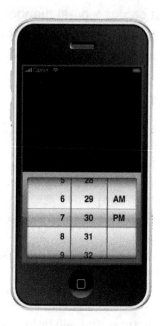

Visual Customization of the Picker Wheel

If you want to customize the appearance of the picker wheel, you can use the following commands. Customization is optional. You can use the default appearance as shown in Project 11.1.

- sheet – The image sheet object for the picker wheel.
- backgroundFrame – The frame number for the background that will sit behind the picker wheel. The image will be stretched to the full width and height of the picker wheel if needed.

- **backgroundWidth, backgroundHeight** – The width and height of the picker wheel background frame image.
- **overlayFrame** – frame number for the glass image or overlay.
- **overlayFrameWidth, overlayFrameHeight** – width and height of the picker wheel overlay frame image.
- **separatorFrame** – The frame number for the divider that separates each column.
- **separatorWidth, separatorHeight** – The width and height of the separator frame image.
- **maskFile** – A mask file used to crop picker wheel columns.

Project 11.1 widget.newPickerWheel Example

In this example, a 3-column time picker wheel is created. First, we will populate the variable minutes, which will be used in the second column to represent minutes, using a for loop. The for loop allows us to create the 0 to 59 elements of the array efficiently.

Next will be using an array within an array. First create the ColumnData array, which will have 3 columns. Next, create a 12-row array for the first column that represents the hour.

config.lua

```lua
application =
{
        content =
        {
                width = 320,
                height = 480,
                scale = "zoomEven"
        },
}
```

main.lua

```lua
local widget = require "widget"

-- setup data that will be used in a column
local minutes = {}
for i=0,59 do
  minutes[i] = i
end

-- create a table to hold all column data
local columnData = {
        { -- column 1
        labels = { "1", "2", "3", "4", "5", "6", "7", "8", "9", "10", "11", "12"
},
        align = "right",
        startIndex = 7,
},
{ -- column 2
        labels = minutes,
        align = "center",
        startIndex = 30,
        },
        {-- column 3
        labels = { "AM", "PM" },
        startIndex = 2,
                }
        }
```

Next we will create a picker wheel using the actual picker wheel call.

```lua
-- Create the actual picker widget with column data
local picker = widget.newPickerWheel{
    id="myPicker",
    top=258,
    columns=columnData
}
```

Finally, we will create a function to report the selected values when the button is tapped.

```
local function showValues( event )
        -- Retrieve the current values from the picker
        local values = picker:getValues()

        -- print the selected values
        print( "Column 1: " .. values[1].value .. "Column 2: " ..
values[2].value .. "Column 3: " .. values[3].value)
end

local getValuesButton = widget.newButton
        {
            left = 10,
            top = 150,
                width = 298,
                height = 56,
                id = "getValues",
            label = "Values",
            onRelease = showValues,
        }
```

widget.newProgressView

The progress view widget can be used in several ways, but is usually associated with either downloading files or showing the load progress of a file. In the example below, I have tied it to the slider widget so that as the slider's value is increased, the progress bar is updated to a new value. Note that the progress view is designed to increase. If you want to use it as a meter it will need to be reset each time the value changes. The progress view receives values between 0 and 1.

Parameters:

- <u>id</u> – optional for specific progress view identification (default is "widget_progressView").
- <u>left, top</u> – specifies the top left corner for the progress view to be created.
- <u>width</u> – specifies the width of the progress view widget.
- <u>isAnimated</u> – optional, to animate the progress. Set to false for immediate updates to the value (default is false).
- <u>fillXOffset</u> – optionally allows you to position the horizontal offset of the fill image.
- <u>fillYOffset</u> – optionally allows you to position the vertical offset of the fill image.

Methods:

- <u>setProgress()</u> – updates the progress view percentage. Receives a value between 0 and 1.
- <u>getProgress()</u> – returns the current value of the progress view.

Visual Customization of a Progress View:

- <u>sheet</u> – The image sheet object for the progress view.
- <u>fillOuterLeftFrame</u> – The frame number for the outer left frame (the background/container).
- <u>fillOuterMiddleFrame</u> – The frame number for the outer middle frame (the background/container).
- <u>fillOuterRightFrame</u> – The frame number for the outer right frame (the background/container).
- <u>fillInnerLeftFrame</u> – The frame number for the inner left frame (the left edge of the fill).
- <u>fillInnerMiddleFrame</u> – The frame number for the inner middle frame (the middle of the fill).
- <u>fillInnerRightFrame</u> – The frame number for the inner right frame (the right edge of the fill).

230

- fillOuterWidth, fillOuterHeight – The width and height of the outer portion of the progress view frame.
- fillWidth, fillHeight – The width and height of the fill frames.

widget.newSlider

The widget.newSlider allows you to create a slider object that can be adjusted in width. This widget is very similar to Apple's iOS slider. It is also very flexible and includes quite a few parameters:

Parameters:

- id – string to identify button (default is "widget_slider").
- left, top – specifies the top left corner for the slider to be created.
- width, height – specifies the width and height of the slider widget.
- value – sets or returns value of the slider between 0 and 100 (default is 50).
- orientation – sets the orientation of the slider to vertical or horizontal (default is horizontal).
- listener - function called every time the slider is touched or moved.

Methods:

- setValue() - returns the handle location by percentage (0 to 100).

Visual Customization of a Progress View:

The slider can be customized in many ways depending on if its being used on a horizontal or vertical slider. The following properties are common to both horizontal and vertical sliders:

231

- <u>sheet</u> – The image sheet object for the progress view.
- <u>frameWidth, frameHeight</u> – the width and height of the slider edge frames.
- <u>handleFrame</u> – the handle/slider frame number.
- <u>handleFrameWidth, handleFrameHeight</u> – width and height of the handle frame.

Horizontal Slider Customization

- <u>leftFrame</u> – left edge frame number for slider.
- <u>middleFrame</u> – middle frame number for slider.
- <u>rightFrame</u> – right edge frame number for slider.
- <u>fillFrame</u> – fill frame number for slider.

Vertical Slider Customization

- <u>topFrame</u> – top edge frame number for slider.
- <u>middleVerticalFrame</u> – middle frame number for slider.
- <u>bottomFrame</u> – bottom frame number for slider.
- <u>fillVerticalFrame</u> – fill frame number for slider.

Project 11.2 Widget Slider & Progress View Example

To implement the slider widget, you will first need to load the widget library with the required command. Unless you want to go through and set all of the various images (which you are welcome to do), I recommend using the pre-defined graphics.

Be sure to set your listener function for your slide event. You can also check for phases "moved" and "released". Moved is a response to the current movement of the slider. Released is the response to when the slider event is completed. In the example below, the listener prints any movement of the slider and updates the progress view. Remember that the progress view will only increase unless it is reset each time.

config.lua

```lua
application =
{
        content =
        {
                width = 320,
                height = 480,
                scale = "zoomEven"
        },
}
```

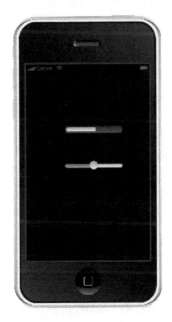

main.lua

```lua
local widget = require("widget")
        -----------------------------------------------
    -- widget.newProgressView()
        -----------------------------------------------
        local newProgressView = widget.newProgressView
        {
```

```
                    left = 100,
                    top = 150,
                    width = 150,
                    isAnimated = true,
        }


                -- The listener for our slider
        local function sliderListener( event )
                -- Update the progress view
                print(event.value)
    -- Must turn event.value into a number between 0 & 1.
             newProgressView:setProgress( event.value/100 )
        end


        ------------------------------------------------
        -- Create a horizontal slider
        ------------------------------------------------
        local horizontalSlider = widget.newSlider
        {
                left = 100,
                top = 232,
                width = 150,
                id = "Horizontal Slider",
                listener = sliderListener,
        }
```

widget.newScrollView

The scroll view widget allows you to create scrolling content areas. It should be noted that if you want a scroll view that does not extend the full height of the screen, you will need to create a bitmap mask that is the width and height of the scroll view that you desire for your app using graphics.newMask(). The scroll view is a fairly straightforward widget with only a few parameters:

Parameters

- id – optional id assigned to the scroll view (default is "widget_scrollView")
- left, top – allows the custom location of scroll view (default is 0 for both values)
- width, height – allows custom width and height of scroll view (default is full width and height of the screen).
- scrollWidth, scrollHeight – required parameter giving the total scrollable area. Cannot be changed after the widget is created.
- topPadding, bottomPadding – optional number of pixels from the top and bottom when the scrolling reaches the end of the scrollable area (default is 0).
- leftPadding, rightPadding - optional number of pixels from the left and right when the scrolling reaches the end of the scrollable area.
- friction – determines how fast the rows travel when flicked up or down (default is 0.972).
- backgroundColor – optional RGBA table for the background of the scroll view (default is white: {1, 1, 1, 1}).
- hideBackground – optional Boolean, hides the background of the scroll view area if set to true (default is false).
- horizontalScrollDisabled – optional Boolean parameter to disable horizontal scrolling.
- verticalScrollDisabled – optional Boolean parameter to disable vertical scrolling.
- isLocked – optional Boolean to keep the scroll view from scrolling.
- hideScrollBar – optional Boolean to hide the scroll bar from view.
- listener – function to listen for scroll view events. Provides two unique events: event.limitReached – when the scroll view reaches one of its limits; and event.direction – returns the direction that scroll view is moving.
- baseDir – optional way of setting the path to the mask file.
- maskFile – optional, used if a custom width and height are set for the scroll view.

Scroll View Methods:

- scrollView:getContentPosition() – returns the current x, y position of the scroll view content. Used to mark the current location (eg. local x, y = scrollView:getContentPosition()).
- scrollView:scrollToPosition(*table*) –scroll to specified y position. Table options include x, y, time, and onComplete.
- scrollView:scrollTo(position, options) – scroll to the top, bottom, left, or right, with the options of time and onComplete.
- insert() – add items to scroll view.

Visual Customization for Scroll View

Scroll view uses a scrollBarOptions table to pass visual customization information.

- sheet – image sheet containing the scroll bar images.
- topFrame – frame number for the top of the scrollBar.
- middleFrame – frame number for the middle of the scrollBar.
- bottomFrame – frame number for the bottom of the scrollBar.

We will look at an implementation of the scroll view in the tab bar example.

widget.newSegmentedControl
The segmented control widget allows you to create a multi-part button that allows the user to select one of the options. Consider it the multiple choice test question of app design!

- id – optional id assigned to the segmented control (default is "widget_segmentedControl").
- left, top – allows custom location of segmented control (default is 0 for both values)
- width, height – sets the width and height of the segmented control's frames. Each segment/frame must be the same width and height and will be loaded from the image sheet.
- segmentWidth – optional sets the segment width (default is 50 pixels).
- segments – a table containing the labels for each segment.
- defaultSegment – allows for the optional setting of a default/selected segment (if not specified, will default to the first segment).
- labelSize – font size for segment labels (default is 12).
- labelFont – font type for segment labels (default is native.systemFont).
- labelXOffset – optional horizontal offset for segment labels.
- labelYOffset – optional vertical offset for segment labels.
- onPress – optional function call when a segment is pressed.

Visual Customization of Segmented Control
- sheet – the image sheet containing the images for your segmented control.
- leftSegmentedFrame, leftSegmentedSelectedFrame – default and pressed frame numbers for the left slice of the segmented control.
- middleSegmentedFrame, middleSegmentedSelectedFrame – default and pressed frame numbers for the middle slice of the segmented control.
- rightSegmentedFrame, rightSegmentedSelectedFrame - right default and pressed frame numbers for the right slice of the segmented control.
- dividerFrame – frame number for the divider line between each segment.

A segmented control demonstration is included in the tab bar example project.

widget.newSpinner

The spinner widget is typically used to show that the application is busy; asking the user to be patient while the app performs needed functions.

Parameters:

- id – optional id assigned to the spinner (default is "widget_spinner").
- left, top – allows the custom location of the spinner (default is 0 for both values).
- width, height – optional, sets the width and height of the spinner frames if you are using a custom imageSheet.
- time – optional, set the time for the spinner animation (default is 1000 milliseconds).
- deltaAngle – optional, sets the delta angle for the spinner rotation per increment.
- incrementEvery – optional, the delay in milliseconds between each segment rotation.

Methods:
- start()- begins the animation of the spinner widget.
- stop() – you guessed it! Stops the spinner animation.

Visual Customization of Spinner
- sheet – the image sheet containing the images for your spinner.
- startFrame – the frame number for the spinner's first frame.

- <u>frameCount</u> – the number of frames in the spinner animation (default is 1).

A spinner demonstration is included in the tab bar example project.

widget.newStepper

The stepper is a simple widget for incrementing or decrementing a value.

Parameters:
- <u>id</u> – optional id assigned to the stepper (default is "widget_stepper").
- <u>left, top</u> – allows the custom location of the stepper (default is 0 for both values).
- <u>width, height</u> – sets the width and height of the stepper frames if you are using a custom imageSheet.
- <u>initialValue</u> – sets the initial value for stepper (default is 0).
- <u>minimumValue</u> – optionally sets the minimum value that the stepper can decrement to (default is 0).
- <u>maximumValue</u> – optionally sets the maximum value that the stepper can increment to.
- <u>onPress</u> – optional function to be called with stepper is pressed. Includes possible event.phases of increment, decrement, minLimit, maxLimit.
- <u>onHold</u> – optional function call while the stepper segment is being held down. Includes possible event.phases of increment, decrement, minLimit, maxLimit.
- <u>value</u> – returns the current value.

Visual Customization of Stepper
- <u>sheet</u> – the image sheet containing the images for your stepper.

239

- <u>defaultFrame</u> – frame number for steppers default (both + and – active).
- <u>noMinusFrame</u> – frame number for minLimit frame (+ active, - greyed out).
- <u>noPlusFrame</u> – frame number for maxLimit frame (+ greyed out, - active).
- <u>minusActiveFrame</u> – frame number with minus pressed or held (- in the pressed state).
- <u>plusActiveFrame</u> – frame number with plus pressed or held (+ in the pressed state).

A stepper demonstration is included in the tab bar example project.

widget.newSwitch

The switch widget is a very flexible tool, able to be displayed as an on/off switch, checkbox, or radio button.

Parameters:
- <u>id</u> – optional id assigned to the switch (default is "widget_switch").
- <u>left, top</u> – allows the custom location of the switch (default is 0 for both values).
- <u>width, height</u> – sets the width and height of the switch frames if you are using a custom imageSheet.
- <u>initialSwitchState</u> – sets the initial value for the switch (default is false/off/deselected).
- <u>style</u> – optionally sets the style of the switch. Options are radio, checkbox, and onOff. (default is onOff).
- <u>onPress</u> – optional function to be called when the switch is pressed.
- <u>onRelease</u> – optional function call when the user releases the switch.

- **onEvent** – optional function call that should only be used if onPress or onRelease are not used.

Methods:
- **setState(options)** – used to set the state of the switch. Options include the table items *isOn, isAnimated, onComplete* .

Visual Customization of Switch

Switch has several possible visual customization options including Radio, Checkbox, and on/off switch. The sheet parameter is used by each of these options.

- **sheet** – the image sheet containing the images for your switch.

Visual Customization of Radio & Checkbox Switch
- **frameOff** – frame number for switch off.
- **frameOn** – frame number for switch on.

Visual Customization of On/Off Switch
- **onOffBackgroundFrame** – frame number for background frame (frame is the image that shows the two colors and on/off text).
- **onOffBackgroundWidth, onOffBackgroundHeight** – frame width and height for image in custom imageSheet.
- **onOffOverlayWidth, onOffOverlayHeight** – frame width and height for overlay.
- **onOffOverlayFrame** – frame number for switch overlay.
- **onOffHandleDefaultFrame** – the frame number for the handle.
- **onOffHandleOverFrame** – the frame number for the handle over the frame.

The switch will be demonstrated in the tab bar project example.

widget.newTableView

The tableView widget allows you to create scrolling lists. This is an example of the third type of table discussed in Chapter 10. With this widget you can control the rendering of the individual rows. You might notice that you are rendering or building each row for view. This gives you a great deal of control over what to include on each row including images and/or text. The tableview widget is very powerful and flexible; with that flexibility comes a few more properties and methods:

Parameters:

- id – optional id assigned to the table view (default is "widget_tableView").
- backgroundColor – RGBA table to set the color of the rectangle that is behind the tableView (default is white {1, 1, 1, 1}).
- left, top – allows custom location of table view (default is 0).

- width, height – allows custom width and height of table view (default width is full width and height of the screen).
- friction – determines how fast the rows travel when flicked up or down (default is 0.972).
- maskFile – allows a custom height through the use of a masking file.
- hideBackground – optional Boolean to hide the background of the widget.
- topPadding, bottomPadding – number of pixels from the top and bottom in a tableView where rows will stop when you reach the top or bottom of the list (default is 0).
- maxVelocity – optional limit to the maximum scrolling speed (default is 2).
- noLines – optional method of hiding lines separating rows.
- isLocked – optional method of locking the table view so that it cannot scroll vertically.
- hideScrollBar – optional method of hiding the scrollbar.
- onRowRender – optional function call on the initial rendering of the table.
- onRowUpdate – optional function call for when previously viewed rows become visible again.
- onRowTouch – optional function call for when a row is touched.
- listener – optional function call to handle all table events.
- baseDir – optional to set a directory for loading the maskFile.

Methods:

- geContentPosition() – returns the current y position of the table view content. Used to mark the current location.
- scrollToY(y position, time) –scroll to specified y position. Time is in milliseconds for how long it takes to scroll to a location (default time is 1500).

- scrollToIndex(index, time) – scrolls table to a specific row. Time is in milliseconds for how long it takes to scroll to the location (default time is 1500).
- insertRow ({parameters}) – used to insert rows into the table view. Accepts as parameters:

insertRow Parameters:

- width, height – allows adjustment of individual rows.
- rowColor – RGBA table to set row color.
- lineColor – RGBA table to set the separator line color.
- isCategory – Boolean specifying the current row as a category.

- deleteRow (row or index) – deletes a specific row.
- deleteAllRows() – you probably guess, it deletes all the rows of the table view.

Row Events – when insertRow method is called the following keys are passed as part of the event table:

- event.name – either tableView_onRender (for onRender listeners) or tableView_onEvent (for onEvent listeners).
- event.tableView – reference to the calling tableView object.
- event.target – reference to the calling row that triggered the event.
- event.view – reference to the display group. If you create a display object for a specific row in your onRender listener function, you MUST insert those objects into the event.view group or they will not render properly and may cause memory leaks.
- event.phase – will either be "press" or "release". You should always test for the phase for onEvent listener functions, and return true on success.

- **event.index** – a number that represents the row's position in the table view.

Project 11.3 widget.newTableView Example

After the required widget, we begin this example by setting up our listeners. The first one will print to the terminal window all table events that occur.

config.lua

```
application =
{
        content =
        {
                width = 320,
                height = 480,
        },
}
```

main.lua

```
local widget = require( "widget" )

-- Listen for tableView events
local function tableViewListener( event )
    local phase = event.phase
    print( event.phase )
end
```

The next two listener functions handle reporting when a row reappears on the screen and reporting when a row is touched. Don't worry; I have a more sophisticated example of using table view later in the book that will show how to create tables that go several screens deep.

```
-- Handle rows becoming visible on screen
```

```
local function onRowUpdate( event )
  local row = event.row

  print( "Row:", row.index, " is now visible" )
end

-- Handle touches on the row
local function onRowTouch( event )
  local phase = event.phase

  if "press" == phase then
    print( "Touched row:", event.target.index )
  end
```

The onRowRender function handles creating the row for the display as the user scrolls through the list.

```
-- Handle row rendering
local function onRowRender( event )
  local phase = event.phase
  local row = event.row

  local rowTitle = display.newText( row, "Row " .. row.index, 0, 0,
nil, 14 )
  rowTitle.x = row.x - ( row.contentWidth * 0.5 ) + (
rowTitle.contentWidth * 0.5 )
  rowTitle.y = row.contentHeight * 0.5
  rowTitle:setFillColor( 0, 0, 0 )
end
```

Time to create our table view widget. I have included the mask-410.png file in the resource folder for Chapter 11.

```
-- Create a tableView
local tableView = widget.newTableView
{
```

```
    top = 100,
    width = 320,
    height = 410,
    maskFile = "mask-410.png",
    listener = tableViewListener,
    onRowRender = onRowRender,
    onRowTouch = onRowTouch,
}
```

Now we will create the row information. In the 25th and 45th rows, categories are created. The final portion of the code handles inserting the row and setting the events and render handlers.

```
-- Create 100 rows
for i = 1, 100 do
    local isCategory = false
    local rowHeight = 40
    local rowColor =
    {
        default = { 1, 1, 1 },
    }
    local lineColor = { .8, .8, .8 }

    -- Make some rows categories
    if i == 25 or i == 50 or i == 75 then
        isCategory = true
        rowHeight = 24
        rowColor =
        {
            default = { .4, .5, .55, .9 },
        }
    end
    -- Insert the row into the tableView
    tableView:insertRow
    {
        isCategory = isCategory,
        rowHeight = rowHeight,
```

```
       rowColor = rowColor,
       lineColor = lineColor,
   }
end

-- delete the tenth row in the tableView
tableView:deleteRow( 10 )
```

widget.newTabBar

The widget.newTabBar allows you to create a customizable tab
bar. Tabs are auto-positioned based on the number of buttons.
While there is no limit to the number of buttons that can be added,
do remember that the button does need to be large enough to tap.
The widget itself only has a few parameters:

Parameters:

- id – string to identify button (default is "widget_tabBar").
- width, height – allows custom width and height of tab bar
  (default width is display.contentWidth, height is 50)
- left, top – allows custom location of the tab bar (default is
  bottom of the screen)
- buttons – table holding the parameters and options for
  each tab button (see Buttons Table).

Method:

- setSelected(*buttonIndex, simulatePress*) – makes a specific button selected. Provide the index number of the button to show as pressed. If you pass a true in the simulatedPress parameter, the app will call the function supplied on onPress.

Buttons Table

- id – optional string to identify button (default is "button").
- label – text that will appear on the button below the icon.
- labelColor – RGBA table showing default and over color states of the label text
- font – allows changing the button label font (default is native.systemFontBold)
- size – the label font size in pixels (default is 10).
- onPress – a function called when the button is tapped.
- selected – Boolean to track if the button is selected (down). Only one button may be down at a time.
- labelXOffset, labelYOffset – optional horizontal and vertical offset to tab bar label.

Buttons can be created from either image files or from an image sheet.

Button Creation from Image Files

- width, height - should match the width/height of your defaultFile/overFile.

- baseDir – optional, sets the base directory where your custom images are located (default is your project folder system.ResourceDirectory).

- defaultFile - the default ("un-pressed") image of the TabBar button.

- overFile -the over ("pressed") image of the TabBar button.

249

Button Creation from Image Sheet

- defaultFrame - the default ("un-pressed") frame index of the TabBar button.

- overFrame - the over ("pressed") frame index of the TabBar button.

Customized ImageSheet Tab Bar Creation

- sheet - the image sheet object for your tab bar.
- backgroundFrame - the background frame number of the tab bar.
- backgroundFrameWidth, - the width/height of the background image of the tab bar.
- tabSelectedLeftFrame - the left edge frame number of the tab bar's selected graphic.
- tabSelectedMiddleFrame - the left edge frame number of the tab bar's selected graphic.
- tabSelectedRightFrame -the left edge frame number of the tab bar's selected graphic.
- tabSelectedFrameWidth, tabSelectedFrameHeight -the width/height of the tab bar selected graphic.

Project 11.4 Widget Tab Bar Example

Since the tab bar was designed to show multiple views or screens, I thought it would be a perfect method to show some of the less complex widgets. In this project, I will use composer to demonstrate the tab bar, which will be used for the calls to show the scroll bar, spinner, stepper, switch, and segmented control widgets. This project is similar to Solar2D Labs Widget Demo (giving credit where it is due!).

config.lua

```
application =
{
        content =
```

```
        {
                width = 320,
                height = 480,
        },
}
```

main.lua

To begin with we will set up a background and load the required widget and composer APIs. We will also set up a gradient for the title bar so that it looks a little flashier.

```lua
-- Set the background to white and hide statusbar
display.setDefault( "background", 1, 1, 1 )
display.setStatusBar(display.HiddenStatusBar)

-- Require the widget & composer libraries
local widget = require( "widget" )
local composer = require( "composer" )

-- Create a gradient to be used by the title bar
local titleGradient = {type = "gradient",
        color1 = { .8, .85, .9, 1 },
        color2 = { .3, .45, .55, 1 },
        direction = "down" }

-- Create a title bar
local titleBar = display.newRect( display.contentWidth/2, 32,
display.contentWidth, 32 )
titleBar.y = titleBar.contentHeight * 0.5
titleBar:setFillColor( titleGradient )

-- Create the title bar text
local titleBarText = display.newText( "Widget Demo", 0, 0,
native.systemFontBold, 16 )
titleBarText.x = titleBar.x
titleBarText.y = titleBar.y
```

Now we are ready to set up the icon bar. I kept it very simple loading image files for each of the 3 tabs.

```
-- Create buttons table for the tab bar
local tabButtons =
{
        {
                width = 32,
                height = 32,
                defaultFile = "tabIcon.png",
                overFile = "tabIcon-down.png",
                label = "Segemented",
                onPress = function()composer.gotoScene( "tab1" );
end,
                selected = true
        },
        {
                width = 32,
                height = 32,
                defaultFile = "tabIcon.png",
                overFile = "tabIcon-down.png",
                label = "ScrollView",
                onPress = function()composer.gotoScene( "tab2" );
end,
        },
        {
                width = 32,
                height = 32,
                defaultFile = "tabIcon.png",
                overFile = "tabIcon-down.png",
                label = "Other",
                onPress = function()composer.gotoScene( "tab3" );
end,
        }
}
```

After defining the tab bar, we can use the definition to create the tabBar widget. Our last step of the main.lua will be to transfer control to tab1.lua.

```
-- Create a tab-bar and place it at the bottom of the screen
local tabBar = widget.newTabBar
{
        top = display.contentHeight - 50,
        width = display.contentWidth,
        buttons = tabButtons
}

-- Start at tab1
composer.gotoScene( "tab1" )
```

tab1.lua

In tab1.lua, we are going to use the segmented control to output the select segment to a status display box. To get things started, we will load widget and composer, and then create a scene to store this composer scene.

```
local widget = require( "widget" )
local composer = require( "composer" )
local scene = composer.newScene()

-- Our scene
function scene:create( event )
        local group = self.view
        print ("Tab 1 Scene")
```

Here we will make a simple rectangle into a status update box. This is a simple method to display changes in the segmented control to the screen so that the user can see what is happening.

```
        -- Status text box
        local statusBox = display.newRect(
display.contentWidth/2, 290, 210, 120 )
        statusBox:setFillColor( 0, 0, 0 )
```

```
        statusBox.alpha = 0.4
        group:insert( statusBox )

        -- Status text
        local statusText = display.newText( "Interact with a widget
to begin!", 80, 300, 200, 0, native.systemFont, 20 )
        statusText.x = statusBox.x
        statusText.y = statusBox.y - ( statusBox.contentHeight *
0.5 ) + ( statusText.contentHeight * 0.5 )
        group:insert( statusText )

        -- widget.newSegmentedControl()
```

Next we will create a function that when one of the segmented
controls is tapped, it will pass which one to the status box.

```
        -- The listener for our segmented control
        local function segmentedControlListener( event )
            local target = event.target

            -- Update the status box text
            statusText.text = "Segmented Control\nSegment
Pressed: " .. target.segmentLabel

            -- Update the status box text position
            statusText.x = statusBox.x
            statusText.y = statusBox.y - ( statusBox.contentHeight *
0.5 ) + ( statusText.contentHeight * 0.5 )
        end
```

Time to create the segmented control:

```
    -- Create a default segmented control (using widget.setTheme)
    local segmentedControl = widget.newSegmentedControl
        {
            left = 10,
            top = 60,
```

```
            segments = { "Aren't", "Segment", "Control", "Widgets",
"Fun?" },
            defaultSegment = 1,
            onPress = segmentedControlListener,
        }
        group:insert( segmentedControl )
        end
```

And that ends our create scene function. Now we just need to call it and return control back to the composer api.

```
scene:addEventListener( "create" )
return scene
```

tab2.lua

In tab2 we will use the scrollView widget to handle a large picture. As before, we will start by loading the required APIs and creating the scene.

```
local widget = require( "widget" )
local composer = require( "composer" )
local scene = composer.newScene()

-- Our scene
function scene:create( event )
        local group = self.view

        -- Display a background
        local background = display.newImage( "background.png",
true )
        group:insert( background )
```

Now for the ScrollView Listener function, which will just report to the terminal any event phases that occur.

```
-- Our scene
```

```
function scene:create( event )
    local group = self.view

    print("Tab 2 Scene")
    -- Our ScrollView listener
    local function scrollListener( event )
        local phase = event.phase
        local direction = event.direction

        -- If the scrollView has reached it's scroll limit
        if event.limitReached then
            if "up" == direction then
                    print( "Reached Top Limit" )
            elseif "down" == direction then
                    print( "Reached Bottom Limit" )
            elseif "left" == direction then
                    print( "Reached Left Limit" )
            elseif "right" == direction then
                    print( "Reached Right Limit" )
            end
        end

        return true
end
```

Now to create the scroll view, loading the mask for the image and setting up the listener.

```
        -- Create a ScrollView
        local scrollView = widget.newScrollView
        {
                left = 10,
                top = 52,
                width = 300,
                height = 350,
                id = "onBottom",
                hideBackground = true,
                horizontalScrollingDisabled = false,
```

```
                    verticalScrollingDisabled = false,
                    maskFile = "scrollViewMask-350.png",
                    listener = scrollListener,
        }
```

Finally, load the image and position it on the screen.

```
        -- Insert an image into the scrollView
        local background = display.newImageRect(
"scrollimage.jpg", 768, 1024 )
        background.x = background.contentWidth * 0.5
        background.y = background.contentHeight * 0.5
        scrollView:insert( background )
        group:insert( scrollView )
end

scene:addEventListener( "create" )

return scene
```

Surprisingly simple! Let's finish up with tab3, which includes the spinner, stepper, and 3 types of switches.

tab3.lua

As before, we will setup the composer structure and use the status box as like we did in tab1.lua.

```
local widget = require( "widget" )
local composer = require( "composer" )
local scene = composer.newScene()

-- Our scene
function scene:create( event )
        local group = self.view
        print("Tab 3 Scene")
        -- Status text box
```

```
        local statusBox = display.newRect(
display.contentWidth/2, 290, 210, 120 )
        statusBox:setFillColor( 0, 0, 0 )
        statusBox.alpha = 0.4
        group:insert( statusBox )

        -- Status text
        local statusText = display.newText( "Interact with a widget
to begin!", 80, 300, 200, 0, native.systemFont, 20 )
        statusText.x = statusBox.x
        statusText.y = statusBox.y - ( statusBox.contentHeight *
0.5 ) + ( statusText.contentHeight * 0.5 )
        group:insert( statusText )
```

Since we are not using a custom spinner widget, adding the spinner is as easy as creating it and telling it where you want it located.

```
        -----------------------------------------------------
        -- widget.newSpinner()
        -----------------------------------------------------

        -- Create a spinner widget
        local spinner = widget.newSpinner
        {
                left = display.contentWidth/2,
                top = 55,
        }
        group:insert( spinner )

        -- Start the spinner animating
        spinner:start()
```

Time to add the stepper widget. We will set up a simple text and increment/decrement according to the user's touches.

```
-------------------------------------
-- widget.newStepper()
-------------------------------------


-- Create some text for the stepper
local currentValue = display.newText( "Value: 00", 165,
105, native.systemFont, 20 )
currentValue:setFillColor( 0 )
group:insert( currentValue )

-- The listener for our stepper
local function stepperListener( event )
  local phase = event.phase

  -- Update the text to reflect the stepper's current value
  currentValue.text = "Value: " .. string.format( "%02d",
event.value )
  end
```

Now to add the stepper widget. As you can see, it is a simple
widget to use!

```
-- Create a stepper
local newStepper = widget.newStepper
{
  left = 115,
  top = 115,
  initialValue = 0,
  minimumValue = 0,
  maximumValue = 50,
  onPress = stepperListener,
}
group:insert( newStepper )
```

Time for the switch widget. We are going to do all three types, so
there will be a little bit of programming to do here. First, we will
configure the listener to update the status box text depending on
what the user taps.

```
            ------------------------------------------------
            -- widget.newSwitch()
            ------------------------------------------------


            -- The listener for our radio switch
            local function radioSwitchListener( event )
                    -- Update the status box text
                    statusText.text = event.target.id.."\nIs on"

                    -- Update the status box text position
                    statusText.x = statusBox.x
                    statusText.y = statusBox.y - (
statusBox.contentHeight * 0.5 ) + ( statusText.contentHeight *
0.5 )
            end

            -- Create some text to label the radio button with
            local radioButtonText = display.newText( "Use?", 60, 160,
native.systemFont, 16 )
            radioButtonText:setTextColor( 0 )
            group:insert( radioButtonText )
```

The Radio Button. Once the style is declared, it is just a matter of
setting the switch state and the listener, and it is ready to go!

```
            -- Create a default radio button (using widget.setTheme)
            local radioButton = widget.newSwitch
            {
                left = 25,
                top = 180,
                style = "radio",
                id = "Radio Button 1",
                initialSwitchState = true,
                onPress = radioSwitchListener,
            }
            group:insert( radioButton )

            local otherRadioButton = widget.newSwitch
```

```
            {
                left = 55,
                top = 180,
                style = "radio",
                id = "Radio Button 2",
                initialSwitchState = false,
                onPress = radioSwitchListener,
            }
            group:insert( otherRadioButton )

            -- Create some text to label the checkbox with
            local checkboxText = display.newText( "Sound?", 140, 160,
native.systemFont, 16 )
            checkboxText:setFillColor( 0 )
            group:insert( checkboxText )

            -- The listener for our checkbox switch
            local function checkboxSwitchListener( event )
                    -- Update the status box text
                    statusText.text = "Checkbox Switch\nIs on?: " ..
tostring( event.target.isOn )

                    -- Update the status box text position
                    statusText.x = statusBox.x
                    statusText.y = statusBox.y - (
statusBox.contentHeight * 0.5 ) + ( statusText.contentHeight *
0.5 )
            end
```

As you can see, the checkbox is even easier than the radio button
(since the radio button requires 2 or more button objects).

```
            -- Create a default checkbox button (using
widget.setTheme)
            local checkboxButton = widget.newSwitch
            {
                left = 120,
                top = 180,
```

```
            style = "checkbox",
            id = "Checkbox button",
            onPress = checkboxSwitchListener,
        }
        group:insert( checkboxButton )

        -- Create some text to label the on/off switch with
        local switchText = display.newText( "Music?", 220, 160,
native.systemFont, 16 )
        switchText:setFillColor( 0 )
        group:insert( switchText )
```

And finally the on/off switch. Like the other switches, it only requires a few parameters to take full use and make your life a lot easier.

```
        -- The listener for our on/off switch
        local function onOffSwitchListener( event )
            -- Update the status box text
            statusText.text = "On/Off Switch\nIs on?: " .. tostring(
event.target.isOn )

            -- Update the status box text position
            statusText.x = statusBox.x
            statusText.y = statusBox.y - ( statusBox.contentHeight *
0.5 ) + ( statusText.contentHeight * 0.5 )
        end

        -- Create a default on/off switch (using widget.setTheme)
        local onOffSwitch = widget.newSwitch
        {
            left = 190,
            top = 180,
            initialSwitchState = true,
            onPress = onOffSwitchListener,
            onRelease = onOffSwitchListener,
        }
        group:insert( onOffSwitch )
```

```
end

scene:addEventListener( "create" )
return scene
```

Removing Widgets

Since widgets are not typical display objects, you must remove widgets manually. You can only use the display.remove() or removeSelf() methods to delete a widget from view. To avoid memory leaks in your program, you must first manually remove any widgets before removing any group that they might be associated with.

```
display.remove(myWidget)
myWidget = nil

display.remove (someGroup)
someGroup = nil
```

This will ensure that memory is conserved as well as prevent your app from crashing.

Summary

Once you become more familiar with using widgets, you will find that they greatly increase your productivity and speed in creating applications. Obviously it will take some practice to become familiar with some of the features available through these apps. To help you gain experience, we will be using many of these widgets throughout the remainder of the textbook.

Assignments

1. Create an app that displays a number between 1 and 100 that updates as the user moves a slider.

2. Rewrite the age app from Chapter 4 to use a picker wheel instead of textfields.

3. Using the newTabBar widget, create an app that allows you to change pages and see what will be served for breakfast, lunch, and dinner (each meal should be a static page).

4. Select one of the previous apps that you have made and replace all buttons in the app with the button widget.

5. (Challenge) Create your own personalized widget theme.

Chapter 12: System Events & Tools

Learning Objectives

When developing apps to sell on the app stores, it is good programming practice to develop your app to properly handle things going wrong (of course, it won't be YOUR app that messes up ;-). In this chapter, we will examine some of the system events and system resources that are available. We will examine:

- How to handle system events
- How to use the accelerometer
- How to use the gyroscope
- How to use the GPS/Compass
- How to use maps in Solar2D
- How to use Alerts for notification

System Events

If you hadn't noticed, your smartphone and tablet are pretty amazing devices. Most of them have many built-in features that make creating sophisticated apps pretty easy. System events are events that are sent by the smartphone or tablet and broadcast for any interested listener to respond. Some key system events that we have previously discussed include orientation change and enterFrame.

A very important system event that you should prepare for is the closing of your app. Whether the user is receiving a phone call, an instant message, or just closing the app to use something else, most apps need to save their data so that they can properly resume. The system will notify your app if any of these cases occur so that it can properly save and resume in the future. A simple way to handle such an event is:

```
local function onSystemEvent(event)
        -- handle unexpected close or interruptions
        if (event.type=="applicationExit" or event.type==
"applicationSuspend") then
                -- save app information (see chapter 13 on how to
save)
                saveStatus()
        elseif(event.type=="applicationResume") then
                loadStatus()
        end
Runtime:addEventListener( "system", onSystemEvent )
```

Accelerometer

Most modern smartphones and many tablet devices can supply accelerometer data (movement in a specific direction) to the app developer. Solar2D has simple event API resources for each.

The accelerometer can measure movement in 3 dimensions. This includes registering shake events and movement in the x, y, or z directions. To use the accelerometer you will need to configure a runtime event:

Runtime:addEventListener("accelerometer", listenerFunction)

Properties available through the accelerometer API include:

- event.isShake – returns true if the device is being shaken.

- event.deltaTime – returns the amount of time in seconds since the last accelerometer event.

- event.xGravity - returns the amount of acceleration in the x direction due to gravity.

266

- event.yGravity – returns the amount of acceleration in the y direction due to gravity.

- event.zGravity – returns the amount of acceleration in the z direction due to gravity.

- event.xInstant – returns the instant acceleration in the x-direction.

- event.yInstant – returns the instant acceleration in the y-direction.

- event.zInstant – returns the instant acceleration in the z-direction.

- system.setAccelerometerInterval() – set frequency of accelerometer events in Hertz (cycles per second). Min. is 10, max 100. Lower is better to conserve battery life.

Wow, that is about as clear as mud. Let's take a look at its use in an app to try to clarify the accelerometer properties. One warning before we get started, the accelerometer does not work in the Solar2D simulator (beyond shake). Moving the simulator window around your screen will not produce an accelerometer event (it was a nice try though). The only accelerometer event that you can simulate in the simulator is the shake event. To see the accelerometer in action you will have to build the app and deploy it to a device.

Let's talk about gravity vs. instant in the API information above. Gravity is the continuous pull of gravity on your device. If you hold your device in the customary portrait view, the primary gravity variable changed will be yGravity. If you tip your device into landscape view, it will be xGravity. And if you lay your phone down (so that you can see the screen, it's kind of pointless to do it the other way), zGravity is what is affected.

Instant is the detection of movement in a direction. If you move the device side to side (assuming you are back in portrait), you will see the xInstant change. If you move it up and down, then it will by yInstant that changes. And if you pretend you are in Sesame Street and do the "Near and Far" routine, zInstant will change.

Project 12.0 Accelerometer

So let's look at an implementation of an app that will show how to use these tools. I developed this app based upon the Solar2D sample app. It has been greatly simplified, which will hopefully help you to see the important bits.

We will get started by hiding the status bar and putting a title at the top of the screen. Next, we will test to see if the app is being run on the simulator or a device.

```
display.setStatusBar(display.HiddenStatusBar )-- hide status bar

-- Displays App title
title = display.newText( "Accelerator", 0, 20, nil, 20 )
title.x = display.contentWidth/2              -- center title
title:setFillColor( 1, 1, 0 )

-- Determine if running on Solar2D Simulator
local isSimulator = "simulator" == system.getInfo("environment")

-- Accelerator is not supported on Simulator
if isSimulator then
        msg = display.newText( "Accelerometer not supported on
Simulator", 0, 55, nil, 13 )
        msg.x = display.contentWidth/2        -- center title
        msg:setFillColor( 1,1,0 )
end

local soundID = audio.loadSound ("beep_wav.wav")
```

Next we will create the text to show changes in gravity and instant
accelerometer feedback. As you can see, I am incrementing y to
make it easier to place the text on the screen.

```
local y = 95
local xgText = display.newText( "gravity x = ", 50, y, nil, 20 )
xgText:setFillColor(1, 1, 1)
local xg = display.newText( "0.0", 220, y, nil, 20 )
xg:setFillColor(1, 1, 1)

y = y + 25
local ygText = display.newText( "gravity y = ", 50, y, nil, 20 )
local yg = display.newText( "0.0", 220, y, nil, 20 )
ygText:setFillColor(1, 1, 1)
yg:setFillColor(1, 1, 1)

y = y + 25
local zgText = display.newText( "gravity z = ", 50, y, nil, 20 )
```

```
local zg = display.newText( "0.0", 220, y, nil, 20 )
zgText:setFillColor(1, 1, 1)
zg:setFillColor(1, 1, 1)

y = y + 50
local xiText = display.newText( "instant x = ", 50, y, nil, 20 )
local xi = display.newText( "0.0", 220, y, nil, 20 )
xiText:setFillColor(1, 1, 1)
xi:setFillColor(1, 1, 1)

y = y + 25
local yiText = display.newText( "instant y = ", 50, y, nil, 20 )
local yi = display.newText( "0.0", 220, y, nil, 20 )
yiText:setFillColor(1, 1, 1)
yi:setFillColor(1, 1, 1)

y = y + 25
local ziText = display.newText( "instant z = ", 50, y, nil, 20 )
local zi = display.newText( "0.0", 220, y, nil, 20 )
ziText:setFillColor(1, 1, 1)
zi:setFillColor(1, 1, 1)
```

To make the app a little more visually appealing, we will include a circle that will eventually be impacted by the gravity property.

```
-- Create a circle that moves with Accelerator events (for visual
effects)
local centerX = display.contentWidth / 2
local centerY = display.contentHeight / 2

Circle = display.newCircle(0, 0, 20)
Circle.x = centerX
Circle.y = centerY
Circle:setFillColor( 0, 0, 1 )            -- blue
```

The next function receives the information from the accelerometer event, receiving which object event happened (xGravity, yGravity, zGravity, xInstant, yInstant, or zInstant), and the new value for that object. While we have mentioned string.format previously, this is an example of using the string format to convert the value supplied by the accelerator and converting it into a value that is understandable. The %1.3f tells formats the text to have at least 1 digit before the decimal and up to 3 after the decimal places in precision. The f tells the app that it is a floating point variable (i.e. it has decimal places).

```
-------------------------------------------------------
-- Hardware Events
-------------------------------------------------------


-- Display the Accerator Values
local function xyzFormat( obj, value)
        obj.text = string.format( "%1.3f", value )

end

-- Called for Accelerator events
-- Update the display with new values
```

Our final function calls the formatting function above, passing the object variable to update and the value based upon the event property. The last step before creating the event listener is to update the circle's location based on changes in gravity (i.e. the tilt of the phone).

```
local function onAccelerate( event )

        -- Format and display the Accelerator values
        --
        xyzFormat( xg, event.xGravity)
        xyzFormat( yg, event.yGravity)
        xyzFormat( zg, event.zGravity)
        xyzFormat( xi, event.xInstant)
        xyzFormat( yi, event.yInstant)
        xyzFormat( zi, event.zInstant)
```

```
            -- Move our object based on the accelerator values
            Circle.x = centerX + (centerX * event.xGravity)
            Circle.y = centerY + (centerY * event.yGravity * -1)
end

-- Add runtime listener
Runtime:addEventListener ("accelerometer", onAccelerate);
```

If you deploy this app to your device, you will notice that it is very sensitive. Minor movements and shifts in how you hold your device have a real impact on the numbers reported.

Gyroscope

The availability of the gyroscope will depend on its availability on the devices that it is deployed to. To use the gyroscope function on iOS devices, you will need to turn it on in the build.settings file with the command:

build.settings

```
settings =
{
        iphone =
        {
                plist =
                {
                        UIRequiredDeviceCapabilities = "gyroscope"
                },
        },
}
```

The properties for the gyroscope include:
 * event.xRotation – rotation around the device's x-axis in radians per second.

- event.yRotation - rotation around the device's y-axis in radians per second.
- event.zRotation - rotation around the device's z-axis in radians per second.
- event.deltaTime – time in seconds since the last gyroscope event.
- system.setGyroscopeInterval() – sets the frequency of gyroscope updates in Hertz (cycles per second). Minimum value is 10, max 100. Lower is better as it conserves battery life.

As with the accelerator API, the gyroscope will not work in the simulator, so you will have to build the next project and deploy it for it to work.

Project 12.1 Gyroscope

Using a similar code as in the accelerometer project, we will now look at how to use the gyroscope. As before, this is a greatly simplified version of the demonstration that comes in the Solar2D sample code folder.

To get started, we will activate the gyroscope for iOS devices in the build.settings file.

build.settings

```
settings =
{
        iphone =
        { plist = { UIRequiredDeviceCapabilities = "gyroscope"
                }, }, }
```

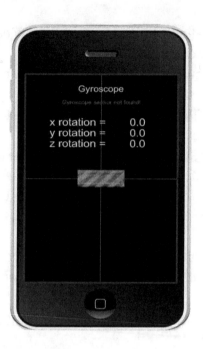

As in the accelerometer project, we will start by setting up our screen, which includes a title, x & y axes lines, and information for the user as they rotate their device.

main.lua

```
-- Project: Ch 12.1 Gyroscope main.lua

-- Hide the status bar.
display.setStatusBar(display.HiddenStatusBar)

-- Draw X and Y axes.
local xAxis = display.newLine(0, display.contentHeight / 2,
display.contentWidth, display.contentHeight / 2)
xAxis:setStrokeColor( 0, 1, 1, .5 )
local yAxis = display.newLine(display.contentWidth / 2, 0,
display.contentWidth / 2, display.contentHeight)
yAxis:setStrokeColor( 0, 1, 1, .5 )

-- Displays App title
```

```lua
local title = display.newText( "Gyroscope", 0, 20, nil, 20 )
title.x = display.contentWidth / 2
title:setFillColor( 1, 1, 0 )

-- Notify the user if the device does not have a gyroscope.
if not system.hasEventSource("gyroscope") then
   local msg = display.newText( "Gyroscope sensor not found!", 0,
55, nil, 13 )
   msg.x = display.contentWidth / 2
   msg:setFillColor( 1, 0, 0 )
end
-----------------------------------------------------
-- Create Text and Display Objects
-----------------------------------------------------

-- Text parameters
local x = 220
local y = 95

local xHeaderLabel = display.newText( "x rotation = ", 50, y, nil, 24
)
xHeaderLabel:setFillColor(1, 1, 1)
local xValueLabel = display.newText( "0.0", x, y, nil, 24 )
xValueLabel:setFillColor(1, 1, 1)
y = y + 25

local yHeaderLabel = display.newText( "y rotation = ", 50, y, nil,
fontSize )
local yValueLabel = display.newText( "0.0", x, y, nil, 24 )
yHeaderLabel:setFillColor(1, 1, 1)
yValueLabel:setFillColor(1, 1, 1)
y = y + 25

local zHeaderLabel = display.newText( "z rotation = ", 50, y, nil, 24
)
local zValueLabel = display.newText( "0.0", x, y, nil, 24 )
zHeaderLabel:setFillColor(1, 1, 1)
zValueLabel:setFillColor(1, 1, 1)
```

As with most things, having a visual representation of what is happening is always nice. We will load a box that will demonstrate the rotations.

```
-- Create an object that moves with gyroscope events.
local centerX = display.contentWidth / 2
local centerY = display.contentHeight / 2
target = display.newImage("target.png", true)
target.x = centerX
target.y = centerY
```

Now we will handle the events for the gyroscope much like we did for the accelerometer.

```
------------------------------------------------------
-- Hardware Events
------------------------------------------------------

-- Display the Gyroscope Values
local function xyzFormat( obj, value )

        obj.text = string.format( "%1.3f", value )
end

-- Called when a gyroscope measurement has been received.
local function onGyroscopeUpdate( event )

        -- Format and display the measurement values.
        xyzFormat(xValueLabel, event.xRotation)
        xyzFormat(yValueLabel, event.yRotation)
        xyzFormat(zValueLabel, event.zRotation)

        -- Move our object based on the measurement values.
        local nextX = target.x + event.yRotation
        local nextY = target.y + event.xRotation
        if nextX < 0 then
```

```
                nextX = 0
        elseif nextX > display.contentWidth then
                nextX = display.contentWidth
        end
        if nextY < 0 then
                nextY = 0
        elseif nextY > display.contentHeight then
                nextY = display.contentHeight
        end
        target.x = nextX
        target.y = nextY

        -- Rotate the graphic box based on the degrees rotated
around the z-axis.
        local deltaRadians = event.zRotation * event.deltaTime
        local deltaDegrees = deltaRadians * (180 / math.pi)
        target:rotate(deltaDegrees)
end

-- Add gyroscope listeners, but only if the device has a gyroscope.
if system.hasEventSource("gyroscope") then
        Runtime:addEventListener("gyroscope",
onGyroscopeUpdate)
end
```

Obviously, the device must have gyroscope capabilities to make use of this app. One of my test devices (an old Nexus One) was not able to perform the operations since it doesn't have this built-in capability.

Alerts

Sometimes when we are creating an app, we need to notify the user of a problem or provide information that they should not ignore. native.showAlert() displays a popup alert box with one or more buttons. The app will remain active in the background but all of the user's activity will be blocked until they respond to the alert dialog. A listener function is used to handle the user's button press in the alert dialog. We will use an alert in our next project example, but for now, here is the API information:

native.showAlert(*title, message [, { buttonLabels } [, listener]]*)

Thus, a showAlert like:

native.showAlert("Mom called", "You are in SO MUCH TROUBLE!", {"Hide Evidence", "I Didn't Do It"})

Results in an alert like

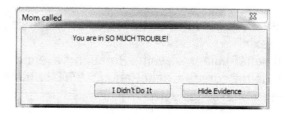

GPS

If you have ever tried to find your way through an area that you are not familiar with, then you know how wonderful applications that help you navigate using GPS services can be. Having recently tried to find my way around near downtown Boston, I can attest to how wonderful these services are to the weary traveler. Need a coffee, restaurant, or gas station? Location aware services make it possible to find the closest vendor and how to get there. Location or GPS events are generated by the GPS hardware within the smartphone with the data being supplied to the runtime object (just like for the Accelerometer and gyroscope). GPS services can supply longitude, latitude, altitude, rate of movement, and direction. You have control over the accuracy of the GPS event.

The GPS location event is based on three possible location services. The most accurate is off of GPS satellites that orbit the Earth (as opposed to Mars, which wouldn't be much help).

Through triangulation, your phone is able to determine your location. The second method, which is used more frequently, is through triangulation using cell towers, which take in to account the amount of time it took the signal to get to the tower, the angle of the signal, etc. The final method is by using wireless routers. This is the least accurate method. Your smartphone uses a combination of these methods to determine location. This is known as Assisted-GPS.

More than any other runtime system, GPS can be a real battery drain. Generally, the higher the accuracy, the more drain. You should also ask your users if location services can be used with the app. Most app stores require the user's approval before their location can be used in your app.

So let's make an app to figure out where we are at! If the app is going to be used on an Android device, you need to include a few permissions in the build.settings file.

Project 12.2 GPS

build.settings

```
settings =
{
   android =
      {
      usesPermissions =
         {       -- Permission to access the GPS.
               "android.permission.ACCESS_FINE_LOCATION",

               -- Permission to retrieve current location from WiFi
or cellular service.
            "android.permission.ACCESS_COARSE_LOCATION",
               },
         },
}
```

Now on to the main lua file. I am again using a simplified version of the app supplied in the sample folder. In this particular app, we will learn our longitude, latitude, speed, direction, and altitude. If it is run in a simulator, it will return a pre-defined location. If you look at the background file included, you will see that the text describing each of the fields is already included. All we need to do is provide the GPS data.

main.lua

```
local currentLatitude = 0
local currentLongitude = 0

display.setStatusBar( display.HiddenStatusBar )

local background = display.newImage("gps_background.png")

local latitude = display.newText( "--", 0, 0, nil, 26 )
latitude.anchorX=0
latitude.anchorY=.5
latitude.x, latitude.y = 125 + latitude.contentWidth * 0.5, 64
latitude:setFillColor(1,.3,.3)

local longitude = display.newText( "--", 0, 0, nil, 26 )
longitude.anchorX=0
longitude.anchorY=.5
longitude.x, longitude.y = 125 + longitude.contentWidth * 0.5,
```

```
latitude.y + 50
longitude:setFillColor(1,.3,.3)

local altitude = display.newText( "--", 0, 0, nil, 26 )
altitude.anchorX=0
altitude.anchorY=.5
altitude.x, altitude.y = 125 + altitude.contentWidth * 0.5,
longitude.y + 50
altitude:setFillColor(1,.3,.3)

local accuracy = display.newText( "--", 0, 0, nil, 26 )
accuracy.anchorX=0
accuracy.anchorY=.5
accuracy.x, accuracy.y = 125 + altitude.contentWidth * 0.5,
altitude.y + 50
accuracy:setFillColor(1,.3,.3)

local speed = display.newText( "--", 0, 0, nil, 26 )
speed.anchorX=0
speed.anchorY=.5
speed.x, speed.y = 125 + speed.contentWidth * 0.5, accuracy.y +
50
speed:setFillColor(1,.3,.3)

local direction = display.newText( "--", 0, 0, nil, 26 )
direction.anchorX=0
direction.anchorY=.5
direction.x, direction.y = 125 + direction.contentWidth * 0.5,
speed.y + 50
direction:setFillColor(1,.3,.3)

local time = display.newText( "--", 0, 0, nil, 26 )
time.anchorX=0
time.anchorY=.5
time.x, time.y = 125 + time.contentWidth * 0.5, direction.y + 50
time:setFillColor(1,.3,.3)
```

Now that we have the variables set up, we can check for potential problems. In the function below, we will use an alert to notify the user of potential problems. If there are no problems, the response from the GPS system will fill in the remaining data.

```
local locationHandler = function( event )

-- Check for error (user may have turned off Location Services)
    if event.errorCode then
        native.showAlert( "GPS Location Error", event.errorMessage,
{"OK"} )
        print( "Location error: " .. tostring( event.errorMessage ) )
    else

        local latitudeText = string.format( '%.4f', event.latitude )
        currentLatitude = latitudeText
        latitude.text = latitudeText
        latitude.x, latitude.y = 125 + latitude.contentWidth * 0.5, 64

        local longitudeText = string.format( '%.4f', event.longitude )
        currentLongitude = longitudeText
        longitude.text = longitudeText
        longitude.x, longitude.y = 125 + longitude.contentWidth * 0.5,
latitude.y + 50

        local altitudeText = string.format( '%.3f', event.altitude )
        altitude.text = altitudeText
        altitude.x, altitude.y = 125 + altitude.contentWidth * 0.5,
longitude.y + 50

        local accuracyText = string.format( '%.3f', event.accuracy )
        accuracy.text = accuracyText
        accuracy.x, accuracy.y = 125 + accuracy.contentWidth * 0.5,
altitude.y + 50

        local speedText = string.format( '%.3f', event.speed )
        speed.text = speedText
        speed.x, speed.y = 125 + speed.contentWidth * 0.5,
accuracy.y + 50

        local directionText = string.format( '%.3f', event.direction )
```

```
        direction.text = directionText
        direction.x, direction.y = 125 + direction.contentWidth * 0.5,
speed.y + 50

        -- Note: event.time is a Unix-style timestamp, expressed in
seconds since Jan. 1, 1970
        local timeText = string.format( '%.0f', event.time )
        time.text = timeText
        time.x, time.y = 125 + time.contentWidth * 0.5, direction.y +
50
            end
    end


-- Determine if running on Solar2D Simulator
local isSimulator = "simulator" == system.getInfo("environment")

-- Location Events is not supported on Simulator
if isSimulator then
            msg = display.newText( "Location events not supported
on Simulator!", 0, 230, "Verdana-Bold", 13 )
            msg.x = display.contentWidth/2      -- center title
            msg:setFillColor( 1, 1, 1 )
    end
```

Now we can call the GPS/location system as a Runtime event.

```
-- Activate location listener
Runtime:addEventListener( "location", locationHandler )
```

As you can see, it is easy to get the data from the smartphone
with Solar2D. The challenge is using the data effectively!

Maps

Having data is one thing. Turning it into information is another.
By using GPS with a map, you can easily determine your location
and how to get to where you want to be or determine what is
available in your local area. Solar2D includes 3 sets of tools for

working with maps: the Map object, mapAddress events, and mapLocation events. Between these three API objects, you can create some neat tools.

Note: Map objects and the associated API only work on Android or iOS devices.

native.newMapView(left, top, width, height)

Map Object

- object:addMarker(latitude, longitude [, options]) – set a marker at the provided location. A title and subtitle can be included in the options table.
- object:getUserLocation() – returns users current GPS location in a table.
- object.isLocationVisible – returns a Boolean if the user's location is currently visible on the map.
- object.isScrollEnabled – allows the user to scroll the map by hand. Set to false if you want to lock the map location.
- object.isZoomEnabled – allows user to use pinch/zoom gestures on the map.
- object.mapType(map string) – sets the map to standard (default) , satellite, or hybrid mode.
- object:nearestAddress(latitude, longitude [, handler]) – returns nearest address on given latitude & longitude. The address is returned as a Map Address event (see below).
- object:removeAllMarkers() – As the name implies, removes pins from the map.
- object:requestLocation(*address string*) – returns the longitude & latitude of an address.
- object:setCenter(latitude, longitude [, isAnimated]) – moves center of map to the given latitude & longitude.
- object:setRegion(latitude, longitude, latitudeSpan, longitudeSpan [, isAnimated]) – moves map region to new location with the center point and horizontal and vertical span (i.e. how much is shown on the screen, or level of zoom) given in degrees of latitude and longitude.

Map Address is created by the object:nearestAddress() and returns the following event fields:
- event.city
- event.cityDetail
- event.country
- event.countryCode
- event.errorMessage
- event.isError
- event.name
- event.postalCode
- event.region
- event.regionDetail
- event.street
- event.streetDetail

Map Location is created by object:requestLocation() and returns the following event fields:
- event.errorMessage
- event.isError
- event.latitude
- event.longitude
- event.name

Project 12.3 Maps

Let's try out the map code for ourselves. Remember, this code will generate an error message in the Solar2D Simulator, so you will have to build and deploy to either the xCode simulator (which will then center on Apple Headquarters), or to a device.

So that the app will work on Android devices, you will need the following permissions in the build.settings file.

build.settings (Android)

```
settings =
{
```

```
    android =
    {
      usesPermissions =
      {
        "android.permission.INTERNET",
        -- Permission to access the GPS.
                "android.permission.ACCESS_FINE_LOCATION",
        -- Permission to retrieve current location from WiFi or cell
service.

        "android.permission.ACCESS_COARSE_LOCATION",
      },
      usesFeatures =
      {
        -- If you set permissions "ACCESS_FINE_LOCATION" and
"ACCESS_COARSE_LOCATION" above,
        -- you may want to set up your app to not require location
services as follows.
        -- Otherwise, devices that do not have location services
(such as a GPS) will be unable
        -- to purchase this app in the app store.
        { name = "android.hardware.location", required = false },
        { name = "android.hardware.location.gps", required = false
},
        { name = "android.hardware.location.network", required =
false }
      },
    },
}
```

Android also requires a **config.lua** file to provide your Google
Maps API key, which you can get from:
https://developers.google.com/maps/documentation/javascript/
get-api-key

```
application =
{
  license =
  {
```

```
    google =
    {
        mapsKey = "YOUR_MAPS_API_KEY",
    },
  },
}
```

build.settings (iOS)

```
settings =
{
   iphone =
   {
      plist =
      {
          NSLocationAlwaysUsageDescription = "This app would like
to use location services.",
          NSLocationWhenInUseUsageDescription = "This app would
like to use location services.",
      },
   },
}
```

Like most Solar2D API tools, using the map feature is very
straightforward. Once the new view is created, we can set the
type of map and its location on the screen. We can also set the
center of the map, retrieve latitude and longitude based on an
address, and then set a marker (or pin) at that location.

main.lua

```
local myMap = native.newMapView(0, 0, display.contentWidth,
display.contentHeight)

myMap.mapType = "hybrid"

myMap.x = display.contentWidth/2
myMap.y = display.contentHeight/2
```

```
-- center on Apple's headquarters to begin
myMap:setCenter( 37.331692, -122.030456 )
local latitude, longitude = mymap:requestLocation( "1900
Embarcadero Rd., Palo Alto, CA 94303" )

myMap:addMarker(latitude,longitude,{title="Solar2D Labs"})
myMap:setCenter( latitude, longitude )
```

Summary

The system tools open up all kinds of possibilities for apps and games (I have at least 5 augmented reality games currently on my personal 'apps to make' list)! I am sure that you see many opportunities for how the smartphone's built-in features can make your app even more useful.

Assignments

1. Create an app that uses the accelerometer to move an object around on the screen. Note: this is the feature many apps use to manage to roll a ball through a maze.

2. Create an app based on the map feature and add a pin for your home address.

3. Add an alert to an app that you have previously made.

4. Using Maps and Location services make an app that shows the map of your current location.

5. Challenge: Create an app that uses the gyroscope feature to keep a round object from rolling off a static beam or line. You will need to use physics and play with the gravity settings for this one!

Chapter 13: File Input/Output

Learning Objectives

I know, I know, you have been wanting to ask the following question for some time now, "How do I save information in my app?" With a few great API resources, we can take care of this problem easily. In this chapter we will learn:

- Where to store files on smartphones and tablets
- The difference between explicit and implicit file input and output
- How to read data from a file
- How to write data to a file
- Using JSON to store and retrieve app data

File I/O Storage Considerations

While we have briefly discussed possible file locations previously, I think it would be a good idea to review. There are three file locations available to app developers through Solar2D:

- system.DocumentsDirectory – should be used for files that need to persist between sessions. When used in the simulator, the user's documents directory is used. You can read and write to this app directory.
- system.ResourceDirectory – is the folder or directory where your assets are stored. Never change anything in this folder! It could invalidate the app and the OS will consider the app malware and refuse to launch. system.ResourceDirectory is assumed (default) when loading assets for your app.
- system.TemporaryDirectory – Just as the name says, is temporary. Only use for in-app data. There is no guarantee that the file will be there the next time the app is used. You can read and write to this directory while the app is active, just don't expect files to persist between sessions.

Generally, you will only use the resource directory for app-specific information that never changes. The documents directory will be used for all types of files that must be updated and persistent between sessions. The temporary directory is those files that are transitory and will not be needed once the app has been closed.

You should think of your apps as being "sandboxed" on any device that they are installed. That means that your files (all of them: images, data, sounds, databases, etc) are stored in a location that is off-limits to any other application that is installed. All of your files will be located in a specific directory for your app.

Reading Data

I am sure that you have noticed that many apps and games take a few seconds (or even minutes) to load. This is primarily due to the need to load a large quantity of data or graphics into memory. By storing data in external files we are able to accomplish several important features.

If security is a concern, either because we are using personal data from those who use our app or the need to safeguard proprietary information, we can encrypt data files making it much more difficult to hack or steal the information. If the data is kept unencrypted, it can be accessed by others.

If I have created a complex game, I will usually need to load a lot of information about the level. While I can program all of the level information into the game, using that approach makes it much more difficult to provide updates, bug fixes, or new levels to the game without resubmitting the app for App Store approval. By storing as much information as possible in external files, I can download updates to my users without needing to go through the approval process again (we will discuss how to download files in

Chapter 15).

Implicit vs. Explicit Files

Lua (and by extension, Solar2D) has two different types of file
input and output: implicit and explicit.

Implicit file operations use standard, predefined files for file input
and output. By default this is the Solar2D Terminal in Solar2D, but
in code is stdin (standard in), stdout (standard out), and stderr
(error reporting). While at first consideration it might seem
strange to think of the Solar2D Terminal as a 'file', it is by
traditional Computer Science considerations. In the 'old' days of
computer usage (i.e. pre-1980s), any operation that wrote or read
information to or from a location was file input or output (file I/O).
In the early days of massive computer systems, to be able to
output information to a terminal was very similar to writing data to
a file or sending the information to a printer. Thus, over time as
programming languages have developed, reading or writing to the
Solar2D Terminal window is still considered a file I/O operation.
Consider it a long-winded way of doing a print command.

Explicit file operations allow the reading and writing of typical (i.e.
not Solar2D Terminal) files including text files and binary files. For
the majority of your file operations, you will be using the explicit
file API tools. The API libraries are differentiated for the two types
of file manipulation. The IO API is implicit, and the file API is
explicit.

Implicit Read

io.type(*filehandle*) – checks whether the file handle is valid.
   Returns the string "file" if the file is open, "closed file" if the file
   is closed (not in use), and nil if the object is not a file handle.
io.open(*filename_path [, mode]*) – opens a file for reading or
   writing in string (default) or binary mode. Will create the file if
   it doesn't already exist. Modes: "r" – read; "w" – write; "a" –

append; "r+" – update, all previous data preserved; "w+" – update, all previous data erased; "a+" – append update, all previous data preserved, writing allowed at the end of file. Mode string can include "b" for binary mode.

io.input(*[file]*) – sets the standard input file (default is Solar2D Terminal)

io.lines(*filename*) – opens the given file in read mode. Returns an iterator (counter) that each time it is called, returns a new line from the file.

io.read(*[fmt]*) – reads the file set by io.input based upon the read format. Generally used with Solar2D Terminal. Use file:read to for files.

io.close() – closes the open file.

io.tmpfile() – creates an empty, temporary file for reading and writing.

Explicit Read

file:read(*[fmt1] [,fmt2] [, ...]*) – reads a file according to the given format. Available formats include: "*n" – reads a number; "*a" – reads the whole file starting at the current position; "*l" – reads the next line (default); number – reads a string with up to the number of characters.

file:lines() – iterates through the file, returning a new line each time it is called.

file:seek(*[mode] [, offset]*) – sets and gets the file position, measured from the beginning of the file. Can be used to get the current file position or set the file position.

file:close() – Close the open file.

Writing Data

io.output(*[file]*) – sets the standard output file (default is Solar2D Terminal).

io.write(*arg1 [, arg2] [, ...]*) – writes the argument to the file. The arguments must be a string or number.

io.flush() – forces the write of any pending io.write commands to the io.output file.

Explicit

file:setvbuf(*mode [, size]*) – sets the buffering mode for file writes. Available modes include: "no" – no buffering (can affect app performance); "full" – output only performed when buffer is full or flush; "line" – buffering occurs until a newline is output. Size argument is in bytes.

file:write(*arg1 [, arg2] [, ...]*) – writes the value of each argument to the file. Arguments must be strings or numbers.

file:flush() – forces the write of any pending file:write commands to the file.

Project 13.0 Reading & Writing to a File

In the following examples we will create simple apps to write and read data to a text file that will be stored in the documents folder of the smartphone or tablet. We will use both implicit and explicit API calls to accomplish our write and read.

One of the first decisions you must make when preparing to write a file is if you need to preserve information that was previously written to the file. When opening the file to write, you must decide if you are over-writing/erasing all previous information ("w"), or appending to previously written data ("a"). When opening a file for writing or appending, if the file does not exist, it will be created.

To keep things simple, I am going to assume that I am not concerned about previously saved files. So, I will use the "w" mode to create or overwrite any previous file.

main.lua

```
-- set the path to the documents directory
pathDest = system.pathForFile( "ch13Write",
system.DocumentsDirectory )

-- open/create the file
local myFile = io.open( pathDest, "w" )

myFile:write("Hi Mom! I made a file")
myFile:flush()
io.close(myFile)
```

When you are finished writing information to the file, you should always flush the data. This will ensure that everything has been written to the file before it is closed.

Now we will add the code to read the data from the file and display it to the screen. After verifying that the file exists, we can load all of the file's contents by using the "*a" parameter.

```
-- check that the file was created
myFile = io.open( pathDest, "r" )
if myFile then
   -- the file exists, read the data
   local contents = myFile:read( "*a" )
   local myOutput ="Contents of \n" .. pathDest .. "\n" .. contents
   io.close(myFile)
   display.newText(myOutput, 450, 150, nil, 16)
end
```

Now that we have successfully created a file, let's look at an example of a file that can be appended.

Project 13.1 Appending & Reading from a File

Building on project 13.0, we will now use the append command. The advantage of this command is data will be added each time we run the program. Thus, if we run the app multiple times, it will continue to add new lines of data. To start using append, we only need replace the "w" with "a" in the initial open command:

```
-- set the path to the documents directory
pathDest = system.pathForFile( "ch13Write",
system.DocumentsDirectory )

-- open/create the file
local myFile = io.open( pathDest, "a" )

myFile:write("Hi Dad! I made a file \n")
myFile:flush()
io.close(myFile)

-- check that the file was created
myFile = io.open( pathDest, "r" )
if myFile then
    -- the file exists, read the data
  local contents = myFile:read( "*a" )
  local myOutput ="Contents of \n" .. pathDest .. "\n" .. contents
  io.close(myFile)
        display.newText(myOutput, 450, 150, nil, 16)
end
```

By adding the "\n" to the end of our write command, we can easily see the additional lines of text since \n forces a new line to the display.

Run this app a few times to see the impact of append.

JSON

You might have heard of JSON (pronounced Jason) before and wondered, "Who is this guy Jason, and what does he have to do with my computer?" JSON stands for JavaScript Object Notation and is a popular method of encoding information for storage. It is considered a lightweight alternative to XML (eXtensible Markup Language) and is fully integrated and supported by Solar2D. JSON data can be very detailed with tables stored within the data.

Now I know what you are thinking: "That's nice, so what?"

Consider this problem: I have been working hard on a mobile game or app and I need to organize the information that will be stored in an easy-to-read format. In other words, JSON is easy to read for the computer and people. Data that has been formatted into a JSON format would look like this:

```
{
        ["First Name"] = "Brian",
        ["Last Name"] = "Burton",
        ["Level"] = 9,
        ["Score"] = 434434,
        ["Location"] = {4.8, 15.16, 23.42},
        ["Avatar"] = "Blue42"
}
```

Now I have information that can be easily passed to the computer app, but is still in a format that most people can easily understand.

Basic JSON commands include decode, encode, and null. JSON is an external library, so it does need to be loaded with *require "json"* before it is use.

json.decode(*json_string*) – decodes the JSON-encoded data structure and returns it as a Lua table object.

json.encode(*json_table*) – encodes and returns the Lua object as a JSON-encoded string.

json.null() – returns a null (decoded as a nil in Lua).

Note that we are using tables when working with JSON! What is encoded and decoded is in the format of an array table. Thus, when I decode a JSON string, it will be in the format of a table with the key being whatever I set (such as "First Name").

Project 13.2 File I/O with JSON

So let's do a simple app to demonstrate how easy it is to use JSON. We will do a more complex application when we get to networking (Chapter 15). We will first require JSON and set up the data. Note that while I am using strings and numbers to pass to the JSON array table, I could just as easily pass variables.

main.lua

```
local json = require "json"
-- JSON script:
local data = {
        ["First Name"] = "Brian",
        ["Last Name"] = "Burton",
        ["Level"] = 9,
        ["Score"] = 434434,
        ["Location"] = {4.8, 15.16, 23.42},
        ["Avatar"] = "Blue42.png"
}
```

Once we have our data loaded, we can encode it easily with the json.encode command. To give you an idea of what it looks like encoded, we will do a print command to show the encoded data.

```
local jsonBlob = json.encode (data)
```

```
print (jsonBlob)
```

Next we will set up our file so that the data can be saved.

```
-- set the path to the documents directory
pathDest = system.pathForFile( "ch13JSON",
system.DocumentsDirectory )

-- open/create the file
local myFile = io.open( pathDest, "w" )

myFile:write(jsonBlob)
myFile:flush()
io.close(myFile)

-- check that the file was created
myFile = io.open( pathDest, "r" )
if myFile then
    -- the file exists, read the data
  local contents = myFile:read( "*a" )

  io.close(myFile)
```

And now we will decode our data. To show how to extract the data from the array table, I have included two display commands to output the data.

```
local myOutput = json.decode(contents)

        display.newText(myOutput["First Name"], 450, 150, nil, 16)
        display.newText(myOutput["Level"], 450, 200, nil, 16)
end
```

Summary

File input and output provide us with the ability to create apps with persistent data. If you have ever had to enter the same data more than once into a mobile application or game, you know how nice data persistence is in an app! We also learned about using JSON to format the data in a user-friendly method.

Assignments

1. Create an app that will allow the user to enter their name and age and store & read the data in an external file.

2. Create an app that will allow the user to enter their name and years in school. The data should be stored in a JSON format.

3. Building on Assignment 1, build an app that checks to see if the file already exists, if it does, welcome the user back to the app and give them a button that will allow them to "logout" and enter new information. Save the new information to the file.

4. Building on Assignment 2, build an app that checks to see if the file already exists, if it does, welcome the user back to the app and give them a button that will allow them to "logout" and enter new information, storing the new information in a JSON format.

Chapter 14 Working with Databases

Learning Objectives

In this chapter we will examine several ways to read and save data to a mobile device. The ability to access external information that is located on your device is critical to many types of data-intensive applications. For the sake of simplicity, we shall keep our focus limited to files that are already located on the device. To that end, we will examine:

- What a Database is and why you would want to use one
- How Databases are structured
- Creating a database for your app
- Reading from a SQLite database
- Writing to a SQLite database

Database Defined

A database in its simplest form is a way to organize a collection of data. Usually, the data being stored is related in some fashion. For example, if I wanted to organize information about students in one of my classes, I could create a database that contained their identification information, how they did on assignments, where they sit, who their best friends are, etc. And just so you know, the word data is plural. When you have only one piece of data, you would use the singular, datum... unless you are talking about the Star Trek character, then it is Data.

Database Software

There are many database programs available to help you create a database. At the personal use end of the spectrum, we have Microsoft Access. For small to mid-size businesses commonly used databases include MySQL and PostgreSQL to databases for huge projects that use Oracle and IBM DB2, and Sybase.

For mobile devices, the database most commonly used is SQLite. Apple began the trend by incorporating SQLite into the early iPhones. Now it is used by almost every smartphone or tablet. For more information on SQLite, I recommend their website: https://www.sqlite.org.

Most databases utilize SQL (Structured Query Language) to handle storing or retrieving information. The basics of SQL are easy to learn (we will cover a few commands in this and later chapters) but can become very complex. There are minor variations of SQL depending on the database, but the basics are fairly consistent across the various databases.

How a Database is Structured

As the purpose of a database is to organize data into a structure, it is a good idea to become familiar with the basic structure of a database. Let me emphasize that this is a simplified presentation of how databases are structured. Let's start at the most basic component and work up.

The simplest part of a database is the field. A field holds one type of data such as an ID number, a name (first, last, or combined), a phone number, etc. When you are creating a field, you specify the type of data that will be stored in the field: String, integer, decimal, Boolean, blob, binary, etc.

When I complete all the fields on a specific subject, it is called a record. In the example below, I can create a record of a student. The student record will have the student's ID, name, current grade level, and classes.

A table is a collection of fields that hold related information. In the example below I have a student table, a class table, a grades

table, and a parent table. Some people like to think of the
information that is created to this point as a spreadsheet, where
the columns would be fields of information, records would be
rows, and the spreadsheet would be the table.

	A	B	C	D	E	F
1	ID	Name	Grade	Class1	Class2	Class3
2	1	Beth	9	312	354	310
3	2	John	10	411	422	310
4	3	Cindy	10	422	454	312

Unfortunately, the spreadsheet analogy quickly breaks down as
we begin to add additional tables and more complex databases.
But for the time being, if it helps you to think of your data
organized as a spreadsheet, by all means, do so!

The container for all of our tables is the database itself. A
database pulls all of this now-organized data and stores it
efficiently as a single file. A database will also usually contain one
or more indexes to help locate the data in a fast and efficient
manner.

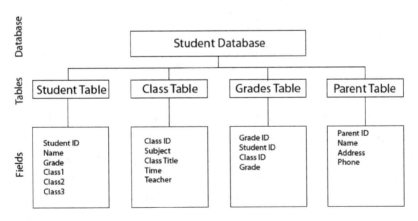

As I mentioned, this is a quick introduction to databases and how
they are organized so that you can create apps that use them. If
you want to go deeper into databases, you will most certainly have
a very lucrative career working with big data and helping

303

organizations manage the information explosion that is occurring today!

How to create a Database

Let's look at how to open or create a database for mobile devices on our PC or Mac, then we will use an existing database for our first app.   One of the advantages of SQLite is that it is in the public domain, so it is freely available to anyone who wishes to use it. There are several great tools available for viewing, creating, or modifying SQLite databases. The one that I use and will demonstrate is a plugin for Firefox. If you would like to use something else, just do a search for SQLite manager. The Firefox plugin can be downloaded from https://github.com/praeclarum/sqlite-net or just do a search in Tools > Add-ons of your favorite browser.

To create a SQLite database with the SQLite Manager, click either File > New Database or the New Database icon. You will get a popup window. Enter a name for your database.

Once you have the database named, it is time to create a table. You can create a new table for the database by selecting Table > Create Table from the menu bar or clicking on the Create Table icon. You will need a name for the table, preferably different from the name of the database and your potential field names.

Time to define your table. Going back to our spreadsheet analogy, think about the names of the different columns (fields) that will be in your table. The first column should always be used for a primary key, which will be used to help keep your data organized. I used the name ID for my primary key. You will next set the data type that will be stored in the field/column. You need to think about the type of information that will be stored in the field. Will it only be numbers? Text (including information such as a phone number or ID number)? Or is the information limited to true or false and should be set to a Boolean?

For the ID field, since it will only be used to keep track of the information entered in this table as an index, I set the data type to Integer. I then checked the Primary Key checkbox so that the database knows this will be used to organize the information in this table. If you would like SQLite to keep track of the Primary Key (which is recommended), you should also check Autoinc, which is auto-increment – meaning it will automatically fill in the next larger integer in the ID for you each time a new record is created.

For the remaining fields of the example table, I created a basic student profile that a school or college might use for tracking. I set each field data type to text except for Graduate, which could be set as a Boolean since it is either true or false.

Once you have created your table, click okay. You are now ready to enter information into your database.

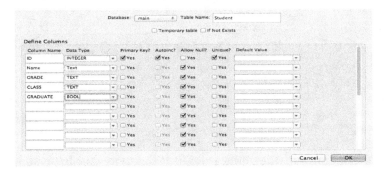

When you click okay, you will be asked to confirm the table creation.

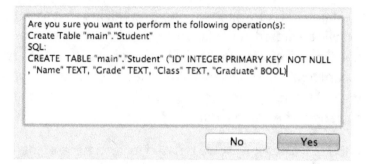

Are you sure you want to perform the following operation(s):
Create Table "main"."Student"
SQL:
CREATE TABLE "main"."Student" ("ID" INTEGER PRIMARY KEY NOT NULL
, "Name" TEXT, "Grade" TEXT, "Class" TEXT, "Graduate" BOOL)|

No   Yes

After the table is created, you will be able to see the table in the
browser. Of course, it doesn't have any data yet, so it will only
show the column or field headings.

Clicking the Add button will open the Add Record window. Go
ahead and create a new record, then click OK.

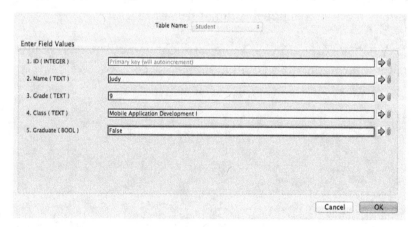

Once the record is added, you will see it listed in your Browse and
Search listing.

That is a quick and dirty introduction to how to create a SQLite database using SQLite Manager. While you may not have a full grasp of what is possible with a database, it should give enough of an understanding to be able to create mobile apps that use pre-existing databases or how to store information in a database.

Working with a Database

Solar2D includes native SQLite support for iOS and a compiled version (adding a mere 300K to your app size) for Android. We are going to continue to keep things simple and use just the basic commands for accessing a local database that is stored on the local smartphone or tablet.

The basic SQLite commands are:

sqlite3.open(*path*) – opens the SQLite file. Note that the path should be the full path to the database, not just the file name to avoid errors.

sqlite3.version() – returns the version of SQLite in use.

fileVariable:exec (*SQL_Command*) – executes a SQL command in the database. Typically used to create tables, insert, update, append or retrieve data from a database.

fileVariable:nrows(*SQL_Command*) – returns successive rows from the SQL statement.

fileVariable:close() – closes the database.

The API for SQLite in Lua is provided by luasqlite3 v0.7. You can find the full documentation on luasqlite3 at http://luasqlite.luaforge.net/lsqlite3.html. Additional information on SQLite can be found at http://www.sqlite.org/lang.html.

LuaSQLite Commands

Luasqlite3 is an external library, thus requiring the use of

local sqlite3 = require "sqlite3"

before any SQLite calls.

Project 14.0: Reading a SQLite Database

For this first database project, we will load an SQLite database with zip code data. This project includes data created by MaxMind, available from http://www.maxmind.com/. I used the SQLite Manager plugin to manage the import and clean up the data for our needs.

The code is fairly straightforward. We will use a standard config.lua and build.settings file:

build.settings

```
settings =
{
        orientation =
        {
                default ="portrait",
                supported =
                {
                        "portrait"
                },
        },
}
```

config.lua

```
application =
{
        content =
        {
                width = 480,
                height = 640,
                scale = "letterbox",
                fps = 30,

        }
}
```

In our main.lua, we will first need to import the sqlite3 framework, set the path to your database file, and open the associated file.

In this example, the database (zip.sqlite) is located in the same folder as my main.lua file to begin with. It is recommended that you do not read from (and never write to) a database stored in the resource directory. Doing so could flag your app as a virus or malware by the operating system! To resolve this problem, we will check to see if a copy of the zip.sqlite database is in the app document folder. If it isn't, we will copy it using IO to read from the resource folder and to write the database to the document folder before opening it.

main.lua

```
--include sqlite
 require "sqlite3"

-- Does the database exist in the documents directory?
local path = system.pathForFile("zip.sqlite",
system.DocumentsDirectory )
```

We now have the variable path set to the location of zip.sqlite (if it exists) in the documents directory. In the next few lines, if there isn't a copy of zip.sqlite in the documents directory, we will use a couple of the file IO commands we have learned previously to copy the file from the resource directory to the docments directory.

Note: To make sure it works on the Windows simulator, be sure to use "rb" and "wb" when copying the file. This forces the Windows simulator to copy the file as a binary instead of a text file. Otherwise, you will get a "Malformed Database File" error (yes, I learned that one the hard way).

```
file = io.open( path, "r" )
  if( file == nil )then
        -- Database doesn't already exist, so copy it from the
resource directory
        pathSource = system.pathForFile( "zip.sqlite",
system.ResourceDirectory )
        fileSource = io.open( pathSource, "rb" )
        contentsSource = fileSource:read( "*a" )

        --Write Destination File in Documents Directory
        pathDest = system.pathForFile( "zip.sqlite",
system.DocumentsDirectory )
        fileDest = io.open( pathDest, "wb" )
        fileDest:write( contentsSource )
        -- Done
        io.close( fileSource )
        io.close( fileDest )
  end

-- One way or another the database exists
db = sqlite3.open( path )
```

Next, we will write some code to handle an applicationExit event, so that the database will be properly closed should the user hit the home button or the phone rings, or something else unexpected happens.

```
-- handle the applicationExit event to close the db
local function onSystemEvent( event )
  if( event.type == "applicationExit ") then
    db:close()
  end
end
```

city, state 000001
Portsmouth, NH 00210
Portsmouth, NH 00211
Portsmouth, NH 00212
Portsmouth, NH 00213
Portsmouth, NH 00214
Portsmouth, NH 00215
Holtsville, NY 00501
Holtsville, NY 00544
Adjuntas, PR 00601
Aguada, PR 00602
Aguadilla, PR 00603
Aguadilla, PR 00604
Aguadilla, PR 00605
Maricao, PR 00606
Aguas Buenas, PR 00607
Aibonito, PR 00609
Anasco, PR 00610
Angeles, PR 00611
Arecibo, PR 00612

Next, we will use a SQL select statement. SELECT tells the
database to return all the rows that meet our search criteria.
Since I am using *, which means wildcard, or "Give me everything!"
that is in the zipcode table, I am going to limit the number of rows
returned to the first 20. We will use a for loop to display the
content of those rows to my device display:

```
local count =0
local sql = "SELECT * FROM zipcode LIMIT 20 "
for row in db:nrows(sql) do
  count = count +1
  local text = row.city.. ", "..row.state.. " "..row.zip
  local t = display.newText(text, 20, 30 +(20 * count),
```

```
native.systemFont, 14)
  t:setFillColor(1, 1, 1)
end
```

And finally, we set up the system event listener for the close event
that was handled earlier.

```
-- system listener for applicationExit
 Runtime:addEventListener ("system", onSystemEvent)
```

And that is how we make an app to read from a database that
already exists. Next, let's save some information to a database.

Project 14.1 Writing to an SQLite Database

In this project, we are going to do one of the most requested types
of apps: an app that can store information in a local database and
retrieve it for later use. We will use a simple form that will be
saved to a SQLite database. For the sake of simplicity, I am going
to limit the database to a single table that is similar to the one we
created earlier in the chapter. We will make use of textfields
(previously discussed in Chapter 4) so that real data can be
entered. As I spend most of my waking hours working with
students, I am going to make this app a simple list of student
information. It could be adapted to any number of different forms
or situations.

I am building this app for a tablet device (specifically the iPad) so
that I have a little more room for data entry. This app will have
three screens: A data entry screen, a list of students in the class,
and a beginning screen that will allow the user to select between
the two other screens. We are going to use composer to move
back and forth between the screens.

To simplify the structure of the finished app, each screen will be stored in its own Lua file. This will give us a total of four Lua files beyond config.lua: main.lua, menu.lua, addStudent.lua, and displayClass.lua.

First, our build.settings and config.lua files:

build.settings

```
settings =
{
        orientation =
        {
                default ="portrait",
                supported =
                {
                        "portrait","portraitUpsideDown"
                },
        },
}
```

config.lua

```
application =
{
        content =
        {
                width = 768,
                height = 1024,
                scale = "letterbox",
        }
}
```

main.lua

When using Composer, the main Lua file primarily serves as a starting place for your app. We begin by loading the Composer and calling the next scene.

```
local composer = require("composer")
composer.gotoScene("menu")
```

menu.lua

The menu.lua file controls the flow between the different pages of our app. It will display two buttons, one that will load the add student screen and one to display the class roster that is stored in the SQLite database. The first portion of the menu.lua file handles the require for widgets (for our buttons) and setting up everything for Composer.

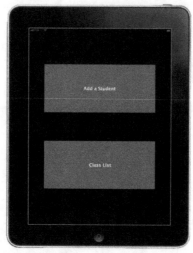

After setting our variables, we can then create widget-based buttons and functions to go to the correct scene.

```
local widget = require ( "widget" )
local composer = require("composer")
local scene = composer.newScene()
local localGroup = display.newGroup()

--Called if the scene hasn't been previously seen
function scene:create( event )

    local displayClass_function = function ( event )
        composer.gotoScene( "displayClass", "fade", 400 )
```

314

```
        end

        local  displayClass_button = widget.newButton{
                defaultFile = "menuButton.png",
                label = " Class List",
                labelColor = {default = { 1,1,1} },
                size = 24,
                emboss=true,
                onRelease = displayClass_function,
                id = "displayClass"
        }

                local addStudent_function = function ( event )
                        composer.gotoScene( "addStudent", "fade",
400 )
                end

                local addStudent_button = widget.newButton{
                        defaultFile = "menuButton.png",
                        label = "Add a Student",
                        labelColor = {default = { 1,1,1} },
                        size = 24,
                        emboss=true,
                        onRelease = addStudent_function,
                        id = "addStudent"
                }

        addStudent_button.x = display.contentWidth/2
        addStudent_button.y = display.contentHeight/2 - 200
        displayClass_button.x = display.contentWidth/2
        displayClass_button.y=display.contentHeight/2 + 200


        localGroup:insert(displayClass_button)
        localGroup:insert(addStudent_button)
end

function scene:show(event)
        localGroup.alpha = 1
```

```
end

function scene:hide(event)
localGroup.alpha = 0
composer.removeScene("scene")
end

-- "create" is called whenever the scene is FIRST called
scene:addEventListener( "create", scene )

-- "show" event is dispatched whenever scene transition has
finished
scene:addEventListener( "show", scene )

-- "hide" event is dispatched before next scene's transition begins
scene:addEventListener( "hide", scene )

return scene
```

addStudent.lua

The addStudent.lua module begins with the required module
statement and then gives a few comments to describe the
function of the file. Adding a few comments on the purpose
program at the beginning of each file is good programming
practice. There is nothing worse than trying to figure out your
program logic six months later when the program needs to be
revised or updated.

We first handle the requires and set up the scene and new group needed in addStudent.lua file. To get started, we will set up the labels and textboxes as a part of our createScene function .

```
--=======================================================--
-- SCENE: addStudent
--=======================================================--
local widget = require ( "widget" )
local composer = require("composer")
local scene = composer.newScene()
local localGroup = display.newGroup()

--include SQLite
require "sqlite3"

--Called if the scene hasn't been previously seen
function scene:create( event )

-- Add textboxes to enter data
-- Labels for textboxes

local title = display.newText(localGroup, "Add A Student",
display.contentWidth/2, 50, native.systemFont, 36)
title:setTextColor(1,1,1)

local nameLabel = display.newText(localGroup, "Name:", 150, 200,
native.systemFont, 24)
nameLabel:setTextColor(1,1,1)
```

```lua
local idLabel = display.newText(localGroup, "ID Number:", 150,
300, native.systemFont, 24)
idLabel:setTextColor(1,1,1)

local seatLabel = display.newText(localGroup, "Seat:", 150, 400,
native.systemFont, 24)
seatLabel:setTextColor(1,1,1)

local gradeLabel = display.newText(localGroup, "Grade:", 150, 500,
native.systemFont, 24)

local studentName = native.newTextField(350, 200, 220, 36)
        studentName.inputType="default"
        localGroup:insert(studentName)

local studentID = native.newTextField(350, 300, 220, 36)
        studentID.inputType="default"
        localGroup:insert(studentID)

local seat = native.newTextField(350, 400, 220, 36)
        seat.inputType="default"
        localGroup:insert(seat)

local studentGrade = native.newTextField(350, 500, 220, 36)
        studentGrade.inputType="default"
        localGroup:insert(studentGrade)
```

All of the actions associated with writing to the database are contained in one function which is called by the submitStudent button. Once the button is clicked, the path is set to students.sqlite which is stored in the device's documents directory. If the file does not already exist, it is created on the first call. By storing the database in the documents directory, it will continue to exist from session to session on the device. The statement to open the database is sqlite3.open(path)

```
-- Setup function for button to submit student data
local submitStudent_function = function ( event )

-- open SQLite database, if it doesn't exist, create database
local path = system.pathForFile("students.sqlite",
system.DocumentsDirectory)
db = sqlite3.open( path )
```

Once the file is open, we need to set up the table that will hold the data. If the table doesn't exist, it will be created. You will notice that we are using standard SQL to define the table (which is called myclass in the example below). The command db:exec(tablesetup) is used to execute the SQL command.

```
-- setup the table if it doesn't exist
local tablesetup = "CREATE TABLE IF NOT EXISTS myclass (id
INTEGER PRIMARY KEY, FullName, SID, ClassSeat, Grade);"
db:exec( tablesetup )
```

After the table is configured, we execute the SQL insert command to pass the contents of the previously created variables to the database. Please note that getting the single quote and double quotes in the right order is critical and is usually the cause of errors in data not being written to the database. The double quotes are used for encapsulating the SQL statement, the single quotes are a part of the SQL statement, as the strings (which all four variables are) must be enclosed in single quotes to pass correctly. The final insert statement after all of the concatenation and quotes would read: "INSERT INTO myclass VALUES(NULL, 'Brian Burton', '0001', 'A5', 'A');" assuming that I was student 0001, sitting in seat A5 and was earning an A in the class.

```
-- save student data to database
local tablefill ="INSERT INTO myclass VALUES (NULL,'" ..
```

```
studentName.text .. "','" .. studentID.text .. "','" .. seat.text .. "','" ..
studentGrade.text .."');"
db:exec( tablefill )
```

After we have executed the SQL insert statement, the database is closed.

```
-- close database
db:close()
```

Now that we have written the data and closed the database, we can prepare the scene to return to menu.lua. First, we must remove the 4 textfields using the removeSelf method (otherwise they will remain on the screen since they are not part of the OpenGL canvas). Then we can call the composer.gotoScene to return to the menu.

```
-- Clear textFields & return to menu screen
studentName:removeSelf()
studentID:removeSelf()
seat:removeSelf()
studentGrade:removeSelf()
composer.gotoScene( "menu", "fade", 400 )
    end -- submitStudent_function
```

Next, we create the addStudent button.

```
local  addStudent_button = widget.newButton{
    defaultFile = "selectButton.png",
    overFile = "selectButton.png",
    label = " Add Student",
    labelColor = {default = {1,1,1}},
    size = 24,
    emboss=true,
    onRelease = submitStudent_function,
```

```
         id = "addStudent"
      }
      addStudent_button.x = display.contentWidth/2
      addStudent_button.y = display.contentHeight-200

      -- add all display items to the local group
      localGroup:insert(addStudent_button)
```

Remember to include a routine to properly close the database should the app unexpectedly close.

```
   -- handle the applicationExit event to close the db
   local function onSystemEvent( event )
      if( event.type == "applicationExit") then
         db:close()
      end
   end

   -- system listener for applicationExit to handle closing
database
   Runtime:addEventListener ("system", onSystemEvent)
end   -- scene:create function
```

With the createScene function finished, we can take care of the other functions needed for composer to work properly. Next, we will take care of the show, which is called when the scene transition has finished.

```
function scene:show(event)
        localGroup.alpha=1
end
```

That just leaves handling what to do when the scene exits and setting up the scene listeners.

```
function scene:hide(event)
```

```
    localGroup.alpha = 0
end

-- "create" is called whenever the scene is FIRST called
scene:addEventListener( "create", scene )

-- "show" event is dispatched whenever scene transition has
finished
scene:addEventListener( "show", scene )

-- "hide" event is dispatched before next scene's transition begins
scene:addEventListener( "hide", scene )
return scene
```

displayClass.lua

The displayClass.lua file handles the displaying of all student data
to the device screen. We will keep this scene very simple, just
displaying the information from the database as a screen text
object, though we could just as easily show it as a Table View or in
some other format.

```
--==========================================--
-- SCENE: displayStudent
--==========================================--
local widget = require ( "widget" )
local composer = require("composer")
local scene = composer.newScene()
local localGroup = display.newGroup()
--include SQLite
require "sqlite3"
```

Next we will set up the create scene which opens the database.

```
function scene:create( event )

  -- open database
  local path = system.pathForFile("students.sqlite",
system.DocumentsDirectory)
  db = sqlite3.open( path )
```

Now we will create the SQL statement that will return all of the fields from the database. We will use the for row in db:nrows(sql) command so that we can step one row at a time through the data. In this case, row is being used as a variable to hold the data that is returned from the db:nrows(sql) command. This allows us to loop through the result set that is returned by the SQL statement and work with each row (or set of data). As you can see, we then take the fields from the row and create a text object that is then displayed to the device screen.

```
local title = display.newText(localGroup, "Class List",
display.contentWidth/2, 5, native.systemFont, 36)
title:setTextColor(1,1,1)

--print all the table contents
local sql = "SELECT * FROM myclass"
```

```
for row in db:nrows(sql) do
   local text = row.FullName.." "..row.SID..", "..row.ClassSeat.."
"..row.Grade
   local t = display.newText(text, 250, 30 * row.id,
native.systemFont, 24)

   t:setTextColor(1,1,1)
   localGroup:insert(t)
end

db:close()
```

Now just a little housekeeping: we create the function and button to handle returning to the menu; add a routine to handle unexpected app closing to close the database properly; and finally return to the director call.

```
-- Setup function for button to load student data
local displayClass_function = function( event )
   -- return to menu screen

   composer.gotoScene( "menu", "slideRight",400 )
end

local  displayClass_button = widget.newButton{
      defaultFile = "selectButton.png",
      overFile = "selectButton.png",
      label = " Return to Menu",
      labelColor = {default = { 1,1,1} },
      fontSize = 24,
      emboss=true,
      onRelease = displayClass_function,
      id = "displayClass"
}

displayClass_button.x = display.contentWidth/2
displayClass_button.y = display.contentHeight-200
```

```
-- add all display items to the local group
localGroup:insert(displayClass_button)

-- handle the applicationExit event to close the db
local function onSystemEvent( event )
   if( event.type == "applicationExit") then
      db:close()
   end
end

-- system listener for applicationExit to handle closing database
   Runtime:addEventListener ("system", onSystemEvent)
end

function scene:show(event)
      localGroup.alpha = 1
end

function scene:hide(event)
   localGroup.alpha = 0
   composer.removeScene("scene")
end

-- "create" is called whenever the scene is FIRST called
scene:addEventListener( "create", scene )

-- "show" event is dispatched whenever scene transition has
finished
scene:addEventListener( "show", scene )

-- "hide" event is dispatched before next scene's transition begins
scene:addEventListener( "hide", scene )

return scene
```

And there we have a basic app that can write and read from a
local database.

Summary

Did I happen to mention that working with databases with your program is considered one of the dividing lines between beginning and experienced programmers? Congratulations, you have leveled up! While working with databases and external files can be challenging in the beginning, the functionality and data storage efficiency that they provide cannot be beat.

Assignments

1) Modify Project 14.1 to include the student's gender and age.

2) Create a database app to store the current date and temperature. The retrieve page should list the dates and temperature.

3) Create a high score app that accepts the name of the game, the name of the player, the high score, and the date the high score was achieved.

4) Augment Project 14.1 to include the ability to update student information (advanced project).

Chapter 15 Network Communications

Learning Objectives

How can we discuss mobile app development without addressing the ability to communicate with a network? In this chapter, we will examine the basic methods used to create network connectivity and how to connect with some of the most popular services. We shall:

- Determine network communication
- Create a network connection
- Connect to a webserver
- Download from a webserver
- Connect to Facebook
- Introduce functions for in-app ads

Network Status

Networking with a mobile device can be a challenge. Users walk in and out of range of wireless connections or switch cell networks on a regular basis; thus it is critical that you have a framework that anticipates these potential networking issues. While it isn't obvious when you are programming due to the efficiency of smartphones and tablets, Solar2D is handling two types of networking: cellular network and wireless (WiFi). The basic network connectivity and reachability can be viewed through the networkStatus event. The networkStatus event can give you information through various properties. To determine the networkStatus, you can use the network.setStatusListener API:

network.setStatusListener(url, listener-function)

Currently the listener only supports named URLs (i.e., you can't use an IP address). To stop the listener, just call the API again, passing *nil* in place of the listener function.

The networkStatus events can return the current status of:

- event.isReachableViaWiFi – returns true if the URL can be reached via WiFi.

- event.isReachableViaCellular – returns true if the URL can be reached via cell network.

- event.address – returns the URL address that is being monitored

- event.isInteractionRequired – returns true if the user needs to interact with the app to complete or stay connected (i.e., they need to enter a password).

- event.isConnectionOnDemand – returns true if the connection will be made automatically.

- event.isReachable – returns true if the host can be reached.

- event.isConnectionRequired – returns true if the connection is active.

Remember, not all tablets have cellular communication. If your app requires a connection to the Internet to work, it is a good idea to check and see if WiFi can reach the desired URL.

Asynchronous Network Requests

An HTTP request is a standard network call, just like what would happen if you type a web address into a web browser. Solar2D SDK contains a full feature of network communication features. With the network API you can make asynchronous HTTP or HTTPS (a secure web connection, usually meaning you have to log in to the remote website) requests to a URL.

HTTP

We will begin with the basics of network communication; establishing a connection using hyper-text transfer protocol (HTTP). As most people are used to seeing and using HTTP through their web browser, using it as part of an app should make sense. The features available with asynchronous HTTP allow you to make regular calls as well as secure socket layer (SSL) calls.

You can use either the built-in network library (which does not need a require) or you can use the socket library (which does need a require). We will begin with the network library:

- network.request(URL, method, listener [, params]) – makes an asynchronous request (either HTTP or HTTPS) to a URL. The time-out for a network is 30 seconds.
    - url – the requested URL
    - method – either GET or POST
    - listener – function to handle the call response. Will return either event.response or event.isError
    - params – a table comprised of params.headers and params.body
- network.download(URL, method, listener [, params], destFilename [, baseDir]) – much like network.request, except it downloads the response as a file instead of storing it in memory. Great for XML/JSON documents, compressed files, sound files, and images.
- display.loadRemoteImage(URL, method, listener [, params], destFilename [, baseDir] [, x, y]) – similar to network download, but specifically designed to load the image from the network.

On Android, you must add the following permission to the "build.settings" file.

```
settings =
{
  android =
  {
```

```
    usesPermissions = {  "android.permission.INTERNET", },
  },
}
```

Project 15.0: Picture Download – Via Network Library

Our first project in this chapter will demonstrate how to download an image from the network using the network library, save the image to the documents directory, then display it to the screen. For this project, I have placed an image on my webserver to demonstrate the download method.

config.lua

```
application =
{
        content =
        {
                width = 480,
                height = 640,
                scale = "letterbox",
                fps = 30,
                antialias = false,
                xalign = "center",
                yalign = "center"
        }
}
```

build.settings

We are adding a new line to the standard build.settings. To the androidPermissions we need to add permission for Internet access.

```
settings =
```

```
{
        androidPermissions =
        { "android.permission.INTERNET" }

}
```

main.lua

I use one button in this app, so we'll use the button widget. The networkListener function is used to check to see if there were any network errors. If there are no errors, then the image is displayed.

```
local widget = require("widget")

local function networkListener (event)
        if (event.isError) then
                print("Network error - download failed")
        else
                testImage = display.newImage("LearningLua.jpg",
system.DocumentsDirectory,10,30);
                testImage.x = display.contentWidth/2
                testImage:scale(.2,.2)
        end
end
```

I will use network.download for this demonstration. First turn on the network activity indicator. This will turn on the spinner on the status bar showing network activity. Now we can set the URL parameter to point at the image on the web server. GET is our HTTP method. The networkListener function is called to handle the image when it is received from the GET call. The final image is saved to the system.DocumentDirectory as LearningLua.jpg.

```
local function loadButtonPress (event)
  native.setActivityIndicator( true )
  network.download("https://burtonsmediagroup.com/wp-
content/uploads/2023/08/Learning-Lua-Book-cover.jpg", "GET",
networkListener, "LearningLua.jpg")
```

```
native.setActivityIndicator( false )

end

-- Load Button
loadButton = widget.newButton{
        defaultFile = "buttonBlue.png",
        overFile = "buttonBlueOver.png",
        onRelease = loadButtonPress,
        label = "Load Picture",
       labelColor = {default = {1,1,1} },
        emboss = true
    }
loadButton.x = display.contentWidth/2
loadButton.y = display.contentHeight - 50
```

Socket

If you are looking for more control over the network interaction, you can use Socket. Full documentation on the Lua Socket is available from
https://docs.coronalabs.com/api/library/socket/index.html.

To demonstrate how LuaSocket works, I have re-worked Project 15.0 as a LuaSocket project to show the differences.

Project 15.1: Picture Download – Via Socket Library

Config.lua and build.settings remain the same. All of the changes occur in main.lua.

main.lua

We will use three requires in this version: widget, socket.http, and ltn12. Socket handles the HTTP request. ltn12 provides the ability to save data to a file (referred to as a 'sink').

After the necessary require statements, we will set the path and create a file to store the image.

```lua
local widget = require("widget")

-- Load the relevant LuaSocket modules
local http = require("socket.http")
local ltn12 = require("ltn12")

-- Create local file for saving data
local path = system.pathForFile( "LearningLua.jpg",
system.DocumentsDirectory )
myFile = io.open( path, "w+b" )
```

In this version of the app, we make a GET request using http.request and provide the sink to handle writing the data to myFile, which is opened in the section above. Finally, the image is displayed from the system.DocumentDirectory where it was saved.

```lua
local function loadButtonPress (event)
   native.setActivityIndicator( true )

   -- Request remote file and save data to local file
   http.request{
      url =
"http://www.BurtonsMediaGroup.com/MobileAppDevelopmentCo
ver.pnghttps://burtonsmediagroup.com/wp-
content/uploads/2023/08/Learning-Lua-Book-cover.jpg",
      sink = ltn12.sink.file(myFile),
   }

   testImage = display.newImage( "LearningLua.jpg",
system.DocumentsDirectory, 10,30);
   testImage.x = display.contentWidth/2
   testImage:scale(.2,.2)
   native.setActivityIndicator( false )
end
```

```
-- Load Button
loadButton = widget.newButton{
        defaultFile = "buttonBlue.png",
        overFile = "buttonBlueOver.png",
        onPress = loadButtonPress,
        label = "Load Picture",
       labelColor = {default={1,1,1}},
        emboss = true
}
loadButton.x = display.contentWidth/2
loadButton.y = display.contentHeight - 50
```

Web Popup

Web Popups allow you to load a webpage (whether local or remote) from within your app. When called, a web popup is loaded on top of your current application, filling the entire screen. By default, the URL is assumed to be the URL of a remote server.

The syntax for a web popup can be either:

native.showWebPopup(url [, options])

or

native.showWebPopup(x, y, width, height, url [, options]).

Parameters include:

- url – the URL of the local or remote web page. By default, this is assumed to be an absolute URL (i.e. use the entire http address).
- x, y – left top corner of the popup.
- width, height – dimensions of the popup window.

Options – optional table/array parameters
- options.baseURL – if set, allows the use of relative URLs.

- options.hasBackground – Boolean that sets an opaque background if true (default is true).
- options.urlRequest – sets a listener function to intercept all urlRequest events for the popup. The listener must return true to keep the popup open (the default return is false).

```
native.showWebPopup( "http://www.BurtonsMediaGroup.com" )

native.showWebPopup( 10, 10, 300, 300,
"https://www.BurtonsMediaGroup.com" )
```

To remove a web popup, use the method:

native.cancelWebPopup()

Web Popup Example

In this example, a webListener function is used to find a webpage that is stored in the system.DocumentsDirectory. If it is not found or an error occurs, the listener will return false, which will cause the web popup to close.

```
local function webListener( event )
    local shouldLoad = true
    local url = event.url
    if 1 == string.find( url, "corona:close" ) then
      -- Close the web popup
      shouldLoad = false
    end

    if event.errorCode then
      -- Error loading page
      print( "Error: " .. tostring( event.errorMessage )
      shouldLoad = false
    end
```

```
      return shouldLoad
end

local options = { hasBackground=false,
baseUrl=system.DocumentsDirectory, urlRequest=webListener }
native.showWebPopup( "localpage1.html", options )
```

Webviews

WebViews load a remote web page into a webView container.
They are different from web popups in that they can be moved,
rotated, and have physics bodies assigned to them. You can also
load html pages into the webView locally.   The webView must be
removed by calling the removeSelf() method.

The syntax for a webview is
native.newWebView(CenterX, CenterY, width, height)

The URL is assigned with
ObjectName:request(URL [,options])

Web Services

Solar2D manages web services through the LuaSocket libraries.
Through the various modules included in these libraries, you can
manage web access (HTTP), send emails (SMTP), upload and
download files (FTP), as well as filter data (using LTN12),
manipulate URLs, and support MIME.

Network access is a huge topic. I could (and might in the future)
write a book that exclusively covered just networking topics. For
the time being, we are going to keep to the basics of networking
and how to implement network features in your apps.

Over the past year a multitude, of libraries and external services have become available to Solar2D. These services are essential to network-based games and apps, so I am also going to briefly introduce these services and explain how to implement them in your game or app. As the APIs change frequently, I recommend that you review the Solar2D documentation for the latest information. https://docs.coronalabs.com/plugin/index.html

Summary

In this chapter, we have examined how to set up basic communications with a web server or proprietary services. Hopefully, you will find these resources a great starting point as you create your network-enabled app.

Assignments

1) Modify Project 15.0 to download an image from your web server.

2) Modify Project 15.1 to download an image or file from your web server.

3) Add a webpopup to an existing app.

4) Create an app to handle simple web navigation using the webview API.

Chapter 16: Head in the Cloud

Learning Objectives

Everywhere we turn today it seems someone in technology is talking about "Cloud" this and "Cloud" that. Utilizing the Cloud has become a very important aspect of mobile and traditional computing. In this chapter, we will:

- Explain what the Cloud is and how it is used
- Discuss the levels of implementation of Cloud computing
- Examine how Cloud computing could be used in mobile applications or games
- Discuss multi-user/player methods within Solar2D SDK

Cloud Computing

There is a lot of hype surrounding cloud computing. The term "Cloud Computing" creates a lot of confusion as to exactly what Cloud Computing is and how it impacts your apps and games. Often times when someone hears the term, they think of things just magically happening on the Internet and they receive the results. Let's begin by defining Cloud Computing so that we don't have any misconceptions. Cloud Computing is using the Internet to access other computing resources to complete your task. Really. That's all it is. Think of it like voice mail on your phone. When you go to check your voicemail, it is located at a remote location and you contact that location to get your messages.

Cloud Computing can vary greatly in what service is being provided by the remote computers. It might be as simple as using Gmail, Hotmail, or Yahoo for your email service or as complex as running a full virtual server remotely through Amazon, Google, or Rackspace.

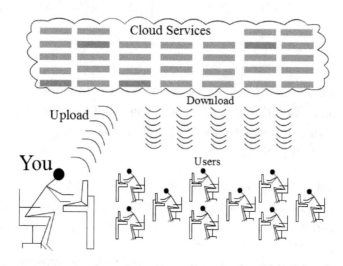

Amazon was one of the first places to begin offering Cloud services with their AWS. It came about through Amazon building an incredible distributed computing server base; large enough to handle Christmas orders on their website without hiccups or delays. Amazon realized that while they needed that much computing power in November and December, the remainder of the year it just sat idle. So they started leasing some of that computer power to others at very reasonable costs. Unlike traditional web hosting where you pay a flat fee for your website, in Cloud Computing, you only pay for what you use in memory, processing, and storage.

One of the things that differentiates Cloud Computing from traditional web hosting is that Cloud Computing is Scalable. Scalable means that if you suddenly have a lot of network traffic, more computer processing power, network bandwidth, memory, and whatever else you need, is made available to your website or app as it is needed. This is because your website or app isn't on one particular computer; it is using shared resources: potentially thousands of computers all interconnected and sharing resources.

Cloud Computing is divided into three general categories:

- SaaS – Software as a Service – provides access to software through your web browser or email software to such resources as email, games, virtual desktops, etc. Examples include Google Apps, Microsoft Office 365, and Salesforce
- PaaS – Platform as a Service – provides a virtual server configured for web hosting, database access, development tools, etc. Examples include AWS Elastic Beanstalk, Google App Engine, and Windows Azure Cloud Services.
- IaaS – Infrastructure as a Service – is the most basic model, that provides access to a cloud of computer resources that you can use to create your own virtual server with your choice of operating system and resources. Examples include Amazon EC2, Google Compute Engine, and Microsoft Azure.

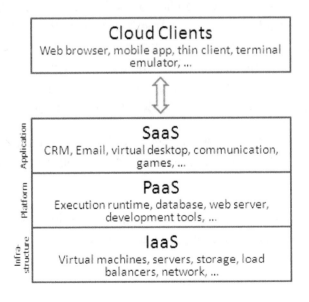

You might be thinking, "Great! Now I understand what a Cloud really is... so what?" I'm glad you asked! When making a mobile app or game, oftentimes you will want or need to take advantage of cloud services to help it be successful. While there are MANY Cloud Computing services available, we are going to look at a few of the most common for your app and game development needs.

Game Services

Both Apple and Google Play game services use the gameNetwork API. While Apple's game center is part of the basic Solar2D SDK, Google Play is a plugin and requires either a Pro or Enterprise License to use.

The gameNetwork API varies according to its use and includes:

- gameNetwork.init(*center [, listener]*) – initiates game services. *Center* will be either "gamecenter" for Apple, or "google" for Google Play.
- gameNetwork.request(*command [, params]*) – sends to or requests information from the game service. Specific *command* differ depending on game services provider and are included under the Apple & Google sections below.
- gameNetwork.show(*command [, data])]*) – sends to or requests information from the game service. Specific *command* differ depending on game services provider and are included under the Apple & Google sections below.

Using the gameNetwork API will enable Solar2D Launchpad, which provides feedback and the use of analytics for your app or game.

Apple Game Center

The Apple Game Center is only available on iOS devices (no Android devices and cannot be used on the Solar2D Simulator). To use the Apple Game Center, you will need to configure the cloud services through iTunes Connect Portal for your app prior to making network calls.

gameNetwork.init("gamecenter" [, initCallback]) –- Initializes iOS

Specific resources available through the game center include:

- gameNetwork.request(*command [, params]*)
  - commands include:
    - setHighScore – used to set a high score for current player. If the score is not higher than the one stored on the server, the server will keep the highest value.
    - loadScores – returns a table based upon playerID, category, or other data.
    - loadLocalPlayer – returns the current player record from Game Center.
    - loadPlayers – returns a list of players with specific player IDs.
    - loadFriends – returns the friends of the currently logged-in user.
    - loadAchievements – returns the user's completed achievements.
    - unlockAchievement – unlocks the specified achievement.
    - resetAchievements – resets all achievements for the current player. There is no undo for this!
    - loadAchievementDescriptions – returns descriptions of the associated achievements.
    - loadFriendRequestMaxNumberOfRecipients – returns Apple's limit on friend requests.
    - loadLeaderboardCategories – returns a list of leaderboard categories for the app.
    - loadPlayerPhoto – returns the player's image from the Apple server.
    - loadAchievementImage – returns the achievement image.
    - loadPlaceholderCompletedAchievementImage – returns a placeholder image generated by Apple for the requested achievement.

- o loadIncompleteAchievementImage – returns the Apple placeholder image for incomplete achievements.

- gameNetwork.show(*command [, params]*) – *commands* include:
    - o "leaderboards" – returns leader board.
    - o "achievements" – returns achievements.
    - o "friendRequest" – returns friend requests.

The *params* table will depend upon the command. Solar2D has been careful to use the same terminology as Apple Game Center to help avoid confusion. For current details on all parameters available for Apple Game Center, check the Solar2D Docs gameNetwork API.

Set High Score

```
gameNetwork.request( "setHighScore",
{
   localPlayerScore = {
category="com.burtonsmediagroup.myGame", value=25 },
   listener=requestCallback
})
```

Load High Scores

```
gameNetwork.request( "loadScores",
{
   leaderboard =
   {
     category="com. burtonsmediagroup.myGame",
     playerScope="Global",   -- Global, FriendsOnly
     timeScope="AllTime",   -- AllTime, Week, Today
     range={1,5}
   },
   listener=requestCallback
```

```
})
```

Google Play Game Services

The Google Play Game Services are only available through the plugin (i.e. only available for those with Pro or Enterprise License) and is only available for Android devices. It does not run on the Solar2D Simulator. At the time of this writing, this is a relatively new service, so be sure to check the Solar2D API for improvements.

gameNetwork.init("google" [, initCallback]) –- Initializes Google Play

Specific resources available through the game center include:

- gameNetwork.request(*command [, params]*)
  - commands include:
    - setHighScore – used to set a high score for the current player. If the score is not higher than the one stored on the server, the server will keep the highest value.
    - loadScores – returns a table based upon playerID, category, or other data.
    - loadLocalPlayer – returns the current player record from Game Center.
    - loadPlayers – returns a list of players with specific player IDs.
    - loadFriends – returns the friends of the currently logged-in user.
    - loadAchievements – returns the user's completed achievements.
    - unlockAchievement – unlocks the specified achievement.
    - loadAchievementDescriptions – returns descriptions of the associated achievements.

- o loadLeaderboardCategories – returns a list of leaderboard categories for the app.
- o isConnected – returns if the user is currently logged into Google Play game services.
- o login – attempts to log the user into Google Play game services.
- o logout – Logs the user out of Google Play game services.

The *params* table will depend upon the command. Solar2D has been careful to use the same terminology as Apple Game Center to help avoid confusion. For current details on all parameters available for Google Play game services, check the Solar2D Docs gameNetwork API.

Set High Score

```
gameNetwork.request( "setHighScore",
{
   localPlayerScore = { category="Cy_sd893DEewf3", value=25 },
   listener=requestCallback
})
```

Load High Scores

```
gameNetwork.request( "loadScores",
{
   leaderboard =
   {
      category="Cy_SLDWING4334h",
      playerScope="Global",    -- Global, FriendsOnly
      timeScope="AllTime",    -- AllTime, Week, Today
      range={1,5},
      playerCentered=true,
   },
   listener=requestCallback
})
```

There are many plugins available that will aid you in developing multiplayer games such as Photon, Amazon Game Circle, Steamworks, and many more. If you are interested in exploring this topic, I recommend visiting the gaming plugin page on the Solar2D website:
https://docs.coronalabs.com/plugin/index.html#gaming

Summary

It cannot be emphasized enough that cloud computing is a rapidly evolving area. You should always check the current documentation for the newest features that are available.

Questions:

1) What is Cloud Computing?
2) Define a "scalable" computing resource.
3) What is a SaaS?
4) What is a PaaS?
5) What is a IaaS?
6) What is the difference between Cloud Computing and hosting your website with a traditional Internet Service Provider?
7) What are some advantages of Cloud Computing?
8) What are some disadvantages of Cloud Computing?
9) List two uses of Saas.
10) Explain why someone might select IaaS over Paas.

Assignments:

1) Modify the Star Explorer project from chapter 9 to have a high score board using either Google Play or Apple Game

Center.

2) Challenge: Add Google Play or Apple Game Center services to one of your apps.

3) Big Challenge: Create a multiplayer game.

Chapter 17: Advanced Graphics

Learning Objectives

In this chapter on using Solar2D, we will examine Graphics 2.0 and create a simple side-scrolling game. I thought long and hard about what to do for this final chapter and then asked the Twitter-verse. The overwhelming response was for a side-scrolling game. So here it is! It seemed appropriate to also discuss some of the capabilities of Graphics 2.0 at the same time:

- Filters, Generators, and Composites
- Liquid Fun
- Learn about parallax scrolling
- Adding a distance meter
- Use physics to simulate jumping

Graphics 2.0

Graphics 2.0 was a major update to the graphics engine for Corona SDK in late 2013. It moved the base graphics engine to OpenGL ES 2.0. This added all types of new capabilities, a major improvement to performance, and a shader-based pipeline for doing some interesting things with graphics.

Paint

Before we dive too deep into some of the special effects available, we need to take a moment to discuss paint. There are several different uses and applications of paint in Corona. The most fundamental is, just as the name implies, like paint. You can select a color using either the traditional {red, green, blue [, alpha]}, or limit it to gray {gray [, alpha]} with the range of each color between 0 and 1.

Paint is not limited to solid colors. You can also use:

- BitmapPaint - which allows you to use a second display object (such as an image) as your fill or image stroke.
- CompositePaint – which allows the selection of multiple textures/images to be used as fills and strokes.
- GradientPaint – used to provide a linear gradient fill or stroke.
- ImageSheetPaint – used to draw your fill or stroke from a specific frame on an image sheet.

Fills - Filters, Composite, and Generators

One of the most exciting tools that is now available to developers is the use of filters, composite, and generators to change or augment your graphics with a minimum of effort. Each of these is slightly different, so let's look at how to apply each of them separately.

Fills

Fills are just like they sound, they 'fill' a vector shape with an image, composite, or effect. To fill an object, create the vector image (display.newCircle, display. newRect, etc), then use the fill property on the object:

```
local myObject = display.newCircle(0, 0, 256)
myObject.x = display.contentCenterX
myObject.y = display.contentCenterY
myObject.fill = {type = "image", filename = "Myphoto.png"}
```

The fill parameters for the type parameter are "image", "composite", and "gradient".

There are so many filter effects available! All filter effects are applied to a single image or texture by using the effect property of **object.fill** or **object.stroke**
myObject.fill.effect = "filter.effect"
myObject.stroke.effect = "filter.effect"

At the time of writing, there are 45 effects available:

- filter.bloom – increases the light saturation of bright areas in an image. Parameters: levels.white (0 to 1; default =0.843), levels.black (0 to 1; default =0.565), levels.gamma(0 to 1; default =1), add.alpha (0 to 1; default =1), blur.horizontal.blurSize (2 to 512; default =8), blur.horizontal.sigma (2 to 512; default =128), blur.vertical.blurSize (2 to 512; default =8), and blur.vertical.sigma (2 to 512; default =128).
- filter.blur – as the name implies, the image will be blurred.
- filter.blurGaussian – A blur function based upon the Gaussian function, resulting in a stronger blur effect in most situations. Parameters: horizontal.blurSize (2 to 512; default =8), horizontal.sigma(2 to 512; default =128), vertical.blurSize (2 to 512; default =8), vertical.sigma (2 to 512; default =128).
- filter.blurHorizontal – A blur effect creates a strong side-to-side effect. Parameters: blurSize (2 to 512; default =8) and sigma (2 to 512; default =8).
- filter.blurVertical – A blur effect that creates an up-and-down streaking effect. Parameters: blurSize (2 to 512; default =8) and sigma (2 to 512; default =8).
- filter.brightness – Brightens the image. Parameter: intensity (0 to 1; default =0).
- filter.bulge – Creates a lens bulging effect of either concave or convex direction. Property: intensity (0 to

351

unlimited; default =1). Values of less than 1 result in a concave (inward bulge), while greater than 1 will result in a convex (outward bulge).

- filter.chromaKey – Sets a portion (or all) of the image to clear (or an alpha of 0) based upon the selected color. Parameters: sensitivity (0 to 1, .4 default), smoothing (0 to 1, 0.1 default), and color (RGBA table). See Project 18.1 below for an example of using the chromaKey filter.
- filter.colorChannelOffset – Moves or separates the colors of the image the specified number of pixels. Parameters: xTexels and yTextels (offset in pixels).
- filter.colorMatrix – Multiplies a source color and adds a bias or offset to the image. Parameters: coefficients (4x4 table of RGBA) and bias (RGBA between -1 and 1).
- filter.colorPolynomial – Applies a cubic polynomial to the image. Parameter: coefficients, (4x4 table of RGBA).
- filter.contrast – Increases or decreases the image contrast. Parameter: contrast, (0 to 4; default =1).
- filter.crosshatch – Creates a crosshatch design based on the original image. Property: grain (0 to unlimited; default =0).
- filter.crystallize – Creates a blurred/crystalized effect based upon the number of tiles or crystals specified. Parameter: numTiles (2 to unlimited; default =16).
- filter.desaturate – Shifts the colors toward the grayscale. Parameter: intensity (0 to 1; default =0.5).
- filter.dissolve – Breaks up the image. Parameter: threshold (0 to 1; default =1).
- filter.duotone – Adds tone of a grayscale image. Parameters: darkColor (RGBA table), lightColor (RGBA table).
- filter.emboss – Creates a greyscale emboss of the image. Parameter: intensity (0 to 4; default =1).

- filter.exposure – Changes exposure or light saturation of the image. Parameter: exposure (-10 to 10; default =0).
- filter. frostedGlass – Applies a blur effect simulating frosted glass. Parameter: scale (1 to unlimited; default =64).
- filter.grayscale – Changes a color image into a grayscale image.
- filter.hue – Adjusts the hue of the image. Parameter: angle (0 to 360; default =0).
- filter.invert – Inverts the colors of the image.
- filter.iris – Changes the center of the image to clear or transparent. Parameters: center (0,0 to 1, 1; default =0.5, 0.5), aperture (0 to 1; default =0), aspectRatio (0 to unlimited; default =1), smoothness (0 to 1; default =0).
- filter.levels – Adjusts the black, white, or gamma levels of the image. Parameters: white (0 to 1; default =0.843), black (0 to 1; default =0.565), and gamma (0 to 1; default =1).
- filter.linearWipe – Adjusts the image so that a portion of it fades to transparency. Parameters: direction ({-1,-1} to {1, 1}; default ={1, 0}), smoothness (0 to 1; default =0), progress (0 to 1; default =0).
- filter.median – Shifts the colors toward the median color in the image, causing a blurring or fading.
- filter.monotone – Shifts the image colors toward a specific color. Parameters: r (0 to 1; default =0), g (0 to 1; default =0), b (0 to 1; default =0), a (0 to 1; default =1).
- filter.opTile – Applies a tiled effect to the image. Parameters: numPixels (0 to unlimited; default =8), angle (0 to 360; default =0), and scale (0 to unlimited; default =2.8).
- filter.pixelate – Creates a pixilated effect on the image. Parameter: numPixels (0 to unlimited; default =4).
- filter.polkaDots – Changes the image into appropriately colored dots. Parameters: numPixels(4 to unlimited;

default =4), dotRadius (0 to 1; default =1), aspectRatio (0 to unlimited; default =1).

- filter.posterize – Shifts the colors of the image to appear more poster-like. Parameter: colorsPerChannel (2 to unlimited; default =4).
- filter.radialWipe – Turns the image to clear in a radial sweep. Parameters: center ({-1, -1} to {1,1}; default ={0.5, 0.5}), smoothness (0 to 1; default =0), axisOrientation (0 to 1; default =0), progress (0 to 1; default =0).
- filter.saturate – Increases the color saturation of the image. Parameter: intensity (0 to 8; default =1).
- filter.scatter – As the name implies, the image becomes scattered or fragmented, the higher the intensity, the more scattered the image becomes. Parameter: intensity (0 to unlimited; default =0.5).
- filter.sepia – Transforms the image to appear like an old photograph. Parameter: intensity (0 to 1; default =1).
- filter. sharpenLuminance – Transforms the image by sharpening the lighter areas. Parameter: sharpness (0 to 1; default=0).
- filter.sobel – Modifies the image to emphasize the edges or transitions.
- filter.straighten – As the name implies, this is used to straighten the image. Parameters: width (1 to unlimited; default=1), height (1 to unlimited; default=1), and angle (0 to 360, default=0).
- filter.swirl – Creates a swirl effect on the image, making it appear that the center of the image has been twisted or is going down a drain. Parameter: intensity (0 to unlimited; default 0).
- filter.vignette – Darkens the outer edge of the image. Parameter: radius (0 to 1; default=0.1).
- filter.vignetteMask – Instead of darkening the edge like vignette, vignetteMask changes the outer edge to clear

(alpha =0). Parameters: innerRadius (0 to 1; default= 0.25) and outerRadius (0 to 1; default=0.8).

- filter.wobble – Creates the appearance of a camera movement or wobble. Parameter: amplitude (none to unlimited; default=10). Note: It is possible to animate the wobble effect using the display.setDrawMode("forceRender")draw mode. This is very processor-intensive and should be turned off when you are finished with the effect.
- filter.woodCut – Changes the image to appear as if it were a woodcut, showing just the edges of objects. Parameter: intensity (0 to 1; default=0.5).
- filter.zoomBlur – Creates a blur effect simulating zooming in on the image. Parameters: u (horizontal origin – 0 to 1; default=0.5), v (vertical origin – 0 to 1; default=0.5), and intensity (0 to 1; default=0.5).

Whew, that is a lot of possible effects! For the full documentation on the effects, check out the Solar2D API: https://docs.coronalabs.com/guide/graphics/effects.html

Here is an example of how to implement one of the effects:

Project 17.0 Filtering with chromaKey

In this example, we will use the chromaKey filter to set an area to transparent.

```
-- create and center object (can be any type of display object)
local bkgd = display.newRect( display.contentCenterX,
display.contentCenterY, display.contentWidth,
display.contentHeight )
bkgd:setFillColor( 1,0,0 )

local myObject = display.newRect( 20, 20, 300, 200)
```

```
myObject:setFillColor(0,1,0,1)
myObject.x = display.contentCenterX
myObject.y = display.contentCenterY

-- set color to be made clear with ChromaKey
myObject.fill.effect = "filter.chromaKey"
myObject.fill.effect.color = {0, 0, 0}
```

In this first version of the program, you should see a green square on a red background.

When we change the value of the last line to:

```
myObject.fill.effect.color = {0, 1, 0}
```

The green square becomes the same color as the background.

With more complex images, this has the effect of rendering a portion of the image transparent.

Composite Effects

Composite Effects are similar to Effects, except that instead of using one image or texture as your fill, you are taking two textures or images, combining them, and then the combined paint or fill is applied to an object. As with Effects, we have quite several possible Composite Effects available. The process to make a composite paint or fill generally follows this pattern:

```
-- Create the object
local object = display.newRect( 100, 100, 160, 160 )

-- Set up the composite paint (distinct images)
local compositePaint = {
    type="composite",
    paint1={ type="image", filename="image01.png" }, -- bottom image
    paint2={ type="image", filename="texture.png" }   -- top image
    }

-- Apply the composite paint as the object's fill
object.fill = compositePaint

-- Set a composite blend as the fill effect
object.fill.effect = "composite.add"
```

The first image loaded (paint1) is considered the bottom image. The second image (paint2) is the top image. Think of it like a stack of photos that you are setting on a table, with the second image set on top of the first, but it can be partially seen, impacting the appearance of the first (bottom) image.

Available composites include:

- composite.add – Adds or overlays the second image to the first. Parameter: alpha (0 to 1; default 1).
- composite.average – Averages the two images. Parameter: alpha (0 to 1; default 1).
- composite.colorBurn – Darker areas of the second image 'burn' or darken the first image. Parameter: alpha (0 to 1; default 1).
- composite.colorDodge – The light areas of the second image lighten the first or bottom image. Parameter: alpha (0 to 1; default 1).
- composite.darken – As the name implies, darken shows whichever pixel is the darkest between the two images, resulting in a darker paint or fill. Parameter: alpha (0 to 1; default 1).
- composite.difference – Subtracts the top image from the bottom or the bottom from the top; whichever results in a positive value. Compositing with a dark top image will result in little to no change; with a light image, the bottom image will be inverted. Parameter: alpha (0 to 1; default 1).
- composite.exclusion – Like difference, exclusion subtracts the top image from the bottom or the bottom from the top; whichever results in a positive value. Compositing with a dark top image will result in little to no change; with a light image, the bottom image will be inverted but with a lower contrast than the difference composite. Parameter: alpha (0 to 1; default 1).
- composite.glow – Similar to colorDodge, but as strong of an impact. The light areas of the top image lighten the bottom image. Parameter: alpha (0 to 1; default 1).
- composite.hardLight – Combines the composite effects of multiply and screen. Dark areas of the bottom image result in a darker top image and light areas of the bottom image result in a brighter top image. Parameter: alpha (0 to 1; default 1).

- composite.hardmix – Forces the color channel to 1 for grey areas that are 0.5 (128) or greater and 0 for grey areas that are less than 0.5 (127). Parameter: alpha (0 to 1; default 1).
- composite.lighten – Shows whichever pixel is brightest between the two images, resulting in a lighter paint or fill. Parameter: alpha (0 to 1; default 1).
- composite.linearLight – The areas of the top image that are light, lighten the bottom image; areas of the top image that are dark, darken the bottom image. Parameter: alpha (0 to 1; default 1).
- composite.multiply – Results in a darker bottom image. The darker the top image is, the greater the impact on the bottom image. Parameter: alpha (0 to 1; default 1).
- composite.negation – Results in the bottom image becoming transparent wherever the top image is light. The lighter the area of the top image, the closer to an alpha of 0 that portion of the image becomes. Parameter: alpha (0 to 1; default 1).
- composite.normalMapWith1DirLight – Applies a rendered directional light to the textures. Parameters: dirLightDirection - specifies when and where the light comes from with a value of 0,0,0 being the origin point of left, top corner, on the same layer as the texture. A z value greater than 0 moves the light in toward the user's perspective in virtual space ({x, y, z}, {0,0,0} to {1,1,1}; default {1,0,0}), dirLightColor – color of the directional light ({r,g,b,a}, {0,0,0,0} to {1,1,1,1}; default {1,1,1,1}), ambientLightIntensity (0 to unlimited; default 0).
- composite.normalMapWith1PointLight - Applies a rendered point light to the textures. Parameters: pointLightPos - specifies when and where the light comes from with a value of 0,0,0 being the origin point of left, top corner, on the same layer as the texture. A z value greater

than 0 moves the light in toward the user's perspective in virtual space ({x, y, z}, {0,0,0} to {1,1,1}; default {1,0,0}), *pointLightColor* – color of the directional light ({r,g,b,a}, {0,0,0,0} to {1,1,1,1}; default {1,1,1,1}), *ambientLightIntensity* (0 to unlimited; default 0), *attenuationFactors* ({0,0,0} to {unlimited, unlimited, unlimited}, default {0.4, 3, 20}).

- composite.overlay – Combines the composite effects of multiply and screen. Dark areas of the top image result in a darker bottom image and light areas of the top image result in a brighter bottom image. Parameter: alpha (0 to 1; default 1).
- composite.phoenix – Dark areas of the texture reverse the colors of the bottom image, the white area is transparent. Parameter: alpha (0 to 1; default 1).
- composite.pinLight – Dark areas of the top layer are treated as transparent or having a pin stuck through it, while light areas are treated as opaque or solid depending on the alpha setting. Parameter: alpha (0 to 1; default 1).
- composite.reflect - The output of reflect is similar to using a colored light on an object. The end product will show the color-saturated with the texture color. Parameter: alpha (0 to 1; default 1).
- composite.screen – The opposite of the multiply composite effect. Results in a brighter bottom image. Parameter: alpha (0 to 1; default 1).
- composite.softLight – Like hardLight, but the effect is not as intense. Combines the composite effects of multiply and screen. Dark areas of the bottom image result in a darker top image and light areas of the bottom image result in a brighter top image. Parameter: alpha (0 to 1; default 1).
- composite.subtract – Subtracts the colors of the top image from the bottom image. Any negative values result

in black being displayed. Parameter: alpha (0 to 1; default 1).

- composite.vividLight – Combines the composite effects of colorDodge and colorBurn with the effect of increasing the contrast of the bottom image. Parameter: alpha (0 to 1; default 1).

Generators

Generators are just what their name implies, they generate a graphic effect automatically. Instead of using a base image to make the change, like with effects, generators are procedurally generated (all programming, no images).   These are easy-to-use tools that allow you to augment your app or change images in a simple and straightforward manner. While not as numerous as filters, I think you will see many ways they can be applied to your app.

- generator.checkerboard – Creates a checkerboard pattern. xStep and yStep determine the size of each square Parameters: color1 ({0,0,0,0} to {1,1,1,1}; default {1,0,0,1}), color2 ({0,0,0,0} to {1,1,1,1}; default {0,0,1,1}), xStep (1 to unlimited; default 3), and yStep (1 to unlimited; default 3).
- generator.lenticularHalo – Applies a halo effect on an object designed to create the illusion of depth. The seed parameter is used to randomly vary the appearance of the halo. Parameters: posX (0 to 1; default 0.5), posY (0 to 1; default 0.5), aspectRatio (0 to unlimited; default 1), and seed (0 to unlimited; default 0).
- generator.linearGradient – Applies a linear gradient to the object. Parameters: color1 ({0,0,0,0} to {1,1,1,1}; default {1,0,0,1}), position1 ({0,0} to {1,1}; default {0,0}), color2 ({0,0,0,0} to {1,1,1,1}; default {1,0,0,1}), position2 ({0,0} to {1,1}; default {1,1}).
- generator.marchingAnts – Applies a moving dotted line around the selected object. Note: "forceRender" draw

mode must be enabled for this effect. This generator has no parameters.

- generator.perlinNoise – Applied to an object to give a more 'real' appearance instead of computer generated. Parameters: color1 ({0,0,0,0} to {1,1,1,1}; default {1,0,0,1}), color2 ({0,0,0,0} to {1,1,1,1}; default {1,0,0,1}), scale (0 to unlimited; default 8).

- generator.radialGradient – Applies a radial gradient onto an object. Paramaters: color1 ({0,0,0,0} to {1,1,1,1}; default {1,0,0,1}), color2 ({0,0,0,0} to {1,1,1,1}; default {1,0,0,1}), center_and_radius – ({center x, center y, inner radius, outer radius}; {0,0,0,0} to {1,1,1,1}; default {0.5, 0.5, 0.125, 0.125}), aspectRatio (0 to unlimited; default 1).

- generator.random – Applies random noise to the object. The generator has no parameters.

- generator.stripes – Applies a stripe pattern to the object. Parameters: periods – table that provides the width in pixels of stripes {w stripe1, w space1, w stripe2, w space2}; default is {1,1,1,1}, angle (0 to 360; default 0), translation – offset of pattern (0 to unlimited; default 0).

- generator.sunbeams – Applies a sunbeam effect to the object. Parameters: posX (0 to 1; default 0.5), posY (0 to 1; default 0.5), aspectRatio (0 to unlimited; default 1), and seed (0 to unlimited; default 0).

Project 17.1 Marching Ants

One of the most useful generators (at least in my opinion) is the marching ants. With the marching ants generator you can create a stroke outline around an object that moves or 'marches' around the object. As mentioned above, to animate the movement of the marching ants, you must set the draw mode to "forceRender" so that the device will redraw the entire scene with each frame refresh. This is a big battery drain and should only be done while the effect is needed.

```
display.setDrawMode( "forceRender" )

local myObject = display.newRect(display.contentCenterX,
display.contentCenterY, 300, 200)
myObject:setFillColor(1,1,1,1)

-- set up the marching ants
myObject.strokeWidth = 2
myObject.stroke.effect = "generator.marchingAnts"
```

Containers

The new graphics engine in Corona gives us another cool feature: containers. Containers function similar to groups for managing groups of objects. One of the big differences between groups and containers is that containers are self-masking. In other words, when you use a container, you can set the size of the container. Any object that is a member of that container that leaves the area of the container will be automatically hidden or masked. Containers allow us to set a stage much easier and more quickly than previous methods. If your app or game is primarily using a specific area of the screen, by setting a container instead of a group, any object that glitches and leaves the area will automatically be hidden from view.

Project 17.2 Containers

```
local myContainer = display.newContainer( 300, 200 )
myContainer.x = display.contentCenterX
myContainer.y = display.contentCenterY
local gradient = { type="gradient", color1={1,0,0}, color2={0.2,0,0},
direction="down" }

local bg = display.newRect( 0, 0, 1000, 1000 )
bg.fill = gradient
myContainer:insert( bg )
local myText = display.newText( "Hello World!", 0, 0,
native.systemFont, 24 )
myContainer:insert( myText )

local function moveText()
    transition.to( myText, {time = 2000, x=myText.x+200} )
end

timer.performWithDelay( 2000, moveText )
```

A couple of things to note about containers. First, when you insert an object into a container, giving the coordinates of 0, 0 will place the new object in the **center** of the container. In our example above, myText is placed at 0, 0, which puts it in the center of the myContainer object.

Second, most devices can only handle a maximum of 3 containers active at any point in time. So use containers when you need them, but don't overuse them!

Liquid Fun

While not truly a graphics but a physics tool, this was just too neat (and recently added) to leave out. Liquid fun became available in Corona as of daily build 2322. Released by Google, Liquid Fun allows you to simulate fluid in the Box2D engine.

Project 17.3 Liquid Fun

```
--Liquid Fun Example

local physics = require( "physics" )
physics.start()

display.setStatusBar( display.HiddenStatusBar )
display.setDefault( "fillColor", 0.5 )

-- Add all physics objects
local left_side_piece = display.newRect( -40,
display.contentHeight-220, 400, 70 )
physics.addBody( left_side_piece, "static" )
left_side_piece.rotation = 80

local center_piece = display.newRect( display.contentCenterX,
display.contentHeight-16, 400, 120 )
physics.addBody( center_piece, "static" )

local right_side_piece = display.newRect(
display.contentWidth+40, display.contentHeight-220, 400, 70 )
physics.addBody( right_side_piece, "static" )
right_side_piece.rotation = -80
```

We start by initializing the physics engine, hiding the status bar, and setting a default fill color. The physics objects in lines 10 through 19 serve as boundaries for the liquid so that it can pool and mix at the bottom. Next, we will set up the particle system used to generate the simulated liquid.

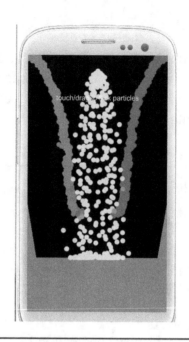

```
-- Create the particle system
local particleSystem = physics.newParticleSystem{
   filename = "particle.png",
   colorMixingStrength = 0.1,
   radius = 3,
   imageRadius = 6
}

-- Paramaters for red particle faucet
local particleParams_red =
{
   flags = { "water", "colorMixing" },
   linearVelocityX = 256,
   linearVelocityY = -480,
   color = { 1, 0, 0.1, 1 },
   x = display.contentWidth * -0.15,
   y = 0,
   lifetime = 8.0,
   radius = 10,
}
```

Using the physics.newParticleSystem, we prepare the Box2D physics. Available parameters for newParticleSystem are:

- **filename** – Required texture file used for an individual particle.
- **baseDir** – Folder where the texture files are stored.
- **radius** – Radius of the generated particle
- **imageRadius** – Allows the image to be rendered with a different radius than the physical body (the radius parameter).
- **pressureStrength** – Pressure is increased in response to compression.
- **dampingStrength** – Slows the velocity of the particle. Larger numbers have more of an impact.
- **elasticStrength** – How quickly the particle returns to its original shape.
- **springStrength** – How quickly a spring particle returns to its original length.
- **viscousStrength** – Slows the velocity of viscous particles.
- **surfaceTensionPressureStrength** – Produces pressure strength on tensile particles (i.e. larger numbers give greater surface tension). Range: 0 to 0.2
- **surfaceTensionNormalStrength** – A smoothing effect for the outline of the particles; gives a more fluid appearance. Larger numbers result in a more water-like appearance. Range: 0 to 0.2
- **repulsiveStrength** – Increases pressure on repulsive particles. Negative numbers result in attraction. Suggested Range: -0.2 to 2.0.
- **powderStrength** – Produces repulsion between powder particles.
- **EjectionStrength** – Particle push from solid particle groups. Larger numbers result in more particles being pushed out of the group.

- staticPressureStrength – Produces static pressure on neighboring particles.
- staicPressureRelaxation – Decreases instability of particles caused by static pressure.
- staticPressureIterations – Changes the number of times the static pressure is calculated. Default: 8.
- colorMixingStrength – Set the speed on how quickly colors will mix. A value of 1.0 will result in an immediate mix, while 0.5 is 50% mixture per simulation step.
- destroyByAge – Boolean variable that allows particle destruction by age when no more particles are created.
- lifetimeGranularity –Sets granularity of particle lifetime in seconds.
- blendEquation – How the blending equation will occur with particles: Values: "subtract", "reverseSubtract", or "disabled".
- blendMode – Set the particle blending mode: Values: "add", "multiply", "screen", or "normal".

A Matter of Perspective

2 ½D, isometric, mode 7, and 3D are all just a matter of perspective when developing games. The Solar2D graphics engine makes it much easier to produce advanced effects and even simulate 3D gameplay on mobile devices.

One of the most common methods to simulate depth in a game is the use of parallax scrolling. The method has been around since the early days of console games and is now commonly used in side-scroller games to give the feeling that the game is taking place in a much larger environment.

Project 17.4 Side Scroller: Parallax Scrolling

Let's begin by defining parallax scrolling. Parallax has many definitions depending on the application. For our situation in creating a mobile side-scrolling game, it is used to give a sense of depth or distance between the camera and the moving objects as they recede into the distance. The method has been around since the early days of game development and is still commonly used in most games.

The parallax scrolling effect is created by using layers. The back layer, or the one farthest from the camera (usually a distant shot of a sun setting, cityscape, or some type of landscape), one or more middle distance objects such as closer buildings, and then close distance which contains our primary character and the immediate obstacles to be overcome.

For our game of a runner, I will use a landscape for the distant shot, intermittent shots for middle distance such as a house, barn, or trees, and then a closer shot of a fence or cornfields. Finally, we need to have a foreground area that will serve as the reference for the parallax scrolling. Each of these distance settings will have a ratio set for it so that we can calculate how much they should move as the foreground moves. You must always have the front-most scene set to 1, else you don't have anything to base the movement ratio on.

Let's start by setting up the config.lua and build.settings files:

build.settings

```
-- build.settings for project: SideScroller

settings =
{
  orientation =
  {
```

```
        default ="landscapeRight",
        supported =
        {
           "landscapeLeft","landscapeRight"
        },
     },
}
```

Since the game is intended to be played as a sidescroller, we will
restrict the orientation to landscapeLeft and landscapeRight.

config.lua

```
-- config.lua for project: SideScroller
application = {
  content = {
          width = 480,
          height = 640
     scale = "letterBox",
     fps = 30,

     imageSuffix = {
       ["@2x"] = 2,
     },
  },
}
```

We are using a standard config.lua for this project.
I want to use composer for scene control for this game. So our
main.lua file just needs to perform some basic setup and call the
splash screen:

main.lua

```
-- Project: SideScroller
-- Description: Simple side scrolling game. .
--
```

```
display.setStatusBar( display.HiddenStatusBar )

local composer = require("composer")

composer.gotoScene( "splash")
```

We will keep the splash screen fairly simple for the moment. Just set up composer and pre-declare the splash variable. In the **create** function we will create a rectangle the size of the screen and set it as a black background. Then create a simple text message and place it in the center of the screen.

We will also set up the scene:show function so that when the background is tapped, we will remove the text and load the next scene.

splash.lua

```
-- splash

local composer = require("composer")
local scene = composer.newScene()
local splash

function scene:create(event)
   splash = display.newRect(0,0, display.contentWidth,
display.contentHeight)
   splash:setFillColor(0,0,0)

   local myText = display.newText("Welcome to my Awesome
Level",0,0,nil,24)
   myText:setFillColor(1, 1, 1)

function scene:show( event )
end
```

```
function scene:hide(event)
end

scene:addEventListener( "create", scene )
scene:addEventListener( "show", scene )
scene:addEventListener( "hide", scene )
return scene
```

1Level.lua

From here forward, we will be working with the 1Level.lua file. This is where we will configure the parallax as well as basic gameplay. We will start by calling composer, setting up our scenes, and getting physics started.

```
-- Side Scroller
-- Graphics 2.0 parallax scrolling
local composer = require("composer")
local scene = composer.newScene()

local physics = require("physics")
physics.start()
physics.setGravity( 0, 9.8 )
--physics.setDrawMode("hybrid")
```

Next, we will set up a few variables that are used throughout the level.

```
function scene:create(event)
   local centerX = display.contentCenterX
   local centerY = display.contentCenterY
   local _W = display.contentWidth
   local _H = display.contentHeight

   -- Define reference points locations anchor points
```

```
local BOTTOM_REF = 1
local LEFT_REF = 0
local baseline = 375
local obj = {} -- used to store parallax objects and obstacles
```

Notice that we simplified keeping track of the anchor points by referencing where they set the anchor point, just to make our lives a little easier. In the last two lines, we set the base of the parallax scrolling (approximately where I want the action to occur) and create a table to hold the objects that will be scrolling across the screen. Time to load some of those objects! First, let's get the background sky loaded and add some text to display how far our runner has run.

```
-- Load the graphics
-- Load the sky and background image.
local sky = display.newImageRect( "sky.png", 1000, 480 )
sky.x = centerX
sky.y = centerY
local distance = 0
local distanceText = display.newText("Distance: "..distance,
100, 40, nil, 24)

obj[1] = display.newImageRect("background.png", 1500, 300)
obj[1].anchorX = LEFT_REF
obj[1].x = -190
obj[1].y = centerY-35
obj[1].dx = 0.01  -- move the background VERY slowly
```

We are also loading our background image that will move as our runner progresses. Nothing should look unusual except the last line. Here we have created a variable within our table to help compute how far the background should move with each iteration. I have it set at .01, which means that for every frame, it will move .01 pixels. The game is set to run at 30 frames per second, so the background should move .3 pixels each second, or approximately 1 pixel to the left every 3.3 seconds.

Next, we will load the road area. I'm using the same graphic five times so that we can slide it. When a piece of road moves off the screen, we move it to the far right and recycle it. There is no sense in using more graphic memory than needed!

```
-- Road has multiple parts so we can slide it
-- When one of the road images is offscreen, move it to the right
of the next one.
local road1 = display.newImageRect("road.png", 325, 45)
road1.anchorX = LEFT_REF
road1.x = -200
road1.y = baseline + 35
local road2 = display.newImageRect("road.png", 325, 45)
road2.anchorX = LEFT_REF
road2.x = 100
road2.y = baseline + 35
local road3 = display.newImageRect("road.png", 325, 45)
road3.anchorX = LEFT_REF
road3.x = 400
road3.y = baseline + 35
local road4 = display.newImageRect("road.png", 325, 45)
road4.anchorX = LEFT_REF
road4.x = 700
road4.y = baseline + 35
local road5 = display.newImageRect("road.png", 325, 45)
road5.anchorX = LEFT_REF
road5.x = 1000
road5.y = baseline + 35
```

With our road in place, we need something for our runner to run on. We COULD set the road, but I think it will be more efficient to create a simple rectangle in the right place and configure it as a static object. Note: I found in my testing that some devices were not showing the screen the way I wanted due to being extra long.

To compensate for this issue, I made the rectangle extra long so that our runner wouldn't fall to their death.

```
local ground = display.newRect( centerX, baseline+40, _W+250,
10 )
  ground.alpha = 0
  physics.addBody( ground, "static" )
```

Time to load our background objects. This is where the parallax becomes important. I am using 3 objects, each traveling at a different speed because of the .dx property (which stands for deltaX, or the change in X position). The value we give dx tells the software how quickly to move the object across the screen. The smaller the number, the further back toward the horizon it is assumed to be. A value of 1 is moving at the same speed as the runner. Thus, if you wanted to add cars zipping past our poor runner, you could set it at a dx of greater than 1.

```
-- Load background objects
obj[2] = display.newImageRect( "barn.png", 204, 200 )
obj[2].xScale = 0.6
obj[2].yScale = 0.6
obj[2].anchorY = BOTTOM_REF
obj[2].x = 200
obj[2].y = baseline+10
obj[2].dx = 0.2

obj[3] = display.newImageRect( "fence.png", 300, 100 )
obj[3].xScale = 0.8
obj[3].yScale = 0.8
obj[3].anchorY = BOTTOM_REF
obj[3].x = 200
obj[3].y = baseline+20
obj[3].dx = 0.3

-- insert obstacles
```

```
    obj[4] = display.newImageRect( "trash cans.png", 50, 50 )
    obj[4].xScale = 1
    obj[4].yScale = 1
    obj[4].anchorY = BOTTOM_REF
    obj[4].x = 20
    obj[4].y = baseline+60
    obj[4].dx = 1
    physics.addBody( obj[4], "dynamic", {density=.5, friction=.5,
bounce=.5 } )
```

Time to load our runner. I modified the green man that comes with the Solar2D animation sample code and made him into a blueman (I always did like that group).

```
    -- A sprite sheet with a green dude
    local sheet = graphics.newImageSheet( "blueman.png", {
width=128, height=128, numFrames=15 } )

    -- play 15 frames every 500 ms
    local blueman = display.newSprite( sheet, { name="man",
start=1, count=15, time=500 } )
    blueman.x = centerX-100
    blueman.y = baseline +40
    blueman:play()
    physics.addBody( blueman, "dynamic", {density=2 } )
    blueman.isFixedRotation=true
```

Parallax

Time to get things moving!   First, we need the current system time so that we can compute how far the scene needs to move. The first time through, we'll capture the system time in **tPrevious** so that it's available for later computations.

The function **move** will take the current event time, subtract the previous time, and compute the time delta (how much time has elapsed). This is in case something slowed the processing of the scene, or the scene processed faster than normal. It will keep everything flowing smoothly across the screen. Once we have **tDelta**, we can also compute the distance. Since our runner is taking a full step every 500 milliseconds, I decided that each time a full second has elapsed, the runner has moved 1 meter forward (which means he has a short stride). This is used to display the distance traveled for text.

```
    -- set parallax scrolling.  Layers must be in back-to-front order
with a distance ratio.
    -- A per-frame event to move the elements
    local tPrevious = system.getTimer()
    local function move(event)
        local tDelta = event.time - tPrevious

        tPrevious = event.time
        distance = distance + (tDelta*.01)

        distanceText.text = "Distance: "..math.round(distance).."
meters"

        local xOffset = ( 0.2 * tDelta )

        road.x = road.x - xOffset
        road2.x = road2.x - xOffset
        road3.x = road3.x - xOffset
        road4.x = road4.x - xOffset
        road5.x = road5.x - xOffset

            if (road1.x ) < -500 then
                    road1.x= 1000
            end
            if (road2.x) < -500 then
                    road2.x= 1000
            end
        if (road3.x ) < -500 then
                road3.x= 1000
```

```
       end
       if (road4.x) < -500 then
              road4.x= 1000
       end
       if (road5.x ) < -500 then
              road5.x= 1000
       end
```

After we compute the distance, we next move the road by just changing the road.x value. Remember, we are only moving a fraction of a pixel per frame, so the movement will look smooth.

After we move the road, we check to see if the road has moved far enough off the screen to move it back to the right. Remember, we want the road off the screen before we move it. If it's not, it will leave a gap in the road on the screen for a few seconds, which is not what we want!

Now it's time to take care of the parallax movement. Using a for loop, we can cycle through all of the objects nice and quick, moving them just like we move the road. We check to see if they are off the screen to the left, and if they are, move them off-screen.

```
    local i
    for i = 1, #obj, 1 do
       obj[i].x = obj[i].x - obj[i].dx * tDelta * 0.2
       if (obj[i].x + obj[i].contentWidth) < 0 then
          obj[i]:translate( display.contentWidth + obj[i].width*2, 0 )
       end
    end

 end
```

Now we just need to take care of the event listener and composer.

```
-- listeners
    Runtime:addEventListener( "enterFrame", move );

end

function scene:show( event )
end

function scene:hide(event)
end

scene:addEventListener( "create", scene )
scene:addEventListener( "show", scene )
scene:addEventListener( "hide", scene )
return scene
```

With the addition of the Runtime event listener, you should be able to now run the game.

But wait! There's more! Won't it be nice if our runner could jump over the trash cans? That would make it a little more entertaining. Let's add a function that will do just that. Insert at line 151 (just before the listeners) a function that will apply a linear impulse to the runner.

Jumping

```
-- handle the controls (tap to jump)
local function jump()
--    print("JUMP!!")
    blueman:applyLinearImpulse( 0, -200, blueman.x, blueman.y )
end
```

And don't forget a tap area and listener to call the jump command:

```
    local tapArea = display.newRect( centerX, centerY, _W+255,
_H+255 )
    tapArea.alpha = .01

    Runtime:addEventListener( "enterFrame", move );
    tapArea:addEventListener( "tap", jump )
```

Fini (maybe)!

Now we're running! We will add one more situation before calling
this game done. Should the runner fail to jump the trash cans and
be pushed to the left of the screen, we'll consider the game over.
Insert these lines in our **move** function before the final end:

```
    -- Finished
    if blueman.x <= -150 then
        blueman:pause()
        physics.stop()
        Runtime:removeEventListener( "enterFrame", move )
        local finished = display.newText("You ran "..distance.."
meters", centerX, centerY, nil, 30)
    end
```

And there we have it, a simple side-scrolling endless runner game!

Summary

If you have ever wondered about the development process that I
use when making a game like this, I wanted to assure you I do not
start at the top line and write to the bottom. The process I use is
to develop one section at a time, such as parallax, then controls,
then sprites, etc.

During that process, I added variables to the beginning of the main file, listeners to the end, and updated previously written sections when something went wrong. Altogether, to get this game written from concept to working version for the book took about 2 weeks of part-time work (I am a professor by day; they expect me to show up and teach my classes).

I should also mention that those 2 weeks of part-time work drew upon over 30 years of programming experience. In other words, if it takes a while to make your game or app, don't be surprised! Making quality apps takes time. But every app you make will contribute to the next app.

Questions

1) Define parallax. How can it be used in game development?
2) Research: What is "Mode 7"? Name at least one game that used Mode 7.
3) Describe the difference between a generated effect, a composite, and an effect.
4) When should a container be used instead of a display group?
5) What does Liquid Fun allow you to simulate?

Assignments

1) Add additional obstacles that must be avoided in Project 17.4: Side Scroller

2) Add additional particle flows to Project 17.3: Liquid Fun

3) Select a composite and apply it to a picture of your choice.

4) Load an image and apply the checkerboard generator to it.

5) Add additional layers to the parallax in Project 17.4: Side Scroller. How does the size of the object impact the perception of distance?

Chapter 18 Future and Beyond

Learning Objectives
- define analytics or metrics
- discuss when to use analytics in your app or game.
- Discuss the future of app development

You say Metrics, I say Analytics

While considering Internet access, it seems appropriate to add the consideration of metrics or analytics. Metrics or Analytics is the process of determining usage app or game usage to measure efficiency, performance, or progress within an app or game.

Over the last ten years, analytics gathering has come under fire for gathering data without the user being aware. While traditional methods of data gathering do not contain personally identifiable information, many app/game developers gather data without letting the user know that data is being collected. This is a big no-no. If you are gathering data, you need to make sure your users are aware of it (usually a statement in the Terms & Agreements is sufficient).

Analytics is handled through the analytics API (don't you love easy-to-remember API calls?). Solar2D has multiple options for helping gather analytics for your apps. We are going to look at one of those services: Flurry Analytics. You can sign up for a Flurry account at http://www.flurry.com.

The API has four commands:

- *flurryAnalytics.init(listener, {apiKey = "yourID"})*

- *flurryAnalytics.logEvent(eventID [,params])*

383

- *flurryAnalytics.startTimedEvent(event [, params])*

- *flurryAnalytics.endTimedEvent(event [, params])*

After you sign up for your Flurry account, you will be able to create your application on Flurry's website. You can choose iPhone, iPad, or Android. This will create an application key which you must enter in the flurryAnalytics.init command.

It should be noted that Flurry now offers a restricted analytics option that is appropriate for use in apps or games that target children. The data gathered is restricted in the type of information gathered and does not include anything that could potentially identify the person using the app but still provides basic usage information.

Note that permissions for Android must be enabled in your build.settings file:

build.settings

```
settings =
{
  plugins =
  {
    ["plugin.flurry.analytics"] =
    {
      publisherId = "com.coronalabs"
    },
  },
}
```

A simple example of using Flurry would be:

main.lua

```
local flurryAnalytics = require( "plugin.flurry.analytics" )

local function flurryListener( event )

  if ( event.phase == "init" ) then  -- Successful initialization
      print( event.provider )
  end
end

-- Initialize the Flurry plugin
flurryAnalytics.init( flurryListener, { apiKey="YOUR_API_KEY" } )
```

The Future of Mobile App Development

Create a vision for the future of mobile app development

You have learned a lot of skills and techniques in this book, but that is not the end of your mobile app development journey. In fact, it is just the beginning. Mobile app development is a field that is constantly changing and growing, and you need to have a vision for the future of mobile app development. Use this vision to then inspire you, guide you, and challenge you to reach your full potential. In this section, we will help you create your own vision for the future of mobile app development.

To create your vision, you need to ask yourself some questions, such as:

- What kind of problems or needs do you want to solve or address with your mobile apps?
- What kind of values or principles do you want to uphold or promote with your mobile apps?
- What kind of impacts or outcomes do you want to achieve or contribute with your mobile apps?

- What kind of innovations or trends do you want to explore or leverage with your mobile apps?
- What kind of skills or competencies do you want to develop or improve with your mobile apps?

These questions will help you identify your purpose, passion, and potential as a mobile app developer. They will also help you define your mission, vision, and goals for the future of mobile app development.

For example, your vision for the future of mobile app development could be:

- To create mobile apps that are innovative, impactful, and sustainable
- To create mobile apps that are inclusive, accessible, and diverse
- To create mobile apps that are aligned with your personal and professional goals

To create mobile apps that make a positive difference in the world

This is just an example. You can (and should) create a vision that reflects your unique interests, values, and aspirations. There is no right or wrong vision, as long as it is clear, realistic, and motivating.

Once you have created your vision, you need to take action to make it happen. You need to plan, execute, evaluate, and improve your mobile app development projects. You need to learn, practice, and apply the latest technologies, tools, and techniques in mobile app development. You need to collaborate, communicate, and network with other mobile app developers, users, and stakeholders. You need to seek feedback, support, and mentorship from experts, peers, and mentors. You need to celebrate your achievements, learn from your failures, and embrace your challenges.

By doing these things, you will be able to create mobile apps that are not only products but also expressions of your vision. You will be able to create mobile apps that are not only functional but also meaningful. You will be able to create mobile apps that are not only successful but also fulfilling. You will be able to create mobile apps that are not only for today but also for tomorrow.

You have come a long way in this book, and we are proud of you. But don't stop here. Keep learning, keep creating, and keep dreaming. The future of mobile app development is in your hands. Make it awesome!

Tips and Resources for Further Learning and Exploration

You have learned a lot of skills and techniques in this book, but there is always more to learn and explore in mobile app development. Mobile app development is a field that is constantly changing and growing, and you need to keep yourself updated and informed about the latest technologies, tools, and trends. Here are some tips and resources that can help you further your learning and exploration in mobile app development:

There are many blogs, books, and articles that cover various topics and aspects of mobile app development. You can find useful tips, tutorials, best practices, case studies, and news from these sources.

Solar2D Discord Channel: (https://discord.com/invite/WMtCemc) This is the official discord of Solar2D, where you can find updates, announcements, and tutorials about Solar2D.

My Solar2D YouTube Channel: Solar2D/Corona SDK Tutorials - YouTube
(https://youtube.com/@profburton)

These are just some of the tips and resources that can help you further your learning and exploration in mobile app development. There are many more that you can find and use, depending on your interests, needs, and goals. The important thing is to keep learning, keep exploring, and keep creating.

You have reached the end of this book, and we are very proud of you. You have completed a comprehensive and practical guide to mobile app development with Solar2D. You have learned a lot of skills and techniques that will help you create amazing mobile apps. You have also created a vision for the future of mobile app development that will inspire you to keep learning, keep exploring, and keep creating. You have done a great job, and we congratulate you on your achievement.

But don't stop here. This book is not the end, but the beginning of your mobile app development journey. Mobile app development is a field that is constantly changing and growing, and you need to keep yourself updated and informed about the latest technologies, tools, and trends. You also need to keep yourself motivated and passionate about creating mobile apps that can change the world for the better.

We wish you all the best in your mobile app development journey. We hope that you will achieve success, happiness, and fulfillment in your mobile app development journey.

Questions

1) Define analytics.
2) When is analytic use appropriate?
3) Research what types of information are illegal to gather in analytics for apps targeting children.
4) What types of information would be useful to you as an app/game developer to gather from analytics?
5) What are the ethical/moral implications of gathering analytics about your app/game users?

Appendix: Publishing to Device

As the publishing requirements are updated frequently, I recommend checking the Solar2D website on publishing should you have any problems https://docs.coronalabs.com/guide/index.html and scroll down to Building and Distributing.

Publishing to an Apple iOS Device

Before we begin deploying to your Apple iOS, I want to remind you that you must be a current Apple Developer with a Standard (most common), University (most common for college students), or Enterprise Developers account. You will need your code signing identity/provisioning certificate already configured through the Apple Developers website to be able to build for the simulator or a device.

When building for an iOS device, you have the option of building to the iOS simulator (the simulator that comes with Xcode) or for a device. Building for the simulator provides you one more opportunity to get the bugs worked out before going through the time-consuming process of deploying to a physical device. When I say time-consuming, this is in comparison to clicking build and having it show in the simulator. It takes a couple of minutes each time you deploy to a physical device, and those minutes add up.

iPhone or iPad changes frequently. For current directions, please visit: Solar2D Documentation — Developer Guides | Building/Distribution

Android OS Device Build

As with iOS, the process to build and publish to Android changes frequently. For the current process, please visit https://docs.coronalabs.com/guide/distribution/androidBuild/index.html

Android Kindle Fire (Amazon) Device Build

Amazon has additional challenges in building for their store. For the latest information on building and releasing for Amazon Kindle Fire devices, please visit

https://docs.coronalabs.com/guide/distribution/kindleBuild/index.html

Mac OS Desktop Build

Apple has specific requirements that are updated regularly. For the most current information, please visit

https://docs.coronalabs.com/guide/distribution/macOSBuild/index.html

Windows Desktop Build

For the latest information on building and releasing for Windows, please visit

https://docs.coronalabs.com/guide/distribution/win32Build/index.html

www.ingramcontent.com/pod-product-compliance
Lightning Source LLC
LaVergne TN
LVHW050144060326
832904LV00004B/165